The Backup Plan Portfolio

The Backup Plan Portfolio

Diversify with gold, real estate, and crypto for protection

Adrian Kassem von Rensselaer

Mindful Pages

Published in 2025

ISBN: 9789371343978 (PB)
ISBN: 9789371343787 (eBook)

Published by

Mindful Pages
Imprint of Alpha Editions LLC
312 W. 2nd St #1834
Casper, WY 82601, USA

This book was developed using advanced writing tools to support the drafting and ideation process. All content has been thoughtfully curated, refined, and reviewed to ensure quality and relevance.

Content

Introduction
The Backup Plan Portfolio

There's a particular stillness that descends after a market collapse. Not merely the quiet that follows the closing bell, nor the strained murmurs of news anchors fumbling through economic carnage. It's an inner silence—the moment one confronts the uncomfortable truth that the mechanisms they entrusted with their future—the pension plan, the index tracker, the neatly curated ETF—were never built to withstand disruption. They were designed for predictability, not resilience. And that silence… it's not just economic. It's existential. It's the sound of once-solid assumptions crumbling under the weight of reality.

This book is for the person who hears that silence and decides: never again.

The Backup Plan Portfolio isn't merely a lesson in diversification—it's a call to reclaim personal agency. It challenges readers to revise their understanding of risk, to take back ownership of their financial trajectory from a system that was never truly built with their security in mind. Let's start from an uncomfortable but vital truth: the financial system is not malfunctioning. In fact, it is operating precisely as intended—to serve its architects first, and its participants, if at all, later. If that observation feels bleak, stay with me. This is not a book of cynicism—it's a blueprint for sovereignty, design, and liberation.

This is not some invitation to speculative mania, nor a pitch for ideological rebellion. Instead, what lies ahead is a measured, intellectually robust exploration of how one might build lasting financial integrity in a world that increasingly disregards yesterday's assurances. The core assets discussed—gold, real estate, and cryptocurrency—are not chosen for their novelty or allure. They are selected for their endurance, their structural independence, and their resistance to systemic decay.

So, what exactly is the problem this book addresses?

At its root, modern life presents us with a peculiar paradox: an abundance of information, yet a drought of clarity. A proliferation of financial tools, yet a deficit of trust. Institutions keep making promises, while individuals increasingly suspect they won't be kept. We've come to associate complexity with security—believing the more layered or obscure a product is, the more insulated it must be. That belief has cost people dearly. Not just in money lost, but in freedom, time, and peace of mind surrendered.

The real peril isn't volatility—it's the illusion that someone else is managing it for you.

Historically, wealth was never an abstract thing. It was land that fed your family, gold that spanned generations, or property you could walk through, touch, and defend. Today, wealth has been digitised, de-personalised—transformed into a game of numbers in a remote server. In this book, you won't find wistful nostalgia, but rather a grounded case for intelligent reversion. A return to assets you can understand, protect, and control—assets that sit beyond the brittle trust scaffolding of highly leveraged intermediaries.

Let's briefly explore the foundation this portfolio rests on.

Gold, first and foremost, offers permanence. It's not a bet—it's a benchmark. Not subject to inflationary whim or monetary conjuring tricks. No committee can print more of it, no bank can cancel it with a keystroke. Its authority lies in its scarcity, and in the centuries of collective human belief that have cemented its role as money. In an era where liquidity is increasingly synthetic and central banks are overextended, gold remains refreshingly unyielding.

Real estate, by contrast, speaks the language of utility. A roof over one's head. An income stream. A tangible asset that can be shaped, leveraged, or fortified through legal and practical strategy. It is not immune to cycles, certainly—but unlike a stock whose fate is sealed in a boardroom, property offers agency. You can walk through it, improve it, rent it out, or defend it in court. There is power in that.

Then there's cryptocurrency—the newest, and for some, the most controversial of the trio. Here, it's important to tune out the hysteria. We're not talking about meme coins or speculative frenzies. We're talking about tools—technologies that provide exits. Exit from capital controls. Exit from inflationary theft. Exit from the opacity of custodial mismanagement. Bitcoin isn't the answer to everything. But it *is* an answer to certain key questions. This book approaches it not with reverence, but with rigour: exploring where it fits, and where it doesn't, in a framework designed for long-term durability.

These three asset classes—gold, property, and crypto—form a structure that is about more than financial returns. It's about diversification not merely across sectors, but across belief systems. Gold assumes nothing of governments. Real estate assumes nothing of the markets. Crypto assumes nothing of legacy infrastructure. Together, they represent a layered redundancy that isn't paranoia—it's prudence.

But perhaps most importantly, this book brings to light a seldom-discussed reality: asset protection is not just about mechanics. It's about psychology. The market may be indifferent, but we are not. Fear, greed, inertia, wishful thinking—these human factors weigh as heavily on portfolios as tax laws or interest rates. True resilience demands more than asset selection. It requires emotional discipline. The steady hand. The patient accumulator. The sceptical optimist. What follows is not just a toolkit, but a vocabulary—a mental architecture to help readers cultivate sound decision-making under pressure.

The Backup Plan Portfolio is not here to upend your existing strategies, but to interrogate them. It invites you to ask hard questions: What if your "safe" assets aren't safe after all? What if your entire plan relies on a long chain of uninterrupted assumptions—stable currency, responsible governance, restrained central banks? Do you have a plan… or just a hope dressed up as one? This book doesn't moralise about risk. It locates it—often in the very places we've been told to feel safest.

This message couldn't come at a more critical time. We are living amid intersecting instabilities: runaway inflation, geopolitical friction, accelerating surveillance, ecological shocks, and fading trust in major institutions. In such a landscape, simplicity feels like a refuge. But that simplicity—"buy the dip," "trust the horizon," "diversify across sectors"—may be precisely what needs to be questioned. What if the dip is not a dip, but a fault line?

That's the heartbeat of this book. While its context is urgent, its philosophy is timeless. Throughout history, economic systems have always cycled through trust and collapse, creation and contraction. Survival doesn't belong to the best predictors. It belongs to those who prepare—not for perfection, but for volatility. That is the core principle behind *The Backup Plan Portfolio.*

To engage with this book is to make a conscious decision. A decision not just about where to invest, but how to think. To become your own reserve bank. Your own strategist. Your own steward of wealth. That's not paranoia—it's maturity. The world is not falling apart, but it *is* rearranging itself. And those who read the new contours early will not merely endure the change—they will shape it.

So here is your invitation. To reconsider not only the location of your money, but its mission. To move from passive allocation to intentional design. From blind trust in complexity to a deliberate embrace of simplicity, structure, and sovereignty.

This book is not for everyone. It is for those who sense that the ground beneath their old assumptions is shifting—and who are ready, calmly and deliberately, to walk in a new direction.

Chapter 1
The Myth of Safe Systems

There's a quiet presumption woven through modern financial thinking, so pervasive that few ever stop to question it: the assumption that what is familiar must, by default, be safe. Fiat currencies, central banks, and sovereign governments—these are the fixtures we've grown up with, the pillars of economic life. Their presence is so entrenched that they've become synonymous with stability itself. The average investor doesn't spend their evenings dissecting central bank minutes or scanning monetary policy statements. They place trust where they're told it belongs. But—as any serious student of history will tell you—trust, while useful, is not the same thing as security. It can be a virtue, yes, but once it calcifies into complacency, it ceases to protect and begins to expose.

This chapter opens with a provocation, not to shock, but to jolt the reader into re-examination: what if these grand financial systems—the ones so widely assumed to be guardians of our wealth—are not safe at all? What if their apparent strength is little more than an illusion, delicately upheld by shared belief and a deep-rooted fear of confronting what lies outside them?

There's no need for conspiracy here. The facts, such as they are, speak for themselves. Consider fiat currency. It is not tethered to gold, not anchored to land, nor backed by tangible goods or services. Its backing is belief—confidence that governments will pay their debts, that central banks will behave sensibly, that inflation will stay within bounds. These aren't guarantees. They are assumptions. And assumptions, as with all belief systems, erode slowly—until, often without warning, they collapse.

Think about the structure of money in our era. For most, currency feels like a neutral instrument, a tool for buying and selling, no more ideological than a measuring cup. But that's a misread. Fiat money is a political tool, issued not in proportion to economic output, but wielded in service of political pressures, emergencies, and shifting economic fashions. There is no hard cap on its creation. Only limits set by political patience and inflationary blowback. And when the public starts to suspect that their money is being drained of value to paper over short-term policy failures, faith begins to fray. Purchasing power doesn't just decline—it evaporates.

This is not a hypothetical scenario. It's a cycle, well-worn and often ignored. Argentina's economy, repeatedly wrecked by currency crises, has forced its citizens into a kind of financial street-smarts borne not of education, but of necessity. Zimbabwe, Lebanon, Venezuela—these are not oddities from far-flung dysfunctions. They are reminders. Lessons, if we choose to heed them. And what's more disconcerting is that the tremors are already making their way through the core economies. Japan's debt now towers above 260% of GDP. The United States has crossed $34 trillion in federal liabilities. The European Central Bank remains mired in a sluggish spiral of stagnation. These aren't background noise—they're the soundtrack of a system that has become abstract to the point of unreality: ballooning debt, anaemic productivity, monetary manoeuvres that resemble stagecraft more than policy.

At the heart of these systems lies not inherent robustness, but the art of coherent storytelling. Governments assure us they're in control: inflation is temporary, debt is sustainable, markets will sort themselves out. Central banks wear the mask of steely calm. The financial sector, meanwhile, packages risk in elegant wrappers—triple-A ratings, well-curated indices, algorithmic portfolios. But beyond the performance, the machinery is increasingly opaque, increasingly brittle. We are entrusting institutions to manage layers of complexity they neither fully understand nor convincingly command.

Worse still, that fragility is often masked by the appearance of diversification. Many investors breathe easy simply because their portfolios contain a mix: a bit of equity, some bonds, perhaps a mutual fund or two. But if every one of those assets is priced in the same currency, and responds to the same macroeconomic levers, what exactly is being diversified? If the whole portfolio hinges on the continued credibility of central banks and fiat infrastructure, the risk isn't spread—it's concentrated. You might as well be betting everything on the same horse and calling it a strategy.

This is why the myth of safe systems is so pernicious. It seduces with the promise of security while leaving real vulnerabilities unaddressed. It tells individuals, families, even institutions, that they are shielded—when in truth they are exposed across multiple vectors: inflation, sovereign debt, institutional dysfunction, and perhaps most subtly, their own psychological inertia. The mantra that "governments won't let it fail" becomes an excuse not to act, not to plan. Yet history doesn't pause to accommodate those who delay preparation until after the breach.

There are precedents, for anyone willing to look. The late 1920s rode a wave of optimism—technological leaps, easy credit, financial deregulation. Until they didn't. The 1970s saw confidence in monetary policy dissolve into stagflation and a gold standard collapse. The 2008 crisis revealed how entangled, and how fragile, the banking sector had become. In every case, people believed the system was sound—right up until it wasn't. Belief gave way to panic. Then came the reckoning.

We are, in many respects, approaching a similar threshold. Excess liquidity. Interest rates distorted by years of emergency policy. Asset prices levitating beyond reason. Markets increasingly driven not by fundamentals but by algorithms and central bank signals. Layer on political instability, social fragmentation, and global volatility, and the picture sharpens. Different instruments, same story. The rhythms may vary, but the structure feels familiar. And so too, inevitably, will the consequences.

But this chapter is not a manifesto of doom. It is a lens—an invitation to see with greater clarity. By dissecting the emotional and institutional dynamics of belief-based finance, the aim here is to strip away the convenient fictions and replace them with frameworks grounded in durability. Because the essence of wealth preservation isn't faith in systems—it's allegiance to structure. Thoughtfully selected, independently valuable assets that do not require institutional competence to retain worth.

Toward that end, we will turn a sharper eye to three illusions that underpin conventional portfolio thinking. The first: fiat durability—the confidence that currencies can be reshaped indefinitely with no consequence. The second: institutional reliability—the belief that those in charge will always act rationally and remain solvent. And the third: diversification—a notion often practised more in form than in function, masking systemic exposure beneath a thin veil of variety.

These are difficult truths, no question. But they're also emancipating. Because once we stop assigning our security to institutions we neither control nor fully understand, we reclaim something vital: our capacity to think and act independently. The power to become not just participants, but designers. Not merely investors, but stewards.

This chapter won't hand you a list of things to fear. That would be far too easy. Instead, it will offer a way to think—more rigorously, more courageously. You needn't abandon markets, nor disengage from the broader economy. But you *should* challenge your assumptions. See the cracks others refuse to acknowledge. Build around what endures.

In the end, the myth of institutional safety isn't kept alive by grand deception—it survives on habit. On the human preference for the path of least resistance, for trusting what has worked so far, for hoping that tomorrow will look like yesterday. This chapter is a challenge to that habit. Not a rejection of the system per se, but a refusal to be confined by it.

Because once you realise that these institutions are not immutable laws but collective constructs—once you see them as belief systems, not certainties—you stop asking if they will last forever. And you start asking, more wisely: *what will I do when they don't?* That shift, quietly made, is where resilience begins. And from there, so does something more lasting.

The Psychology of Dependence

There is a deeply unsettling truth at the heart of modern finance: many people trust systems that have repeatedly failed them. They do so not because they are uninformed, nor necessarily because they are naive, but because they are human—driven as much by emotion and social dynamics as by logic or evidence. The enduring faith in institutional safety nets—state pensions, fiat currencies, national banks, regulated investment schemes—persists not despite history, but in *defiance* of it.

This chapter asks a difficult but necessary question: *Why do we cling to these institutions, even after they have proven untrustworthy?* The answer, as we will see, lies not in the numbers, but in the narratives. Hope, denial, and social conformity do not merely colour individual decisions; they *anchor* entire societies in financial behaviours that are fundamentally misaligned with reality.

To understand this psychological dependence, we must first appreciate the emotional terrain it occupies. Money is never just money. It is safety, identity, power, agency, and, for many, self-worth. Institutions that promise to protect one's financial future are, by extension, guardians of one's existential stability. To question them is not merely an intellectual exercise—it is an act of psychological upheaval. It invites uncertainty where there was previously structure, and for most, that invitation is unwelcome.

Consider the phenomenon of *optimism bias*—the cognitive tendency to believe that negative events are less likely to happen to oneself than to others. In financial behaviour, this manifests as a persistent faith that "our country won't collapse," "our banks are different," or "our generation's pensions will be honoured." Even as inflation eats away at purchasing power, as national debts climb past sustainable thresholds, and as banks require ever more complex regulations to stay solvent, many continue to behave as though the future will resemble the past. This is not irrationality in the purest sense; it is *defensive rationalisation*. Hope is cheaper than preparation.

This psychological insulation is reinforced by *normalcy bias*, the internalised belief that because something has never happened to *us*, it won't. This bias does not just delay reaction to systemic risk; it actively suppresses our willingness to *see* the warning signs. Citizens of pre-crisis Venezuela or Cyprus did not wake up one day to a financial apocalypse; they lived for months, sometimes years, in a state of suspended disbelief, even as capital controls, hyperinflation, and institutional rot became increasingly visible. Denial is not passive—it is performative. People mimic calm because calmness itself becomes currency.

But perhaps the most insidious psychological force underpinning dependence on institutional safety nets is *social proof*. Human beings are profoundly influenced by the behaviour and attitudes of those around them, particularly in situations of uncertainty. If everyone in your social and professional circles contributes to a pension fund, holds most of their savings in fiat currency, and trusts their bank's solvency, *you will too*. The power of consensus cannot be overstated. It is not just behavioural—it is epistemological. We take social agreement as a substitute for independent verification. If no one is sounding the alarm, we assume there is no fire.

This conformity is particularly dangerous when the institutions themselves are engaged in narrative management. Governments and central banks have long relied on *rhetorical stability* to maintain market calm—forward guidance, confidence signalling, even selective transparency. Markets do not just react to interest rates or employment figures; they react to tone, posture, language. When the Federal Reserve says inflation is "transitory," or when a central bank insists a banking crisis is "contained," they are not making predictions—they are issuing *emotional prescriptions*. Their goal is not to inform but to soothe.

And people comply, often willingly. There is a kind of quiet relief in being told that things are under control. This deference becomes especially acute in times of broader societal stress—during recessions, pandemics, or geopolitical instability—when individuals are most in need of reassurance and least equipped to evaluate risk. In such conditions, the psychological reward of trust outweighs the intellectual discomfort of scrutiny.

The effect is that institutions become *emotional surrogates*. Central banks take on the role of paternal protectors, governments become financial caregivers, and regulatory bodies serve as moral referees. Dependence, then, is not merely a failure of critical thinking—it is a displacement of responsibility. Individuals outsource financial vigilance to entities they assume are better informed, better resourced, and better motivated to act on their behalf. But these assumptions often fail to withstand scrutiny.

History offers ample evidence of the costs of such trust. The Argentine peso has collapsed multiple times within a single generation. In 2001, Argentina froze bank accounts, confiscated savings, and restructured sovereign debt, leaving millions financially stranded. Yet to this day, many Argentinians continue to hold pesos, open domestic accounts, and appeal to the same state apparatus that once betrayed them. Not because they have forgotten, but because the alternatives are psychologically taxing and socially marginal. Similarly, the Cypriot banking crisis of 2013—where depositors in certain banks were forced to "bail in" their own institutions—should have been a watershed moment in rethinking custodial risk. And yet, little structural behavioural change followed among global retail savers.

This behavioural inertia points to a deeper truth: *reliance on institutional systems is not sustained by evidence, but by emotional convenience*. It is easier to believe that the system will hold than to reckon with the possibility that it might not. It is easier to criticise those who prepare—gold holders, Bitcoin proponents, real estate decentralisers—as paranoid or fringe than to interrogate one's own fragilities.

But perhaps the most troubling consequence of this psychological dependence is that it limits innovation in personal finance. When the majority trust that retirement will be handled by a pension system, that currency will hold value because it always has, and that banks will never become inaccessible, *they do not build backup plans*. They do not develop the habits, acquire the knowledge, or seek the autonomy that more resilient wealth design demands. The psychological architecture of dependence stunts intellectual and strategic growth. It leaves people not just exposed, but *unprepared* to imagine life outside the safety net.

To move beyond this dependence, individuals must be willing to confront discomfort—intellectually and emotionally. This involves three essential shifts. First, a revaluation of risk: understanding that systemic risk is often invisible until it is not, and that diversification must include systems as well as sectors. Second, the cultivation of epistemic humility: acknowledging that just because something hasn't happened does not mean it cannot, and that historical memory should be a guide, not a museum. And third, the restoration of personal agency: refusing to outsource financial sovereignty to systems that are neither infallible nor immune from conflict, capture, or collapse.

This does not mean abandoning all institutional engagement, nor does it imply retreat into cynicism. Rather, it is a call to *mature engagement*—to participate with eyes open, safeguards in place, and exit options identified. To hold assets outside the banking system is not an act of rebellion; it is an act of prudence. To explore crypto custody or foreign property is not extremism; it is *contingency planning.* These are the behaviours of adults who understand that complexity is not the same as control.

The psychology of dependence is ultimately about stories—stories we are told, stories we repeat, and stories we internalise. Breaking from those narratives requires a deeper story: one of autonomy, foresight, and a deliberate refusal to confuse stability with permanence. Only then can individuals begin to construct a financial life that is not only technically diversified, but *structurally liberated* from the myths that keep so many complacent.

It is not easy to walk away from the comfort of consensus. But history belongs to those who do.

The Fragile Architecture of Trust

If the modern economy were a machine, its most essential component wouldn't be oil, capital, or labour—it would be belief. Not belief in a divine sense, but the quietly powerful, socially reinforced trust that currencies will hold value, that banks will honour withdrawals, and that governments will act as rational stewards of public resources. This trust is so deeply woven into the mechanics of everyday life that it is almost invisible. Yet it is *astonishingly fragile.* The global financial system rests not on immutable truths, but on *shared confidence*—confidence that can shift suddenly, with consequences that reverberate far beyond markets.

Fiat currency, commercial banking, and central governance are often discussed as if they were structurally secure systems—rational, regulated, and responsive. But this perception obscures a more uncomfortable reality: these institutions derive stability not from intrinsic qualities, but from *perceived legitimacy*. They are, in essence, consensus-based belief systems, closer to social contracts than engineered fortresses. When enough people believe, they function. When that belief erodes—even incrementally—the edifice begins to crack.

To understand why, we must begin with money itself. Fiat currency—by definition—has no intrinsic value. It is not backed by gold, silver, or any tangible commodity. Its worth is a function of state decree and public trust. A £20 note is worth £20 not because of the paper or ink, but because we collectively *agree* to treat it as such. This agreement is not legally optional; it is economically necessary. And yet, it is not indestructible. It can be damaged by inflation, undermined by reckless policy, or rendered meaningless by political collapse.

The 20th and early 21st centuries are replete with examples of this dynamic in motion. The German mark during the Weimar Republic, the Zimbabwean dollar under Mugabe, the Venezuelan bolívar in the last decade—each began as a functioning national currency. Each succumbed to hyperinflation when state mismanagement intersected with a loss of public confidence. The pattern is not linear; it is cascading. Trust holds until it doesn't—and once breached, restoration becomes nearly impossible without radical reform.

The same logic applies to the banking system. Commercial banks operate on what is effectively a trust-based promise: that depositors will not all demand their money at once. This is the cornerstone of *fractional reserve banking*, a system in which banks keep only a small fraction of their depositors' funds on hand, lending out the rest in pursuit of profit. This model works brilliantly—until it doesn't. Bank runs are not caused by insolvency in the technical sense, but by *expectations of insolvency*. Fear, not fact, is the primary accelerant.

Consider Northern Rock in 2007. A reasonably well-capitalised British bank, it collapsed not because it was bankrupt on paper, but because depositors lost faith in its liquidity and withdrew funds en masse. The bank's downfall triggered broader distrust in the financial sector and presaged the global crisis that would erupt the following year. Central to this cascade was not the collapse of balance sheets, but the collapse of *narratives*—the belief that banks were fundamentally sound, that regulators were competent, and that depositors need not worry.

This architecture of belief extends upwards to central banks and sovereign governments. These institutions enjoy what economists call "monopoly power" over currency issuance and monetary policy. But their authority is only as strong as the legitimacy they project. The Bank of England, the European Central Bank, the Federal Reserve—each depends on its reputation for impartiality, expertise, and coherence. When that reputation falters, so does the efficacy of its actions. Interest rate announcements and quantitative easing lose potency if markets begin to doubt the competence or intent behind them.

We witnessed the precarious nature of this trust during the UK's "mini-budget" crisis in September 2022. The Truss government proposed aggressive, unfunded tax cuts without clear economic rationale or market signalling. The pound dropped precipitously. Gilt yields spiked. The Bank of England was forced into emergency bond-buying to stabilise pensions. The entire episode lasted mere days, but it laid bare how quickly markets can punish perceived institutional incoherence. The fragility was not in the budget numbers alone, but in the *belief* that the UK government and central bank were aligned, rational actors. That belief evaporated—and with it, market confidence.

These examples underscore a broader point: *trust is not a renewable resource; it is a contingent one.* It is not guaranteed by status, longevity, or even legality. It must be earned and maintained through consistency, transparency, and restraint. Yet many of the world's most powerful financial actors treat it as a given—as something automatic, rather than something that can be forfeited.

This creates a dangerous asymmetry. Institutions are granted expansive powers under the assumption of trustworthiness, but the mechanisms to rebuild that trust once it is broken are weak or non-existent. Citizens and investors have little recourse when central banks pivot without warning, when governments restructure debt, or when banks close overnight under duress. The social contract is implicit, not enforceable. And this asymmetry is growing more acute as financial complexity accelerates.

Today's financial architecture is more opaque than ever. Algorithmic trading, shadow banking, synthetic derivatives—these are not instruments that invite public comprehension or confidence. They demand a level of trust in institutional competence that is increasingly difficult to justify. When the 2008 crisis revealed that banks did not fully understand their own risk exposure, or that regulators were asleep at the wheel, public faith should have collapsed more comprehensively. That it did not speaks less to institutional strength than to collective inertia. People *need* to believe. The alternative is too destabilising to contemplate.

And so we arrive at the central paradox: *the more fragile the system, the more belief it requires*. Fiat money must be believed in more devoutly than gold-backed currency. Banks must be trusted more explicitly than decentralised, self-custodied systems. Governments must inspire more confidence even as their fiscal positions deteriorate. The whole structure is a kind of inverse pyramid—balanced not on hard assets or enforceable contracts, but on the psychology of the masses.

This is not a call for alarmism. Institutions still matter. They enable coordination, enforce contracts, and facilitate stability when functioning well. But to ignore their contingent nature is to confuse power with permanence. Every major economic collapse of the last century has been preceded not by war or catastrophe, but by *misplaced faith*—faith in unsustainable policies, dishonest accounting, or institutions that failed to adapt.

What, then, are the practical implications of understanding institutions as belief systems?

First, individuals must design their financial lives with *structural independence* in mind. This means holding assets that do not rely entirely on the continuity of institutional trust—physical gold, real property, decentralised crypto, or offshore mechanisms governed by alternative jurisdictions. Second, it means evaluating policy not by its intent, but by its *credibility*. Who is making the decision? Under what constraints? With what track record? Finally, it means cultivating a deeper financial literacy—not just of markets, but of the *behavioural and institutional dynamics* that underpin them.

Trust is necessary for modern economies to function. But blind trust is not resilience. It is exposure. Recognising the fragile architecture of institutional legitimacy is not cynicism—it is realism. And it is the starting point for building a portfolio, and a worldview, that does not depend on the uninterrupted competence of others.

If the modern financial system is held together by trust, then the intelligent actor does not seek to destroy it. They seek to *hedge it*. Not out of fear, but out of understanding. Because systems built on perception are not protected by permanence. They are protected by *preparedness*.

The Return of Economic Unpredictability

Economic stability is often remembered more vividly than it is understood. The decades following the Second World War, particularly the stretch from the 1950s through the early 2000s in many developed economies, cultivated a deep-seated belief in the manageability of macroeconomic systems. Growth was expected. Inflation, when it occurred, was temporary. Recessions were cyclical, not existential. Policymakers were presumed to be rational custodians of progress, armed with fiscal levers and monetary tools that, when deployed skilfully, could prevent catastrophe. But this confidence—resting heavily on a handful of favourable decades—was always a fragile inheritance. It downplayed the deeper truth revealed repeatedly throughout history: that *economic order is more often the exception than the rule.* And when disorder returns, it rarely knocks—it breaks the door down.

We are living through a reintroduction. What was once dismissed as outlier volatility—currency collapse, sovereign debt crises, runaway inflation—is beginning to reappear not just in the global periphery, but in the very economies that long styled themselves as anchors of stability. The United States, the eurozone, the United Kingdom, Japan—none are immune. Inflation, once declared dead, has reasserted itself. Public debt levels have reached peacetime highs. Central banks, once viewed as dispassionate technocrats, now oscillate between stimulus and correction in increasingly reactive cycles. Volatility is no longer confined to emerging markets or crisis headlines; it is embedded in the financial architecture of the developed world.

To make sense of this return, we must revisit what history has been trying to tell us all along. Economic collapses do not begin with panic—they begin with *overreach*. Governments overextend their promises, central banks overestimate their models, and populations over-trust the appearance of stability. This pattern, visible across centuries and continents, is not ideological. It is behavioural. When a nation begins to believe that rules no longer apply—that deficits do not matter, that currencies are infinitely elastic, that growth can be engineered without cost—it sets in motion forces that eventually exceed its control.

Take the case of the Roman Empire in the third century CE. Facing military overspending and a collapsing tax base, Roman emperors began to debase their currency—the denarius—replacing silver with cheaper metals while maintaining face value. For a time, the illusion held. But inflation surged, trade collapsed, and the empire fractured. The economic mismanagement was not born of ignorance but of political necessity, justified by short-term gains. The echoes are unmistakable in modern fiscal debates where long-term solvency is routinely sacrificed for electoral expediency.

Fast forward to the 20th century, and the same anatomy recurs. The Weimar Republic in post-World War I Germany is often reduced to a cautionary tale about printing money. But beneath the hyperinflation lies a story of political paralysis, war reparations, and a desperate attempt to preserve legitimacy through financial distortion. The consequences were not merely economic; they were psychological and cultural. When citizens lose trust in their currency, they do not simply adjust their budgets—they change their worldview.

The late 1990s Asian financial crisis offered another iteration. Triggered by unsustainable borrowing and rigid exchange-rate regimes, countries like Thailand, Indonesia, and South Korea experienced capital flight, currency collapse, and deep recessions. For years prior, these nations were celebrated as economic miracles—proof that globalisation and rapid development could coexist without structural risk. That optimism proved misplaced, as hot money evaporated, IMF programmes enforced austerity, and entire middle classes saw their wealth evaporate almost overnight.

And yet perhaps the most illustrative case for today's reader is the 2008 global financial crisis. At its core was a system that believed it had outgrown unpredictability. Derivatives were engineered to distribute risk, central banks provided unlimited liquidity, and housing prices were presumed to rise indefinitely. The collapse was not the product of one bad actor or one faulty product—it was the culmination of *systemic faith in the unbreakability of the system itself.* Credit ratings, regulatory frameworks, and interbank lending all depended on mutual trust that, once questioned, became irrecoverable.

Today, we see strikingly similar patterns resurfacing under different guises. Public and private debt levels have ballooned far beyond pre-2008 benchmarks. Asset bubbles—particularly in equities, real estate, and speculative digital assets—have been fuelled by more than a decade of near-zero interest rates and central bank balance sheet expansion. Policymakers, faced with the political costs of contraction, have repeatedly opted to delay structural correction. The belief that "this time is different" lingers in investor memos and public policy alike.

But economic history is not circular; it is *patterned.* It does not repeat like a script, but it rhymes through incentives, responses, and constraints. Every collapse has its own vocabulary, but the grammar remains constant: *overreach, denial, delay, rupture.* And the rupture always seems impossible until it is already under way.

The global response to the COVID-19 pandemic further deepened this trajectory. Emergency spending, which was necessary in many respects, also entrenched a new precedent: that vast fiscal deficits could be run without immediate consequence. Central banks stepped in to monetise debt on an extraordinary scale. Bond markets, placated by low yields and faith in institutional control, absorbed the shock. But the longer-term costs are now emerging. Inflation has returned, wages have struggled to keep pace, and public trust in both economic stewardship and future security is fraying.

This raises a critical question: *Why does unpredictability return, even in systems designed to suppress it?* The answer lies in the limits of technocracy. Economic models, however sophisticated, are abstractions of behaviour, not replacements for it. They function within assumed boundaries—stable politics, cooperative global trade, rational consumers. When those boundaries shift, the models fail. Yet policy continues to rely on them, creating a widening gap between projected outcomes and lived realities.

Moreover, the illusion of control often generates complacency. Low volatility is mistaken for low risk. Stability becomes self-reinforcing until it breeds the very conditions—leverage, speculation, concentrated bets—that guarantee instability. The current fragility of the global economy is not due to randomness; it is the *product* of decisions made in pursuit of order.

This is not a call to abandon markets or reject globalisation. But it is a warning against the seductive certainty that has gripped much of the financial and policy elite for too long. Economic unpredictability is not a bug in the system—it is a signal that the system has exceeded its design limits.

What, then, should the intelligent reader do with this understanding?

First, recognise that predictability was always more precarious than it appeared. A generation raised on central bank omnipotence and fiscal firepower must now recalibrate its assumptions. Diversification is no longer a matter of asset classes within one paradigm; it must now encompass *entire paradigms*—different monetary systems, alternative jurisdictions, decentralised technologies, and non-correlated stores of value.

Second, cultivate institutional scepticism—not as cynicism, but as strategic maturity. Do not assume that governments will always act coherently, that currencies will always behave predictably, or that markets will always reflect fundamentals. Build resilience accordingly.

Third, reconnect economic thinking with historical memory. There is nothing radical about preparing for unpredictability. It is, in fact, the most *rational* response to a world where overreach and denial remain evergreen features of governance.

The return of economic unpredictability is not a singular crisis; it is a structural condition. It demands more than financial literacy—it requires *strategic realism*. And those who understand the cycles of trust, overconfidence, and collapse will not only survive it—they will design around it. That, ultimately, is what this book proposes. Not a rejection of the system, but an upgrade in perspective—one rooted in history, informed by current signals, and prepared for what happens when the improbable becomes inevitable.

False Diversification

There is perhaps no concept more lauded—and more misunderstood—in modern portfolio theory than diversification. It is the mantra of wealth managers, the comfort blanket of retail investors, and the default prescription of financial advisors seeking to reduce exposure. Diversify, and you'll be safe. Spread your bets, and you'll lower your risk. These reassurances are so culturally embedded they rarely receive serious scrutiny. Yet, upon closer examination, many portfolios that appear diversified on the surface are in fact *concentrated expressions of systemic fragility*. They are diversified in form, but not in function. This is what we must now call out with precision: *false diversification.*

False diversification is not a matter of poor mathematics or naive asset allocation. It is subtler than that. It arises when investors hold a broad mix of assets that are all—directly or indirectly—anchored to the same economic engine, priced in the same currency, influenced by the same monetary policy, and vulnerable to the same institutional risks. Superficially, it may appear that risk has been spread across different vehicles—stocks, bonds, REITs, mutual funds—but structurally, these assets are often just different branches of the same tree. When the trunk shakes, all the branches fall.

To grasp this, we must begin by interrogating what diversification is *meant* to achieve. At its core, diversification is about reducing *unsystematic* risk—the idiosyncratic volatility of individual companies, sectors, or asset classes. This principle holds firm within a single system. A portfolio that includes both energy and technology equities, for example, may better withstand a sector-specific downturn. But diversification across similar systemic exposures does *nothing* to hedge *systematic* risk—the risk of collapse or dysfunction within the entire system itself.

This became brutally clear in 2008. Many portfolios deemed "diversified" collapsed in unison. Equities fell, corporate bonds followed, real estate plunged, and even traditionally conservative assets like money market funds required government intervention to remain solvent. What investors discovered was that their supposed diversification was *correlated dependency*. Everything was tied to the same underlying assumptions: functioning credit markets, stable currencies, and uninterrupted liquidity. When those assumptions broke down, correlations that were historically uncorrelated moved sharply together.

The illusion of safety had been manufactured through statistical back-testing and historical models that presumed normal distributions and ignored fat-tail events. But crises are never statistical anomalies—they are structural awakenings. When trust falters at the systemic level, even the most balanced portfolio within that system becomes vulnerable. You cannot hedge systemic collapse with instruments that are themselves part of the system.

False diversification is further exacerbated by the dominance of fiat currencies in global pricing. A portfolio might include emerging market ETFs, U.S. Treasury bonds, European equities, and real estate investment trusts from Asia. On paper, this appears geographically and sectorally diverse. But if every one of these assets is denominated in U.S. dollars or another fiat currency—subject to inflation, central bank intervention, and sovereign debt risk—they are all exposed to *monetary debasement* and *currency failure.* A global basket of fiat-priced assets does not escape fiat vulnerability; it amplifies it.

This is not merely a theoretical concern. In recent years, the purchasing power of major currencies has quietly deteriorated, masked by nominal asset appreciation. Central banks, in response to successive crises, have inflated their balance sheets to levels that would have been politically unthinkable just a generation ago. Quantitative easing, yield curve control, and artificially low interest rates have distorted asset prices across the board. Under these conditions, traditional diversification fails not because the theory is wrong, but because the environment has changed. When central bank policy becomes the dominant force across all asset classes, independence between them collapses.

We must also consider the behavioural and institutional components of false diversification. Many retail investors, guided by conventional wisdom and modern portfolio theory, rely heavily on index funds and ETFs. These instruments promise low cost, broad exposure, and passive risk management. But their composition is inherently systemic. The S&P 500, for instance, is deeply concentrated in a handful of mega-cap tech firms. Its performance is tightly correlated with broader market sentiment, U.S. monetary policy, and credit availability. During a systemic crisis, it is not a hedge—it is a thermometer.

Similarly, bond portfolios that include sovereign debt are often assumed to be safe counterweights to equity exposure. Yet sovereign bonds carry their own systemic risk: inflation, interest rate spikes, or even selective default. The notion that government bonds are "risk-free" is a cultural myth, not a financial truth. When interest rates rise sharply—as witnessed in 2022 and 2023—bond portfolios can suffer severe mark-to-market losses, particularly when duration is long and yields are artificially suppressed by policy.

Even real estate, often touted as a tangible hedge against market instability, can become a channel of false diversification. Real estate investment trusts (REITs), for example, are heavily influenced by capital markets, credit conditions, and monetary policy. Private property, meanwhile, is vulnerable to taxation, regulation, and geopolitical risk. In many countries, real estate booms have been sustained by low interest rates and central bank liquidity—conditions that cannot be assumed to persist indefinitely. When those factors reverse, real estate can become highly illiquid, even in supposedly stable jurisdictions.

What this means is that diversification, if not structurally informed, becomes a form of *risk disguise*. It soothes the investor with variety while exposing them to concentration they do not see. A truly resilient portfolio does not merely spread capital across different sectors; it allocates capital across *different assumptions*. This is the core insight that separates robust diversification from its false counterpart.

To illustrate: gold is not correlated to equities, not reliant on central bank credibility, and not subject to counterparty default. It operates on a different set of premises. Cryptoassets like Bitcoin, though volatile and still evolving, offer monetary characteristics that are deliberately decoupled from state control. Certain types of international real estate—held in politically diverse jurisdictions—can offer exposure to uncorrelated legal and fiscal environments. These assets are not merely different in asset class—they are different in *systemic alignment*. They do not assume the continued solvency, rationality, or stability of the same institutions that manage fiat liquidity, public debt, and equity issuance.

Diversification, then, must be redefined. It is not an aesthetic of variety. It is a design of *redundancy and independence*. The purpose is not to optimise for return under ideal conditions, but to maintain functionality under adverse ones. In a world of rising geopolitical tensions, institutional fragility, and financial repression, false diversification offers only the illusion of preparedness. True diversification asks harder questions: *What happens if the system fails? What if fiat confidence breaks? What if inflation is not transitory, but structural?*

This may seem like a pessimistic framing, but it is in fact a disciplined one. Resilience is not born of fear; it is born of clarity. Investors who build portfolios across *systems*—fiat and non-fiat, centralised and decentralised, regulated and sovereign-independent—are not doomsayers. They are realists. They are preparing not for collapse, but for continuity under disruption.

To move from false diversification to structural resilience, investors must interrogate each asset not just for what it earns, but for what it *assumes*. Does it assume liquidity? Credibility? Policy coherence? Legal stability? When those assumptions are tested—as history promises they will be—the architecture of the portfolio will matter more than the names in it.

The financial industry has excelled at marketing complexity. But the future will reward *clarity of architecture*. In a fragile world, resilience is not a product—it is a perspective. And it begins by seeing through the façade of diversification that flatters, but does not fortify.

Chapter 2
The Philosophy of Financial Sovereignty

Every financial system—regardless of its digital prowess or historical weight—depends, in the end, on your quiet assent. You agree, often without much thought, to store your life's work in a currency whose rules are set by others. You accept terms crafted by entities you didn't vote for, enforced through mechanisms you cannot inspect. You rely on a machinery so vast and opaque that its inner workings are more myth than method. And for most, this isn't just convenient—it's invisible. Yet that invisibility is beginning to fray. Increasingly, the real question isn't whether to participate in the system, but whether one is still free to walk away from it.

So this chapter begins from a premise that may sound bold, even subversive: you have the right to opt out. Not out of cynicism or anger, but as a matter of principle. Financial sovereignty isn't simply about exotic asset allocations or hedging strategies—it's a philosophical claim. It demands an answer to a deceptively simple question: who owns your labour, your savings, your risk profile, your future? It challenges the quiet assumption that one must comply with centralised systems merely because they've always been there. And it advances a moral argument—beyond the technical or tactical—for developing viable alternatives when the incumbent frameworks cease to deserve your allegiance.

At its core, financial sovereignty means retaining the option to say no. No to obfuscated policy. No to inflation that punishes savers to reward spendthrifts. No to institutional fragility disguised as stability. And above all, no to the notion that wealth is whatever central banks decree it to be. To opt out is not to disengage from society—it is to ask more of it. It is a deliberate act of reclaiming agency over how you store, move, and manifest value. That kind of agency is not a luxury. It's foundational.

Take, for example, the distinction between currency and value—terms often used interchangeably, yet fundamentally different. Currency is a convention, an agreement. It functions only so long as enough people believe in it. Value, on the other hand, can stand on its own. A tract of farmland, a bar of gold, a piece of code, or a learned skill—these hold significance whether or not a central database recognises them. Wealth, when understood correctly, isn't a string of digits on a glowing screen. It's something you can stand on, build with, or trade even if the system itself goes dark.

This distinction between intrinsic and extrinsic forms of wealth lies at the heart of financial self-determination. Fiat currency is extrinsic—it holds value only by decree. Equities, though dynamic, rely on the machinery of exchanges and the mood of markets. Bank deposits, for all their seeming solidity, are contingent IOUs. By contrast, sovereign financial strategies seek assets defined by intrinsic features: physical custody, decentralisation, portability, or utility that endures without third-party validation. The question isn't whether money will still exist in a crisis—it's whether your form of it will still be meaningful.

Yet to embrace sovereignty is to shoulder a particular kind of burden. It's not just a shift in portfolio construction—it's a shift in accountability. You gain control, yes—but also responsibility. When you hold your own private keys, you hold your own risk. There's no claims desk for mislaid seed phrases. No helpline if your decentralised asset becomes irretrievable. No central banker to blame when your gold, too cleverly hidden, becomes irrecoverable. Sovereignty does not coddle. It expects preparedness. It rewards attention. And it forces a reckoning with a deeply modern delusion: that someone else should bear the consequences of your economic life.

This burden—though weighty—is also clarifying. It fosters a mindset rooted in caution, yes, but also in competence. It weeds out naivety and replaces it with strategic curiosity. Sovereignty makes students of us all, not because we are forced to learn, but because we choose to understand what was previously ignored. It isn't driven by a fear of collapse so much as a refusal to be caught unready.

What's more, mainstream financial thinking rarely touches the ethical fibres that sovereignty lays bare. We're told to diversify, contribute, dollar-cost average—as though these habits are apolitical, neutral, even virtuous. But little is said about the moral hazards beneath them. What does it mean, ethically, to invest in a system where governments are rewarded for debasing their obligations? Or where banks, incentivised to leverage to the hilt, expect the public to absorb their missteps? Sovereignty invites a different question: Is the system worthy of our dependency? And if not, then what?

To pose such questions isn't to retreat into cynicism—it's to engage with reality at a deeper level. The sovereign actor isn't disengaged from the world—they're simply no longer passive within it. They remain active, informed, pragmatic. They don't reject institutions outright, but they insist those institutions earn their trust. They build pathways of value that don't require permission slips to function.

History is generous with its warnings. In 2013, Cypriots saw their savings confiscated overnight under the banner of stability. In 2016, Indians watched the vast majority of their cash holdings turned to wastepaper within a single evening. In Lebanon, a collapsing regime began throttling withdrawals, as official exchange rates lost touch with lived reality. In each case, citizens were reminded—often brutally—that access does not mean ownership. That rights without enforcement are merely conveniences.

And yet, today's tools allow for more than just lamentation. The architecture for exit has evolved. Cryptocurrencies, when used judiciously, enable private transfer of value without central intermediaries. Tokenised assets offer ownership unfettered by national borders. Physical bullion, offshore structures, and well-placed real estate holdings act as bulwarks against fiscal overreach. These aren't rebellious gestures—they are rational hedges. They are instruments of sovereignty for those who refuse to let tomorrow be dictated solely by institutions with yesterday's interests in mind.

Are these methods without risk? Certainly not. Crypto can be exploited. Properties can be expropriated. Laws, as ever, are one regime away from rewriting. But sovereignty was never about eliminating risk—it was about owning it. True resilience doesn't come from the illusion of safety. It comes from redundancy, from layered design, from the quiet discipline of diversified jurisdiction and decentralised access.

This chapter doesn't offer financial advice in the conventional sense. What it offers is a reframing. It holds up a mirror to the contracts—often silent—we've made with the systems that govern our financial lives. It asks whether those contracts still serve us, or whether they merely bind us to a fading past. It challenges us to exchange complacency for control, and trust for understanding. Because the truth is, financial sovereignty isn't a niche concern—it's the bedrock of any serious attempt at lasting autonomy.

You'll come away not merely with a list of instruments, but with a lens. A way of seeing the financial landscape with new eyes—one that perceives value as something active and chosen, not merely inherited or assigned. One that views markets not as inevitabilities, but as agreements. And one that treats the act of opting out not as escapism, but as an affirmation of one's ability to build better.

If the prior chapter dismantled our illusions of security, this one lays down the scaffolding for deliberate independence. Because wealth that isn't sovereign is never truly yours—it's on lease, subject to the goodwill of systems you don't control. And waiting for permission to exit is not a plan. Knowing how to leave, and where to land, is.

Wealth as Self-Defence

Most financial advice is framed around aspiration. Invest for retirement. Build generational wealth. Maximise returns. The language is upward-facing—steeped in optimism, growth, and long-term planning. Rarely does anyone tell you, plainly, that financial planning is first and foremost *self-defence*. Not metaphorically, not abstractly, but concretely: a means of protecting yourself against coercion, instability, and theft—whether by inflation, regulation, institutional collapse, or policy manipulation. In a world where monetary policy is increasingly experimental and governments are comfortable blurring the lines between taxation and confiscation, wealth is no longer merely a sign of success. It is a form of *personal infrastructure*—a firewall between your autonomy and the arbitrary pressures of a volatile system.

This reframing is essential. Too often, the pursuit of financial literacy is treated as a lifestyle enhancement rather than a security imperative. But security, in its broadest and most urgent sense, is the core function of intelligent asset management. When you hold resources that can survive currency debasement, withstand capital controls, and remain liquid in hostile or uncertain jurisdictions, you are not "rich" in the conventional sense. You are *fortified.* And that distinction can be the difference between resilience and exposure when the system begins to fail those who assumed it would protect them.

Let us begin with inflation. It is often dismissed as a background annoyance—an unavoidable side effect of economic growth. Central banks describe it as manageable, even necessary. But inflation, at its core, is *a dilution of your claim on value.* When a currency loses purchasing power, your savings are being quietly devalued. You are being taxed without a vote. Your labour—stored in money—is being eroded not by accident, but by design. This is not a fringe observation. It is a structural reality. Governments inflate because it's easier than raising taxes and more politically palatable than austerity. And most citizens endure it passively because they have few alternatives.

Wealth as self-defence begins with rejecting this passivity. It means holding at least some of your capital in forms that cannot be debased by a central authority—whether that's physical assets like gold, decentralised digital currencies like Bitcoin, or real estate in jurisdictions that cannot unilaterally confiscate it. This is not speculation. It is insulation. You are not betting on collapse—you are building a structure that does not collapse *with* everything else.

But inflation is only one threat. Regulation—particularly in response to crisis—is another. The financial history of the 20th and 21st centuries is littered with examples of governments responding to economic instability by *tightening control over capital.* In 1933, the United States issued Executive Order 6102, criminalising the private ownership of gold and forcing citizens to sell it to the government at a fixed price. In the aftermath of the 2008 financial crisis, capital controls were reintroduced in multiple European nations, most notably in Cyprus, where bank accounts were frozen and depositors were forced to "bail in" failing institutions. More recently, governments have experimented with transaction monitoring, asset seizure, and retroactive tax policy to fill fiscal gaps in the wake of COVID-19 stimulus spending.

None of this is theoretical. It is precedent. And if history teaches anything, it is this: *the more financially fragile a state becomes, the more aggressively it seeks to control the private wealth of its citizens.* In such environments, wealth is not merely something you own—it is something that can be *taken.* To treat financial planning as self-defence, therefore, is to design your capital not just for appreciation, but for *access, mobility, and legal resilience.*

This changes how we define a "safe" asset. Conventional portfolios often lean heavily on institutional vehicles—pension funds, equities, bank savings, government bonds. These assets are praised for their historical returns, liquidity, and perceived safety. But their underlying condition is *permission.* You need the system to remain functional. You need regulators to remain rational. You need financial institutions to remain solvent. That is a long list of dependencies—and dependencies are vulnerabilities.

By contrast, a sovereign wealth structure privileges *independence over optimisation.* It accepts that a 7% annual return means nothing if you cannot access your capital when needed, or if your account is frozen because of political instability, social unrest, or policy shifts. It understands that *yield without control is risk, not return.*

Consider the growing trend toward programmable finance and central bank digital currencies (CBDCs). While proponents point to the efficiency and transparency of these systems, critics—rightly—highlight the enormous power they grant to issuing authorities. A CBDC can, in theory, be coded to expire, restricted by geography, or denied to specific individuals. If this becomes the standard framework for currency, financial autonomy is no longer a matter of wealth, but of *permission granted.* In that future, the distinction between personal finance and personal freedom collapses. Only those with sovereign tools will retain both.

This is where the philosophical and psychological dimensions of financial self-defence come into sharp focus. To prepare for adversity, you must *believe it is possible.* Most people do not. They assume the worst is behind us, that democracies don't confiscate, and that "it can't happen here." But these are beliefs, not data. And they reflect a form of emotional dependence on institutions that have, time and again, failed their own populations under pressure.

Financial planning as ambition leads to speculation, overexposure, and performance-chasing. Planning as self-defence fosters clarity, selectivity, and realism. It's not about fear. It's about optionality. If your assets are jurisdictionally diversified, legally insulated, and functionally liquid, you are not hostage to policy swings, financial repression, or institutional decay. You can wait out a crisis. You can move. You can say no.

But let us be clear: this posture is not passive. It demands knowledge of law, access to international markets, digital literacy, and a high tolerance for personal responsibility. It is not enough to own the right assets—you must also *understand their vulnerabilities*, protect their custody, and structure them for long-term resilience. This is why most people don't pursue financial sovereignty. It is intellectually and operationally demanding. And it carries no guarantee of immediate reward. But in the right conditions—the ones that matter most—it is the only preparation that works.

The wealth-as-self-defence mindset also alters how we talk about legacy and inheritance. It is not about passing on a number. It is about passing on *capability*—a structure that works independently of trust in governments or markets. A son or daughter who inherits capital but not the mindset to defend it is no safer than one who inherits nothing. Self-defence is not just what you store—it is what you *teach*.

So what are the principles that guide this way of thinking?

First, *visibility is vulnerability*. The more visible your assets are to any one government, the more subject they are to future policy risk.

Second, *liquidity is location-dependent.* What is liquid in one jurisdiction may be inaccessible in another. Cash, crypto, and physical assets have different profiles depending on where and how you intend to use them.

Third, *legal control beats nominal ownership.* If your assets are owned in structures you don't control—funds, pensions, intermediated platforms—they can be frozen, taxed, or diluted with little recourse.

And finally, *self-reliance must be designed, not assumed.* You are not sovereign because you wish to be. You are sovereign because you've planned not to need permission.

In the end, wealth is not your defence because of what it can buy—it is your defence because of what it can *protect you from.* A well-structured portfolio is not a symbol of ambition, but a *quiet refusal to be at the mercy of fragility.* It is not about outperforming someone else. It is about outlasting what most others haven't even begun to imagine.

When the rules change—and they always do—the difference between resilience and regret will not be income. It will be *preparation.* And that begins with seeing wealth not as luxury, status, or speculative vehicle, but as something far more grounded: *your defence against what you cannot predict and no longer trust.*

The Right to Opt Out

A truly free society must allow not only the right to participate in public systems, but the right to *refuse them* when they become coercive, dysfunctional, or fundamentally unaccountable. This principle—the right to opt out—is not merely economic in character. It is political, ethical, and deeply personal. It is the quiet but forceful assertion that consent to a system is not permanent, and that legitimacy cannot be claimed from tradition, scale, or monopoly alone. In finance, this right finds its sharpest edge in decentralised assets—tools that allow individuals to exit legacy structures without permission. These tools are often dismissed as speculative, subversive, or impractical. But at their core, they embody something more radical and essential: *the ethics of exit.*

To opt out is not to reject society. It is to reject *compulsion.* It is to say that systems must earn our participation through transparency, accountability, and alignment with our interests—not demand it through force, inertia, or manufactured dependence. Historically, exit has been a powerful mechanism of reform. When individuals or groups walk away from institutions—whether religious, political, educational, or economic—they force those institutions to reckon with their own legitimacy. They introduce competition where monopoly once reigned. They restore agency where compliance was assumed.

In the context of money and finance, opting out is increasingly feasible—but still culturally fraught. Traditional financial institutions are deeply intertwined with state authority. National currencies are not just economic tools; they are sovereign symbols. Banking systems are tied to regulatory apparatuses. Taxation regimes are constructed on the assumption that all value flows through observable, controllable channels. To opt out of these systems, even partially, is to invite scrutiny. But scrutiny should not be mistaken for immorality. *The freedom to choose how one stores, transacts, and preserves value is a foundational right*, not a technical loophole.

This is where decentralised assets—particularly cryptocurrencies like Bitcoin—challenge the dominant framework. Bitcoin is not simply an alternative currency. It is an opt-out mechanism from a fiat system that requires perpetual inflation, centralised control, and implicit trust in opaque monetary policy. It operates independently of borders, intermediaries, and institutional permission. And that independence is *not* a flaw—it is the point. It forces the uncomfortable but necessary question: *Why should individuals be compelled to rely on financial systems that do not reliably serve their interests, or worse, systematically erode them?*

Critics of decentralised finance often characterise it as anarchic or destabilising. But this critique is based on the assumption that current systems are stable, fair, and ethically grounded. That assumption does not withstand serious scrutiny. Consider the silent confiscation of value through inflation—an unvoted tax on savers and wage earners. Or the increasing use of financial surveillance under the banner of anti-money laundering, which often criminalises privacy rather than crime. Or the weaponisation of payment infrastructure, where individuals and organisations are deplatformed not by court order, but by policy fiat. These are not hypotheticals—they are well-documented features of modern financial governance. *To opt out is to create a peaceful alternative—not to burn the house down, but to build another one outside its reach.*

Historically, those who lacked the ability to exit were the easiest to exploit. Serfs in medieval Europe could not leave their land. Subjects under monarchies could not challenge taxation. Citizens in closed economies had no alternative to their devalued currency. The right to exit is the ultimate check on power. It shifts the burden of justification back to the institution. *If people are leaving, the system must ask why*—not punish their departure. In this light, decentralised assets are not just technical innovations; they are *institutional feedback loops*. They express discontent in measurable, irreversible terms. Every transaction conducted outside the banking system is a vote cast for autonomy.

The moral argument for opt-out finance becomes even clearer when viewed through the lens of coercion. In most modern democracies, participation in fiat currency systems is compulsory. Legal tender laws enforce their use in contracts. Taxes must be paid in state currency. Regulatory regimes require banks to report client behaviour. The individual is treated not as a sovereign economic actor, but as a node within a network they did not design and cannot easily leave. And yet, when individuals *do* seek to exit—even partially—they are often met with moral suspicion: "What do you have to hide?" "Why not trust the system?" These questions reveal how deeply compliance has been normalised. But in a healthy society, the burden of proof should rest not with the individual who desires independence, but with the institution that demands control.

This does not mean all exits are ethically equal. Using decentralised assets to shield criminal behaviour is not a defence of sovereignty—it is a corruption of it. But neither should criminal abuse be used to discredit the tools themselves. Cars can be used for escape, but we do not ban roads. Phones can coordinate crime, but we do not outlaw communication. *The ethical use of opt-out mechanisms must be judged by intent and impact—not by the fear of misuse.*

Nor does opting out imply absolute disengagement. Most people who use decentralised assets still participate in traditional systems to some degree. They pay taxes. They use fiat when necessary. They abide by law. But they also *diversify their risk*. They build parallel strategies. They ensure that if the dominant system becomes intolerable—through mismanagement, overreach, or collapse—they have *options*. This posture is not subversive. It is prudent. It is the same reasoning that drives individuals to hold foreign passports, own land in different jurisdictions, or study in multiple languages. *Optionality is not disloyalty. It is preparation.*

This brings us to the deeper philosophical insight: opting out is not only a right, but a responsibility. If you have the tools, the knowledge, and the access to build independent financial systems—for yourself, your family, or your community—it is ethically coherent to use them. Dependency on flawed systems is not a virtue. And blind trust in central authority, especially when that trust is repeatedly betrayed, is not maturity—it is inertia.

The right to opt out is not exercised through slogans. It is exercised through *design*. It is encoded in the tools we build, the assets we hold, the networks we join, and the habits we cultivate. And it requires more than ideology—it requires competence. To be sovereign in the financial domain is not to shout about freedom. It is to understand cryptography, legal jurisdictions, asset custody, and counterparty risk. It is to be *unimpressed by centralisation* not because it is evil, but because it is brittle. It is to ask not whether something is permitted, but whether it is defensible.

The systems we inherit are not the systems we must remain loyal to. Participation without consent is compliance. And the option to exit—peacefully, legally, and strategically—is the highest expression of a mature society. Decentralised assets offer that option in tangible form. They are not answers to every problem, but they represent a powerful new question: *What if you didn't need permission to protect yourself?*

The right to opt out is not the rejection of order—it is the insistence that order must respect the individual. It is not isolationism—it is interdependence by choice, not mandate. And it is not a radical dream. It is a current reality for those who understand that freedom is not something you wait to be granted. It is something you design into your life while you still have the choice.

Value Beyond Currency

Wealth is not a number. It is not a balance on a screen, a market valuation, or a multi-coloured dashboard in a trading app. These are proxies—sometimes useful, often deceptive. The modern financial system encourages the illusion that value is whatever a central server says it is at a given moment. But beneath that illusion lies a deeper truth: *true wealth must endure beyond the system that accounts for it.* It must possess significance independent of political decrees, market sentiment, or institutional permission. To understand this distinction—between extrinsic and intrinsic value—is not simply an academic exercise. It is a practical necessity for anyone seeking to preserve autonomy in an increasingly fragile economic environment.

Let's begin with the most basic observation: most people measure wealth in units of fiat currency. Pounds, dollars, euros, yen. This is not irrational—it is convenient. Fiat currencies are universally accepted, easy to transact, and required for obligations such as taxes, debt payments, and basic consumption. But the value of a fiat currency is not absolute. It is a contingent agreement between the state and its population, backed by the credibility of its issuers and the continued compliance of its users. When either of these factors breaks down—through inflation, capital controls, or political dysfunction—the perceived wealth denominated in that currency can evaporate without warning.

History offers numerous examples. In Zimbabwe, billionaires could not afford bread. In Weimar Germany, wages were paid twice a day so that workers could spend them before they became worthless. In Venezuela, bolívar balances remained numerically intact even as their purchasing power collapsed. In each case, wealth measured by *number* remained constant, but its *function* disintegrated. That disjunction—between quantity and utility—is the essence of extrinsic value.

Extrinsic value is derivative. It depends on a system to validate it. It is not false, but it is fragile. Stocks are extrinsically valued: their price depends on markets, liquidity, sentiment, and regulatory stability. Bank balances are extrinsically valuable: they are digits on a ledger maintained by an institution that assumes continued solvency. Government bonds, pension entitlements, even retirement portfolios built on passive index strategies—all depend on frameworks that are themselves exposed to centralised policy risk, inflationary drift, or structural dysfunction. When trust in those frameworks is undermined, the assets built upon them become brittle.

Contrast this with *intrinsic value*—assets or capabilities whose worth is not defined by external systems. A productive plot of land. A functioning well. A bar of gold. A decentralised digital asset secured by distributed consensus. A set of skills that generate value across contexts and borders. These are not speculative hedges—they are *anchors*. Their utility or desirability does not vanish when fiat collapses, governments default, or platforms go offline. They can operate without translation. They persist without permission.

Intrinsic value, by definition, is *less dependent*. It does not eliminate risk, but it displaces it away from central failure points. Owning gold does not protect you from theft or confiscation, but it insulates you from currency devaluation. Holding Bitcoin does not guarantee price stability, but it ensures *custodial independence* and *portability*. Owning productive land does not hedge against drought or policy interference, but it provides direct access to a tangible, useful asset. These assets function even when accounting systems fail. They store energy, utility, and optionality—three characteristics that survive across regimes.

This is not a romantic return to barter or an argument for abandoning financial sophistication. It is a sober reevaluation of *what counts as wealth*. A million pounds in an inaccessible account is not wealth. A well-diversified but illiquid portfolio during a capital freeze is not wealth. A pension that can be restructured by legislative decree is not secure. Real wealth *works* under pressure. It translates into control, choice, and stability—*not only when systems function, but especially when they don't.*

This reframing also calls for intellectual honesty in assessing the risks of purely digital, institution-bound wealth. Most people assume their bank balances are sacrosanct, that their brokerage accounts are insulated, and that price feeds reflect reality. But in truth, these are abstractions governed by infrastructure you do not own. Your money is a promise made by a counterparty you must trust. Your assets are entries in databases you do not control. If those systems are interrupted, redefined, or selectively enforced—as they have been in countless historical and contemporary cases—you are not a "holder" of wealth. You are a *dependent.*

The decentralised asset space offers an alternative not just technologically, but philosophically. Bitcoin, for instance, is not valuable because of its price—its price is volatile, often erratic. It is valuable because *its existence does not depend on any one state, institution, or individual.* It is auditable, portable, and functionally neutral. It allows for exit, resilience, and voluntary participation. Its value proposition is not "number go up," but *value without permission.* That distinction matters. It may not replace fiat in all its functions, but it renders fiat *optional.* And in doing so, it introduces a form of wealth that survives across systems.

The broader insight is this: *value that can be revoked is not true wealth.* If your assets can be frozen by a banking glitch, devalued by monetary policy, or rendered worthless by regulatory whim, then you are not sovereign—you are merely included. And inclusion without autonomy is a fragile privilege. True wealth is *design-agnostic.* It works across borders, beyond borders, and even without borders.

This also applies to non-financial assets. Skills, relationships, reputational capital—these can have more real-world value than many so-called "safe" investments. A skilled electrician or software developer will likely remain valuable regardless of currency fluctuations. A tight-knit, trusted community can provide resources, information, and support during institutional breakdown. These forms of wealth do not appear on financial statements, but they are *assets in the deepest sense*. They generate optionality under stress.

None of this is a rejection of conventional finance. It is a recalibration. Fiat currency is useful. Stock markets are productive. Credit can be leveraged responsibly. But these tools must be understood as *conditional*. Their value is predicated on continued participation in a system that may not always be aligned with your interests. The task is not to abandon them but to *supplement them* with assets, strategies, and structures that remain functional when those conditions change.

This perspective also demands a more nuanced understanding of liquidity. Many investors chase liquidity without recognising that liquidity is *contextual*. A market may be liquid today and frozen tomorrow. A highly liquid stock may be worthless during a trading halt. A fully funded pension may be politically restructured in the face of budget constraints. Liquidity that disappears under stress is not a feature—it is a liability. Intrinsic value, while sometimes less liquid in peacetime, becomes more functional in periods of dislocation. It endures.

Ultimately, value beyond currency is not a speculative theory—it is a strategic posture. It asks: *What will still matter when the lights flicker?* What holds value without verification? What assets give you time, choice, and mobility when systems fail to deliver clarity? These questions are not hypothetical. They are increasingly relevant in a world of rising geopolitical risk, fiscal instability, and institutional mistrust.

To build wealth that endures is not to chase returns—it is to *curate permanence*. It is to hold fewer illusions about the permanence of digits and more curiosity about the durability of things. It is to treat your portfolio not as a list of numbers, but as a living system designed to function without perfect conditions.

Because the real test of wealth is not how it performs in a spreadsheet. It is how it protects, enables, and sustains you *when the world that measures it begins to fail*. And that is why value must always be built on something deeper than currency. It must be built on *what lasts when nothing else does.*

Sovereignty and Responsibility

The language of sovereignty—especially in finance—is seductive. It suggests control, mastery, and independence. But sovereignty without responsibility is not autonomy. It's theatre. Owning your wealth in the sovereign sense—beyond banks, beyond permissioned systems, beyond the curated limitations of institutional finance—means owning not only your outcomes but your *judgements*. Your decisions. Your timing. Your failures and your foresight. There are no helpdesks in true financial independence. That is its cost—and its power.

The cultural narrative around money has, for decades, encouraged a kind of infantilisation. Financial institutions present themselves as custodians. Governments act as paternal protectors. Retirement schemes are managed by professionals. "Diversify, dollar-cost average, trust the market," is the modern catechism. If something fails, it is externalised—blamed on policy, timing, or global factors. Sovereign finance breaks this framework. It forces the individual to engage directly with *cause and effect.* You are no longer a client. You are the architect—and the consequences, for better or worse, are yours.

This shift is not cosmetic; it is structural. Traditional finance is designed to diffuse responsibility. When you place funds in a pension, you are outsourcing strategy. When you buy into a mutual fund, you are delegating selection. When you hold fiat in a regulated bank, you are trusting not only the bank, but the monetary policy that governs it. These are not inherently bad choices. But they are *choices of delegation*, not of sovereignty. Sovereignty begins when that delegation is questioned, withdrawn, or replaced with active intent.

Consider, for instance, the self-custody of digital assets. In crypto, holding your private keys means no third party can freeze, seize, or reverse your funds. But it also means *you alone are responsible for not losing them.* There is no password reset. There is no regulator to call.

There is no mechanism to reverse a mistaken transaction. To those steeped in legacy systems, this sounds reckless. But to those who understand sovereignty, it is simply the honest expression of accountability. If you want to control your money absolutely, *you must be absolutely accountable for it.*

This is where vigilance enters. Sovereignty is not a static condition—it is a practice. Systems evolve. Threats shift. Tools change. Legal frameworks adapt. To remain sovereign, you must remain aware. Not paranoid, not reactionary—but informed and adaptive. The sovereign individual does not rely on autopilot. They do not assume that yesterday's structure guarantees tomorrow's safety. They monitor, they reassess, they recalibrate. Vigilance is not anxiety; it is *discipline* in the presence of complexity.

There is a philosophical tension here, and it's worth examining. On the one hand, modern societies are built to reduce individual burden. Division of labour, expert management, legal recourse—all are designed to allow people to function without having to master every system they depend on. On the other hand, those same efficiencies create dependencies. And in financial matters, dependency is risk. When systems fail—through collapse, corruption, or policy shift—those who outsourced responsibility suffer the most. The paradox is that *the more seamless a system feels, the more fragile its users become.* Sovereignty resolves this paradox not by rejecting systems, but by refusing to be helpless within them.

Real-world examples illustrate this vividly. In 2013, Cypriot bank depositors woke to find their funds inaccessible. Some accounts were "bailed in" to recapitalise failing banks. This was legal, announced overnight, and non-negotiable. Those who had relied entirely on domestic banks had no recourse. Those with funds in decentralised assets, international accounts, or physical reserves had options. The difference was not wealth—it was *structure and responsibility.*

Or consider the 2022 collapse of centralised crypto platforms such as Celsius and FTX. Many users believed their assets were secure because they appeared in a dashboard. But those assets were not held in custody. They were liabilities of a third party—subject to leverage, rehypothecation, and management error. When the platforms failed, users lost everything. Not because they lacked resources, but because they had not *taken responsibility for custody*. Again, the distinction between asset ownership and *actual control* proved decisive.

Sovereignty also reframes how we interpret risk. Traditional risk frameworks are statistical—value at risk, standard deviation, Sharpe ratios. These are useful in stable environments, but they obscure *existential risk*: the risk that the system itself fails or redefines the rules mid-game. Sovereign individuals account for this by holding uncorrelated assets, diversifying across jurisdictions, and structuring wealth in ways that are *hard to revoke*. This is not alarmism. It is *layered risk design* based on the sober observation that institutions, however robust, are not infallible.

There is also a moral dimension to financial responsibility. When you take ownership of your decisions, you are no longer entitled to externalise blame. If your investment fails, it is not the algorithm's fault. If you overexpose to an asset class, it is not the market's betrayal. This mindset is confronting. It strips away the comfort of deflection. But it also cultivates maturity. Sovereignty is not just about protecting wealth—it is about growing into the kind of person who can *handle* that protection with integrity.

In this way, financial sovereignty becomes an internal practice as much as an external structure. It demands clarity of values: What matters enough to protect? What are you unwilling to delegate? Where do you draw the line between acceptable loss and intolerable exposure? These are not just technical questions. They are questions of *identity and responsibility*. The sovereign individual is not defined by what they own—but by how they own it, and what they're prepared to do to defend it.

There will always be trade-offs. The more autonomy you claim, the more infrastructure you must build for yourself. You must understand legal frameworks. You must manage cross-border complexity. You must safeguard your access, your keys, your liquidity. Mistakes will be made. You may under-diversify, over-trust a tool, or misread a regulatory trend. But *you will learn*. Because the cost of your mistake is yours to carry—and *that is what produces competence.*

This also means that victories are real. When you successfully protect capital in a downturn, that is not luck—it is the result of prior vigilance. When your portfolio survives systemic volatility, it reflects your architecture. When your assets are accessible despite legal uncertainty, you are not just fortunate—you are *sovereign.* The satisfaction is not just financial. It is psychological. It is the calm of knowing that you are not waiting for rescue. You are not dependent on an institution's mercy. You are *prepared.*

To live this way is not for everyone. Most people are conditioned to seek convenience over control. But for those willing to accept the cost, financial sovereignty is transformative. It builds confidence without arrogance. It replaces outrage with action. And it frames wealth not as a prize, but as a *responsibility worth defending.*

The sovereign individual does not seek perfection. They seek *resilience.* They do not fantasise about control—they prepare for volatility. And when mistakes happen—and they will—they do not outsource the blame. They ask: *What did I miss? What do I now know? What will I change next time?* In doing so, they become not just owners of capital, but *masters of its consequences.*

In the end, sovereignty is not defined by what you've escaped. It's defined by *what you're willing to carry.* Ownership is easy when things go well. Responsibility begins when they don't. And that, more than any asset class or allocation strategy, is the foundation of enduring wealth.

Chapter 3
Designing Your Backup Plan Portfolio

Every portfolio tells a story. More than a spreadsheet of holdings or a neat pie chart, it's a declaration—quiet perhaps, but deeply revealing—of how you see the world. Each investment, whether a modest rental flat, a tranche of sovereign bonds, or a crypto wallet tucked away in cold storage, reflects assumptions. Assumptions about stability, trust, power, and the arc of history. A portfolio is never just numbers—it is the behavioural fingerprint of its owner. Beneath its structure lie intuitions about danger, optimism, control, and escape. This chapter doesn't hand you a formula. It proposes a framework: a way to architect your Backup Plan Portfolio—one built not merely to grow, but to endure; one that is as mentally coherent as it is materially resilient, and that can weather shifts in law, politics, markets, or mood.

The conventional portfolio model—the so-called 60/40 split, or its many cousins—was born for a different era. It was crafted for continuity, not collapse. Its architecture leans on assumptions: that institutions will remain upright, that markets will remain liquid, that monetary authorities will act with discipline. These aren't foolish beliefs. They're just brittle. And the moment they fracture, the tidy logic of traditional allocation begins to fail you.

A backup portfolio, if it is to serve its name, must prepare for rupture—not in some apocalyptic sense, but in the practical understanding that systems fail. Markets seize up. Banks shut their doors. Borders harden. Capital controls appear overnight. You are not simply investing; you are negotiating with the unknown. Your assets must not only seek returns—they must function when assumptions no longer hold. That means classifying them not just by what they are, but by what they do: what they hedge, how they behave under stress, and what psychological ballast they offer when the waters get rough.

This is where thinking in archetypes becomes vital. Assets play roles. Some are guardians. Others are hunters. Defensive assets hold the line—they store value, resist seizure, and offer access when all else locks up. Gold bullion. Agricultural land. Crypto held with self-custody. A banknote in a neutral currency stashed abroad. Even an international trust, well-constructed, can stand as a defensive sentinel. These instruments are rarely glamorous. Their returns are slow, if they come at all. But when the sky darkens, they are the tools you'll wish you had sharpened.

On the other hand, offensive assets drive growth. They take the field. Equities, leveraged property, early-stage tokens, venture capital—all can offer upside, but with fragility. They're designed to expand your future, not protect your present. Mistaking them for protection is a common, and costly, error. Volatility feels like dynamism—until you need safety, and find instead exposure.

Crafting a resilient portfolio isn't about equalising these forces. It's about deliberately shaping an imbalance that fits you. There is no golden ratio. What matters is the congruence between your assets and your unique profile of vulnerabilities: where you live, how you earn, which laws shield you (or don't), how much ambiguity you can stomach. A software developer in Argentina has very different pressures than a Norwegian civil servant or a Malaysian retiree with adult children abroad. Risk isn't abstract—it is circumstantial.

This mapping of personal fragility is, in many ways, the real work. What would happen if your primary currency lost 40% of its value overnight? What if your income stream dried up for six months? What if your government froze capital flows, or changed the rules on ownership? These are not intellectual exercises. They are dress rehearsals. A resilient portfolio is built not just to diversify return, but to disperse control, custody, and dependency.

It also demands a clear view of time. Liquidity and longevity often pull in opposite directions. Liquid assets—digital cash, stablecoins, even some precious metals—offer speed and flexibility. Long-duration assets—timberland, private equity, hard real estate—offer permanence. You will need both. Liquidity buys you time to think, to act, to breathe. Longevity sustains you when the crisis becomes chronic. Bridging the two requires intentional layering: nested structures, staggered timelines, multi-tiered access. This is not diversification as Wall Street teaches it. It's continuity planning, plain and simple.

By now, if you've been following the book's arc, the groundwork is familiar. We've examined how financial systems are upheld by narrative and compliance, not inevitability. The Backup Plan Portfolio is where that understanding becomes embodied. This isn't theory anymore—it's muscle memory. You are not just moving assets around. You are shifting your dependence away from fragile defaults, and re-rooting it in a structure you control.

This chapter guides you through that transition—not with spreadsheets, but with mental models. We'll delve into the emotional functions of assets: why some bring peace, others anxiety. We'll look at lived case studies—how ordinary people in politically volatile or economically unstable contexts have preserved wealth, sometimes with tools others overlook: dual citizenships, legacy planning, multi-sovereign accounts, even vaults in neutral jurisdictions. We'll examine how custody, legal rights, and over-reliance on a single authority can quietly become existential risks.

What matters most is not what you hold—it's whether your holdings match your life. The elegant charts from your wealth manager may look convincing, but they rarely account for things like jurisdictional risk, familial obligations, or implicit political bets. A divorced parent in New Delhi, an expat entrepreneur in Nairobi, or a third-generation farmer in Alberta will each need radically different approaches, even if their net worths are identical. Design begins where generalisation ends.

By the time you finish this chapter, you won't be handed a portfolio to copy. You'll have something more lasting: a cognitive lens. A new way of seeing your financial ecosystem—not as a frozen balance sheet, but as a dynamic structure with roles, tensions, and escape hatches. You'll see that each asset can serve a function—some to stabilise, others to stretch. Some to protect you now, others to protect the ones who follow you.

Because this isn't about outperforming a benchmark. It's about staying upright when the benchmark itself no longer applies.

Resilience isn't a return metric. It's a design philosophy. And it starts, always, with the simple, sometimes unsettling question: what does your life actually require?

Your Backup Plan Portfolio is not just a hedge. It is a declaration. A decision to reject fragility disguised as efficiency. A quiet promise that you will not be caught unready. And with that, the real work begins.

The Three Pillars Approach

A well-structured backup portfolio does not begin with speculation—it begins with structure. Amid financial unpredictability and institutional decay, the goal is not merely to accumulate returns but to *engineer resilience.* The Three Pillars Approach offers a pragmatic framework for wealth preservation and strategic autonomy. It is not an abstract theory, but a refined allocation philosophy that balances historical precedent, tangible utility, and adaptive potential. Each pillar—gold, real estate, and crypto—anchors a different dimension of trust, function, and future-proofing. Together, they represent a triadic hedge against systemic fragility, policy volatility, and technological disruption.

Gold is the first pillar—not because it grows wealth quickly, but because it preserves wealth reliably. For more than 5,000 years, gold has functioned not as a speculative asset but as a *monetary constant.* It is apolitical, non-digital, and free from counterparty risk. Its value does not rely on contractual enforcement, government solvency, or technological infrastructure. Whether during currency collapses in Weimar Germany, capital controls in Argentina, or inflationary spirals in Zimbabwe, gold has served as an asset of last resort when paper currencies failed to hold purchasing power. It is the historical anchor of the Three Pillars, offering continuity across regimes, cultures, and crises.

The modern financial industry often diminishes gold's relevance. It does not produce cash flows. It does not innovate. It is seen, mistakenly, as inert. But that is precisely its function: *to stand still when everything else moves.* It does not need to outperform equities or real estate. It only needs to retain value when the instruments of trust—currencies, bonds, and central banks—lose coherence. Its utility lies not in appreciation, but in *preservation.* It is a defensive pillar, a ballast against monetary abuse and fiscal irresponsibility. No digital dashboard, regulatory freeze, or institutional fraud can alter its materiality. This permanence is not a weakness. It is its core strength.

Real estate, the second pillar, is grounded in utility and legal identity. It is both shelter and status. Unlike gold, which is transportable and private, real estate is rooted—geographically, legally, and socially. It offers tangible utility: you can live in it, rent it, borrow against it. Real estate generates yield through use and capital appreciation through scarcity. But more than that, it connects wealth to *location.* In doing so, it exposes the investor to jurisdictional risk—but it also offers a foothold in political systems, immigration frameworks, and tax regimes.

This duality is what makes real estate unique in the backup plan portfolio. It is not purely financial; it is also *civic.* Owning property often grants access to residence permits, legal standing, and regulatory rights unavailable to renters or expatriated investors. In Portugal, Greece, and several Caribbean nations, property ownership is the gateway to residency or citizenship. In Singapore or Switzerland, real estate acts as a de facto vote of confidence in state governance and urban planning. When chosen carefully—away from overheated, debt-saturated markets—real estate can act not just as an asset, but as *infrastructure* for sovereignty. However, its value is conditional on local law, economic stability, and political climate. It requires diligence, legal awareness, and sometimes, diversification across borders.

The third pillar—cryptoassets—is the most recent and the most controversial. It is also the most *structurally transformative.* Bitcoin, Ethereum, and decentralised finance protocols challenge the very assumptions of central banking, custody, and transnational capital flow. Unlike gold or real estate, crypto is natively digital, globally accessible, and permissionless. It allows users to store and transmit value without intermediaries, creating a system that is less dependent on banks, borders, or bureaucracy. For those seeking a future-facing hedge against institutional overreach, it is unmatched in design.

Critics dismiss crypto as volatile, speculative, and unregulated. And indeed, in its early forms, it is all those things. But the volatility is not incidental—it is part of the *price discovery process* for an entirely new monetary paradigm. Bitcoin, the flagship asset, offers a hard-capped supply and decentralised architecture that no nation-state can inflate, seize, or debase. Ethereum expands that vision to programmable contracts, decentralised applications, and algorithmic trust. Both have survived crashes, bans, and scandals—not because they are perfect, but because they are *anti-fragile.* The more they are attacked and survive, the more robust they become.

Crypto is not a replacement for gold or real estate—it is a *complement.* It introduces flexibility, mobility, and censorship resistance into a portfolio that otherwise depends on geography and tradition. It is the pillar of optionality. While gold preserves, and real estate roots, crypto allows the investor to move—to route around capital controls, to transact without gatekeepers, and to adapt to regulatory flux in real time. The key, however, is understanding *custody and exposure.* Crypto held on centralised exchanges is not sovereign. Only assets held in self-custodied wallets, with full control of private keys, qualify as truly decentralised stores of wealth. This introduces a new layer of personal responsibility—a theme explored earlier in this book.

Together, these three pillars form a non-correlated framework. Their strengths compensate for each other's weaknesses. Gold is unyielding but inert. Real estate is tangible but jurisdiction-bound. Crypto is fluid but volatile. Used in proportion, they offer layered protection: *historical continuity*, *functional stability*, and *technological agility.* This trichotomy reflects the multidimensional nature of modern risk. Inflation is not the only threat. Nor is taxation, nor regulation, nor social upheaval. The true threat is *concentration of exposure*—to a single system, a single geography, or a single paradigm. The Three Pillars exist to break that concentration.

This framework is also psychologically coherent. Gold reassures the traditionalist. Real estate satisfies the pragmatist. Crypto empowers the reformer. Each asset speaks to a different orientation toward time, control, and trust. The goal is not to choose between them, but to integrate them into a *philosophical architecture of wealth.* In doing so, the portfolio becomes more than a set of investments. It becomes an expression of agency—designed not just to survive volatility, but to *withstand coercion.*

This is what makes the Three Pillars more than an allocation model. It is a methodology for financial independence in a post-trust era. It does not chase performance; it curates *resilience.* It recognises that central banks, housing markets, and digital protocols will all be tested in the coming decades—and that no single pillar can carry the weight of long-term security alone. The strength lies in the structure. Gold grounds. Real estate houses. Crypto liberates.

The chapters ahead will explore each of these in depth—delving into acquisition strategies, legal frameworks, custody practices, and jurisdictional considerations. But their integration begins here. A well-designed Backup Plan Portfolio does not merely contain gold, property, and crypto. It *balances* them. It uses each as a counterweight to the others. And it treats them not as products to be consumed, but as instruments to be mastered.

This is not just a call for diversification. It is a call for *design.* Because the future will not reward the well-informed—it will reward the well-prepared. And preparation, as this framework makes clear, begins with three questions: What will preserve my purchasing power? What will house my function? What will protect my freedom?

Gold. Real estate. Crypto.

The Three Pillars—built to withstand collapse, navigate transition, and embrace transformation.

Asset Archetypes: Defensive vs Offensive

To the average investor, an asset is either performing or it isn't. Return on investment—whether measured in price appreciation, rental income, dividends, or token staking rewards—is often treated as the definitive metric. But this fixation on numerical returns, while important, obscures something far more foundational: the *role* an asset plays in the architecture of one's financial sovereignty. Not all assets are created to grow. Some are created to guard. The mature investor does not simply ask "What will this earn?" but "What will this protect? What will this enable? What will this offset?" A resilient portfolio is not a spreadsheet of projections—it is a map of intentions. It reflects the investor's vulnerabilities, ambitions, and thresholds for uncertainty. And to construct that map intelligently, we must first distinguish between *defensive* and *offensive* asset archetypes.

Defensive assets are characterised not by their yield, but by their *function under stress*. They are designed to preserve value, provide liquidity during crises, or buffer volatility. Their strategic role is not to outperform bull markets, but to *survive bear markets intact*. Gold, high-quality sovereign bonds, cash equivalents, and certain insurance products fall into this category. These instruments are often underwhelming in times of prosperity, yet become invaluable when everything else falters. Their utility is countercyclical. They offer peace of mind, not exuberance.

Take gold, for instance. It generates no yield. It does not innovate. But it does not default, either. It does not require trust in any government, central bank, or legal system. During Argentina's 2001 currency collapse, it wasn't the equities or real estate that proved immediately useful—it was gold, dollar bills, and durable goods. Similarly, U.S. Treasury bonds, despite being denominated in fiat, retain defensive characteristics due to their deep liquidity and government backing—*so long as the issuing government remains credible*. Even cash, often dismissed for its inflationary decay, serves a defensive purpose in the short term: agility. It gives the holder time to think, reposition, or escape.

Contrast this with offensive assets. These are the engines of capital growth. They are designed to compound wealth, expand purchasing power, and fuel generational uplift. Stocks, private equity, entrepreneurial ventures, cryptoassets, and growth-oriented real estate exemplify this category. Offensive assets are forward-leaning. They carry greater risk, but also greater reward—assuming conditions remain favourable. They are not designed to shield. They are designed to *advance*.

Tech stocks are a textbook example. In times of optimism, they outpace defensive plays by wide margins. But when sentiment sours, they often fall the hardest. Cryptocurrency, too—especially outside of Bitcoin—is deeply offensive in nature. Its value is speculative, its volatility extreme. But it offers transformative upside, particularly in decentralised finance or Layer 1 infrastructure plays. Owning these assets is not merely about tolerating risk—it is about *understanding what kind of risk* one is underwriting. Offensive assets are expressions of conviction. They require timing, thesis, and adaptability.

Real estate defies easy classification, because it straddles both sides depending on its form. A mortgage-free agricultural property in a politically stable region can be highly defensive: it offers utility, barter potential, and long-term store-of-value traits. A highly leveraged investment condo in a speculative urban market, by contrast, is decisively offensive. The investor must evaluate not just the *category* of the asset class, but the *configuration* of the asset itself. Context shapes role.

What distinguishes a strong portfolio is not how many asset classes it touches, but *how clearly the investor understands what each asset is meant to do.* A collection of assets with impressive paper returns but overlapping vulnerabilities is not diversification—it's concentration under a different name. If your equities, your real estate, and your pension fund all depend on a robust fiat currency, low interest rates, and functioning banking infrastructure, then you are not diversified. You are merely decoratively exposed to the same systemic assumptions.

Understanding asset archetypes sharpens judgment. It prevents over-optimising for growth at the expense of protection. It also guards against the opposite mistake: hoarding too much in defensive assets and thereby surrendering to purchasing power erosion over time. Every portfolio is a blend of security and ambition. The proportions should reflect the investor's life phase, cash flow profile, jurisdictional stability, and emotional capacity for volatility. A 60-year-old retiree in a fragile political environment might prioritise defensiveness. A 35-year-old entrepreneur with offshore income and mobile citizenship might lean heavily into offence. There is no perfect balance—only *contextual alignment.*

Psychologically, defensive assets offer emotional ballast. When markets collapse, headlines scream, and liquidity dries up, the presence of gold bars in a safe, cash under a mattress, or a modest property in a low-debt region can prevent panic. It becomes easier to make rational decisions when part of your wealth is *not at the mercy of other people's risk models*. That calm is not quantifiable on a balance sheet, but it is one of the most powerful forces in financial behaviour. Similarly, offensive assets allow the investor to participate in progress. To fund innovation. To bet intelligently on the future. They create not just financial returns, but a sense of engagement with the world's potential trajectories. That too is a kind of wealth.

The tension between these archetypes is not a flaw—it is the portfolio's *engine*. Each dampens the other's extremes. Defensive assets sacrifice return in exchange for reliability. Offensive assets sacrifice reliability in exchange for return. In unison, they create a system that is not purely reactive, but *strategically resilient*. The investor ceases to be a gambler or hoarder and becomes a *designer of outcomes*—someone who thinks in layers, contingencies, and time horizons.

Critically, this framework extends beyond finance. In a broader sense, defensive thinking guards autonomy: skills, health, citizenship options, and legal insulation. Offensive thinking grows opportunity: education, innovation, networks, and influence. The best backup plans blend both. A passport is defensive. A startup is offensive. A well-stocked pantry is defensive. A scalable business is offensive. Financial assets are only one domain of sovereignty. But they mirror the same strategic postures.

To close, understanding assets by their *strategic role*, not just by their yield, is the mark of a mature investor. It elevates wealth from a numbers game to a structural endeavour. It enables decisions that are coherent, not reactive. And it lays the groundwork for building a Backup Plan Portfolio that can withstand not just market cycles, but *civilisational swings*. The question is not merely what to own. The question is *what role each asset plays when the world stops playing by the rules you were told to expect*.

This is not semantics. It is survival architecture. And it begins by asking, with clarity and courage: Which assets guard? Which assets grow? And how much of each do I need—not just to thrive, but to *remain free*?

Liquidity vs Longevity

The modern investor faces a quiet but consequential dilemma: how to allocate resources between what is *immediately accessible* and what is *permanently reliable*. While portfolio theory often speaks in terms of volatility, yield, and correlation, it less frequently confronts the *temporal utility* of assets—what they are able to do for you, *when* you need them most. Liquidity and longevity are not opposites; they are complements in tension. Together, they form a strategic axis of decision-making that is as psychological as it is financial. The art lies not in choosing one over the other, but in understanding *how each serves a fundamentally different purpose*, and how to balance them in a world where both short-term shocks and long-term erosion are increasingly likely.

Liquidity refers to the ability to convert an asset into spendable value without significant delay or loss. It is speed, simplicity, and certainty of access. Cash in a bank account. A gold coin in your drawer. Bitcoin in a self-custodied wallet. These are forms of liquidity. They allow movement, response, and escape. Liquidity is what feeds you in a crisis, helps you seize an unexpected opportunity, or shields you from institutional dysfunction. It is freedom in compressed time.

Longevity, by contrast, refers to an asset's capacity to *endure*. It is the measure of value that survives not just quarterly downturns but generational transitions, political transformations, or systemic resets. Longevity is embodied in things that cannot be easily debased, deleted, or dissolved by external events. A debt-free plot of land. A diversified vault of precious metals. A private key stored offline and passed down securely. These assets may not be quick to liquidate, but their resilience across time is what makes them indispensable. They are not designed for today—they are designed for *continuity*.

The mistake many investors make is to mistake one for the other. The cryptocurrency exchange account may appear liquid until withdrawals are frozen during a liquidity crunch. The property may seem long-lasting until local laws shift, taxes rise, or political unrest renders its use impractical. Fiat currency appears supremely liquid—until inflation eats away its purchasing power so subtly that, over a decade, it has silently halved your wealth. *Neither category is inherently safe.* Each contains vulnerabilities that must be understood in context.

A resilient Backup Plan Portfolio, therefore, treats liquidity and longevity as *functions*, not features. It does not ask, "What's the best-performing asset?" It asks, "What could I *rely* on, and *when*?" Imagine three cascading levels of financial disruption. In the first, you need fast access to cash to cover an emergency. In the second, you face a longer economic freeze, where markets seize, banks impose limits, and mobility becomes constrained. In the third, you're navigating a deep systemic crisis—currency debasement, civil disorder, or regime change. Each scenario calls upon different layers of your portfolio. If you've optimised only for liquidity, you may find yourself eroded by time. If you've optimised only for longevity, you may not survive the week. This is not just a financial equation. It is a *sequencing problem*—a choreography of access and preservation.

To explore this further, consider the psychology of financial time. Liquidity appeals to *urgency*, to our need for immediacy, flexibility, and reaction. It soothes the anxiety of unknowns. Longevity, on the other hand, speaks to *legacy*, to our desire to anchor value beyond the individual and into the intergenerational. One is about navigation. The other is about preservation. It is not difficult to see how our age of instant gratification overweights liquidity. We want to know we can click, transfer, move. But true wealth—*durable* wealth—asks us to think not only of our needs but of the shape of the world decades from now.

This balance becomes even more complex when we factor in *jurisdictional and systemic trust.* If your liquidity is denominated in a currency managed by a government with a history of capital controls or inflationary policy, its apparent utility can become a trap. If your long-term stores of value are custodial—held on your behalf by institutions—then their longevity is not intrinsic but *conditional.* It exists only so long as the system deems you eligible to access it.

Hence, the need for *sovereign-grade design*: liquidity you can control, longevity you can pass down *outside institutional permission structures.*

One illuminating historical example is the experience of wealth preservation during the collapse of the Soviet Union. Those who held roubles or state bonds saw their holdings rendered worthless. Those who had physical assets—gold, land, tools, or tradable goods—fared far better. But more instructive still were those who balanced both: liquid stores to buy their way through transitional hardship, and enduring assets that regained value once a new order emerged. The lesson is not merely about asset classes; it is about *strategic temporal layering.*

In modern application, the need for liquidity is obvious. It pays your rent. It funds your exit strategy. It keeps your business solvent. But the need for longevity is less visceral, even though it's more dangerous to neglect. A financially literate individual must therefore reverse-engineer their asset stack around *personal timelines of vulnerability.* For example, a tech worker in a politically volatile country might prioritise portable, liquid assets like decentralised crypto or foreign-denominated stablecoins. A retiree in a stable country with declining trust in central banking might lean into gold, foreign real estate, or family trusts. The allocation isn't merely about market cycles—it's about *life design under duress.*

This also raises ethical and philosophical dimensions. Longevity assets often require foresight, patience, and discipline. They signal a belief that value must outlive the self. That wealth is not just consumption power, but *continuity power.* Liquid assets, by contrast, reveal our survivalist instincts, our readiness to act and adapt. The right balance requires not only economic acumen but *moral clarity* about what we're protecting, who we're protecting it for, and what kind of life we are building with it.

Critically, the tension between liquidity and longevity is not static. It shifts as your context shifts. What was once an optimal allocation may become brittle under new conditions. The rapid monetisation of real estate, the emergence of new decentralised financial tools, or the introduction of central bank digital currencies may recalibrate what's considered liquid or enduring. For example, Bitcoin, once considered fringe and illiquid, has matured into a partially liquid store of value for those with the infrastructure to use it sovereignly. But without self-custody, it remains vulnerable to third-party risks. Similarly, physical gold remains a cornerstone of long-term preservation—*but only if stored accessibly*. It is not merely about what you own, but how, where, and under what terms.

So how should the thoughtful investor proceed? Begin with clarity: map your needs by timeline. Immediate (0–6 months), mid-term (6 months–5 years), and long-term (5 years–lifetime or beyond). Then align your assets with those timelines not just in terms of maturity, but in *access and resilience*. Ask: *What can I reach in a day? What can I liquidate in a crisis? What will survive me? What do I want my children to inherit intact, not just in value but in meaning?*

That final question is often the most neglected. Longevity is not just about what endures, but what *should* endure. Wealth passed down unthinkingly can become a burden. Wealth built for continuity—with intentionality, clarity, and structural foresight—becomes a gift. Liquid wealth is a tool. Long-term wealth is a signal. It tells your family, community, and future self what you considered worth preserving.

Ultimately, a Backup Plan Portfolio that fails to reconcile liquidity and longevity is not a backup plan at all—it's a fragmented hope. The serious investor—especially one seeking autonomy in uncertain times—must treat this axis not as a secondary consideration, but as a *core design principle*. Because when systems break, the two questions that matter most are: *Can I move?* and *What will still matter once the dust settles?* Liquidity answers the first. Longevity answers the second. And only both, in tandem, can offer the kind of resilience that outlives volatility, ideology, and time itself.

Your Personal Risk Map

Financial advice too often arrives pre-packaged in formulas: allocate X% to equities, Y% to fixed income, and the rest in cash or alternatives. The implication is universal applicability—a one-size-fits-all wisdom handed down from abstract economic models. But real lives are not statistical averages. Real people live amid real pressures, and those pressures differ radically depending on where you live, how you earn, whom you answer to, and what you fear. *A meaningful financial strategy begins not with spreadsheets, but with personal context.* The first step in designing a resilient Backup Plan Portfolio is not choosing the right assets; it is understanding your *exposures*—geographic, professional, legal, and emotional. These are not academic variables; they are existential ones.

This is where the concept of a **Personal Risk Map** becomes essential. Unlike generic asset allocation models, a personal risk map helps you visualise your life as a system of vulnerabilities. It asks you to interrogate your environment, your dependencies, and your blind spots. It replaces the language of market risk with something more intimate: *What could go wrong, for me?* This is not an exercise in paranoia. It is an exercise in clarity. If wealth is a shield—as we've previously argued—then the shape of that shield must correspond to the contours of your actual threats. A titanium wall is no good if the arrow comes from behind.

Start with **geographic risk**. Where you live is not merely a backdrop—it is a nexus of policies, infrastructure, and political temperament that can either amplify or mute financial vulnerability. Are you in a country with high inflation, capital controls, or authoritarian tendencies? Then fiat savings and local bank deposits may be systemically exposed, regardless of your diligence. Are you in a jurisdiction prone to natural disasters, energy instability, or fragile supply chains? Then your backup plan must account for *operational continuity*, not just financial continuity. For instance, a citizen of Argentina or Lebanon in the past decade would have benefited not from clever stock picks, but from *capital mobility and jurisdictional diversification*—access to stable currencies, foreign-held assets, and secure digital tools. Your address is not neutral; it is a risk variable.

Next, consider **professional risk**. How do you earn your income—and how vulnerable is that stream? If you are salaried by a single employer, your exposure is concentration. If you are self-employed in a volatile sector—say, digital media or freelance design—your risk lies in income irregularity and platform dependence. If you're a public figure, your exposure may include reputational fragility. If you work in a highly regulated industry, your livelihood may hinge on legal interpretations over which you have little control. Income is often treated as a fixed input in financial planning, but in reality, it is often the most *fragile variable.* A robust personal risk map evaluates not just the amount of income but its *stability*, its *dependency chains*, and its *substitutability* in crisis conditions.

Legal risk is another critical dimension. What are the rules governing your property, data, and mobility? Are you vulnerable to asset seizure, tax overreach, sudden regulatory shifts, or unjust enforcement? Are you a citizen of a country that claims the right to tax global income? Do you hold dual citizenships or visas that could complicate your financial obligations or restrict your movements? Legal structures can be invisible until they aren't—until you try to move capital across borders, or inherit an asset, or contest a claim. The wealthy often employ teams of lawyers to navigate this terrain; you must at least *map* it. For example, American citizens face unique global tax reporting obligations—making certain investment vehicles abroad financially dangerous, even if they seem advantageous locally. The risk is not criminality, but *non-compliance through ignorance.* That ignorance can be expensive.

Then there's **emotional risk**, which is almost never discussed in financial planning, and yet it quietly shapes every decision. What is your tolerance for volatility—not just in theory, but in practice? How do you behave under pressure? Do you panic at downturns, or cling to assets out of nostalgia? Do you overspend when anxious, or freeze when required to act decisively? Do you have family members who are financially dependent on you, or emotionally entangled with your financial decisions? These are not abstract questions. They directly affect the structure and allocation of your portfolio. An asset that is theoretically optimal but triggers personal instability is *not resilient* for you. Conversely, an asset that generates calm and clarity—even if suboptimal on paper—may be a *keystone of psychological stability* in your broader wealth system.

To make this framework actionable, imagine constructing a four-quadrant matrix: Geographic, Professional, Legal, Emotional. In each quadrant, list your primary exposures. Be specific. "Political unrest" is too vague. "Dependent on a single banking system" is better. "High tax risk in my country" can be refined to "new legislation threatens capital gains shelter on retirement savings." The goal is to *name* your vulnerabilities. Once you name them, you can plan against them. This is not a once-and-done exercise. It should be reviewed as your life evolves—when you change careers, relocate, marry, divorce, become a parent, or inherit responsibility.

The Personal Risk Map is not about fear; it is about *agency*. It transforms amorphous anxiety into structured insight. It also reveals the limits of mainstream financial advice. Most portfolios are built for theoretical averages: 30-year investment horizons, 5–6% returns, normal distribution of volatility. But your life is not average. You may face sudden relocations, health events, or regime changes. You may live in a country where the rule of law is eroding. You may work in a sector disrupted by AI. None of these risks appear on a Monte Carlo simulation. Yet they are the actual determinants of financial continuity.

Once your risk map is drawn, your portfolio design should evolve to *counterbalance* its vulnerabilities. If you are geographically exposed, you need asset diversification across jurisdictions—offshore accounts, second passports, decentralised currencies. If you are professionally exposed, you need income redundancy—side businesses, passive revenue streams, or upskilling into adjacent sectors. If you are legally exposed, you need clarity: competent legal advice, conservative structuring, and exit strategies. If you are emotionally exposed, you need simplicity—fewer moving parts, clearer rules, and trusted systems that won't buckle under cognitive stress. Your portfolio is not a trophy; it is a tool. Its purpose is not just to grow, but to protect—*you*, your family, your freedom to act.

Real-world examples underscore the point. In 2013, Cypriot bank account holders—many of whom had followed conventional financial wisdom—were blindsided by a government-imposed "bail-in," which appropriated deposits over €100,000 to rescue failing banks. Their error wasn't imprudence; it was *context-blindness*. A personal risk map would have revealed a deep reliance on a single banking jurisdiction during a fiscal crisis—a fragility not visible in nominal portfolio metrics. Likewise, during the Venezuelan hyperinflation crisis, families that survived intact were often those who had *pre-positioned value* outside the country—whether in the form of foreign property, stored cryptocurrencies, or stable foreign income. Risk wasn't avoided through financial engineering; it was mitigated through *life design*.

In advanced economies, the illusion of systemic stability often delays the construction of personal risk maps. But the 2008 financial crisis, the COVID-19 policy shocks, and the weaponisation of the financial system in geopolitical conflict have made clear that *there is no neutral ground*. Being unprepared is not safer—it's just more comfortable until it's not.

This subchapter asks the reader to do something most people avoid: to sit down and trace their personal fault lines—not because collapse is imminent, but because *uncertainty is inevitable*. Your Personal Risk Map is not a prediction tool; it is a *preparedness tool*. Its value lies in making the invisible visible, and the complex navigable.

If wealth is to serve as self-defence—as argued elsewhere in this book—then the risk map is the blueprint for where to place your armour. Without it, even a well-funded portfolio is vulnerable in all the wrong places. With it, even a modest portfolio can become strategically robust. This is the real pivot point from passive investing to *sovereign wealth architecture*—from reacting to markets to *designing for resilience*. And in a world where risks are multiplying and systems are fragmenting, *clarity is no longer optional. It is a form of capital in itself*.

Chapter 4
Gold – The Memory of Money

Few materials on Earth carry the same paradoxical gravity as gold. Chemically inert, yet historically alive; emotionally charged, yet culturally impartial—it straddles contradiction. Across epochs and empires, gold has served as both currency and myth, valued not just for what it is, but for what it evokes. In today's climate of digitised finance, algorithmic velocity, and evaporating privacy, its re-emergence is not loud, but purposeful. Not because gold has changed, but because the world around it has moved so fast that stillness—real, tangible, sovereign stillness—has become a form of strategy.

This chapter isn't here to romanticise gold as a relic of crowns and conquest. Rather, it sets out to reframe its continued relevance—psychologically, philosophically, and yes, financially—in an age ruled by abstraction. When wealth becomes no more than code in a server, visible to algorithms, governed by policy, and modifiable with a keystroke, the analogue weight of gold offers something rare: autonomy. Its recent revival in the collective financial psyche is not merely an inflation hedge; it's something deeper. It's a growing rejection of dependency—on systems, on permissions, on shifting rules that may no longer feel secure.

Economists have often called gold "dead money," especially during speculative peaks when equity markets thrive and fiat confidence holds. But the current reappraisal is different—it's not just being whispered among the tinfoil-hatted fringes or gold-bug doomsayers. This time, it's the coders, fund managers, and citizens of brittle democracies who are reconsidering it. When money becomes programmable, it also becomes revocable. In such a world, to own value that cannot be reversed or retracted is no longer an eccentricity. It is a philosophical line in the sand.

What gives gold its real pull is not yield—it pays none. Nor is it growth—it offers no quarterly report or upside potential. What it offers is something far more elusive: independence without infrastructure. It needs no network to validate its worth, no intermediary to authorise its use. It cannot be locked, reversed, seized digitally, or reduced to ones and zeros. That may sound like a limitation—but in the current climate of monetary experimentation, geopolitical fragmentation, and central bank distortion, it starts to look like a feature. Gold demands patience, and in return, it delivers resilience. That makes it one of the very few assets with enduring relevance across not just market cycles, but regime shifts.

Still, holding gold today is no longer a straightforward act. The form you choose—bullion in a private vault, ETFs managed through financial platforms, or tokenised gold riding on a blockchain—carries implications that go far beyond storage. Each format signals a different worldview: about custody, about sovereignty, about how much control you're willing to surrender for convenience. This chapter will dig into those implications, examining how they align with your broader investment philosophy and your personal threshold for systemic risk.

But let's pause for a moment on the emotional question: Why, in a world of speed and screens, does gold *feel* safe? The answer is less about economics than about identity. Gold is stable, heavy, slow—it resists decay. In a world where everything flickers and updates and evaporates, that resistance is grounding. Its very existence suggests continuity, and with it, a certain comfort. Of course, this emotional appeal can mislead; just because gold feels eternal doesn't mean one should hold it passively, without thought. To use it well is to grasp both its objective utility and its psychological pull.

The financial industry often worships abstraction: frictionless transactions, leveraged instruments, compounding complexity. Yet there's a cost to this elegance—it removes us from physical reality. Gold reintroduces that friction. You can't high-frequency trade a gold bar. It makes you slow down, think. And that deliberation, in an era of manic optimisation, is precisely where its strategic value lies.

Let's be honest, though—gold isn't perfect. It can be taxed. It can be confiscated. It can, under certain conditions, even be manipulated. It may not deliver stellar returns in the short run. But what it *does* provide—uniquely, consistently—is persistence. It outlasts. That alone earns it a place in any serious Backup Plan Portfolio. It's not that gold wins every time. It's that it's still there the next time.

Over the coming pages, we'll examine three key dimensions of gold's role in modern financial life. First, we'll look at *Gold in a Digital Age*: how it functions as a physical counterbalance to the rising tide of programmable finance and monetary experimentation. Then we'll turn to the practical challenge of *Owning Gold Without Owning a Safe*, assessing custodial strategies, digital alternatives, and what's really at stake in your method of storage. Lastly, we'll explore *Gold and the Psychology of Permanence*—the deeper emotional and existential role it plays as both hedge and anchor.

Gold is not about hoping for collapse. It is about recognising that systems fail, that trust can vanish suddenly, and that rebuilding confidence is always slower than losing it. In a world cascading toward more opacity, more velocity, more reliance on unseen hands, sometimes the most radical choice is the simplest one: to hold something that exists entirely on its own terms.

By the end of this chapter, you'll have more than a technical grasp of how to include gold in a well-structured portfolio. You'll gain a sharper awareness of what it symbolises—and why it endures. Gold stands not just as a store of value, but as a quiet act of resistance. A material memory of what money once meant. And perhaps, if we pay attention, what it might mean again.

Why Gold Still Matters

There is a peculiar kind of arrogance that creeps into civilisations at their peak—a belief that technological progress renders foundational truths obsolete. Paper replaces metal. Code replaces paper. Then, inevitably, comes the moment when systems fracture and abstraction fails. It is in these moments, historical and modern alike, that humanity rediscovers what it already knew: *gold still matters*. Not because it is ancient, but because it is fundamentally *incorruptible* in ways most financial instruments are not.

To dismiss gold as an anachronism is to misunderstand the role it has played—not just as a commodity or hedge, but as a *civilisational constant.* From Mesopotamia to the Federal Reserve, from ancient tombs to central bank vaults, gold has served as a unifying metric of trust. It is not backed by a promise; it *is* the promise. And that distinction—between something with value and something that *is* value—explains why it continues to endure even as the world shifts into the intangible and algorithmic.

To understand why gold still matters, we must begin not with charts or price histories, but with human nature. For over 5,000 years, societies have converged—without collusion and across cultures—on gold as the ultimate reference point of value. This convergence is not arbitrary. Gold possesses an unparalleled combination of physical and psychological attributes: it is scarce but not too scarce; durable but malleable; portable but difficult to counterfeit. Unlike fiat money, it requires no centralised authority for validation. And unlike cryptocurrencies, it does not require electricity or internet access to exist.

Gold is, in essence, value made visible—permanent, portable, and immune to political whim.

Throughout history, whenever political systems collapsed or currencies hyperinflated, gold functioned as the fallback layer of financial sanity. When the Roman denarius was debased to near worthlessness in the 3rd century CE, people hoarded solid aurei. During the Wiemar Republic's collapse in 1923, a loaf of bread might have cost 200 billion marks—but it could still be bought with a small gold coin. In Zimbabwe's 2008 hyperinflationary spiral, and Venezuela's ongoing crisis, similar dynamics played out. And when trust evaporated during the 2008 global financial crisis, central banks didn't flee to innovation—they bought gold.

Critics often argue that gold is "unproductive"—that it generates no yield, pays no interest, and sits inert in vaults. But this critique conflates *utility* with *resilience.* Gold's role is not to generate returns but to preserve purchasing power across decades—and, in many cases, generations. In a diversified portfolio, gold is not a growth asset; it is a continuity asset. Its primary function is to remain *outside the system* when that system is in flux, or worse, in freefall.

This is particularly relevant in our current environment, where the digitisation of money has made assets more mobile, but also more fragile. Today, wealth is largely composed of electronic entries subject to surveillance, restriction, and deletion. Banks can freeze accounts. Governments can impose capital controls. Platforms can de-platform. In such a world, gold's analog nature becomes a form of insurance—not against volatility, but against *compliance dependency*. It is one of the few financial instruments that cannot be turned off remotely.

There is also a philosophical dimension at play. In a world increasingly obsessed with speed, liquidity, and leverage, gold stands as a monument to patience and discipline. It reminds investors that not all value must be *used* to be meaningful. Some value is preserved *precisely by being unused.* A kilo of gold sitting quietly in a vault is not idle—it is vigilant. It says, "I do not trust your spreadsheet. I trust permanence."

Gold's continuing relevance is also confirmed by those who understand systems most intimately. Central banks—the very institutions that issue fiat currency—are among the largest holders of gold. Their actions betray a pragmatic truth: when trust in monetary theory meets the limits of geopolitical reality, gold remains the fallback asset. Russia, China, and India have all accelerated their gold accumulation over the past decade. These are not sentimental moves. They are strategic hedges against a future in which the dominance of the US dollar may be contested, and sanctions may weaponise the financial system.

Importantly, gold does not require belief in any particular economic thesis. Whether one expects inflation or deflation, gold offers a measure of optionality. It tends to appreciate when monetary policy veers into extremity—either through reckless stimulus or aggressive tightening. It acts as a counterweight to policy failure, not a bet on any specific policy path. For this reason, it can serve as a form of *meta-diversification*, hedging not only against market risk but against systemic malfunction.

The digital age has not obsoleted gold—it has created new avenues for its expression. Tokenised gold platforms, for example, allow fractional ownership and blockchain-based verification of vaulted assets. While still nascent and fraught with custody risks, such innovations bridge the reliability of gold with the accessibility of modern finance. But even these advances ultimately orbit the same premise: that *gold's value lies in its independence from trust-based systems.* Blockchain may decentralise verification. Gold decentralises value.

That said, owning gold wisely requires understanding its limitations. It is not immune to theft, confiscation, or taxation. Its liquidity can be impaired in crisis scenarios. And its pricing, especially in ETF and futures markets, is increasingly influenced by speculative flows rather than fundamentals. Yet none of these issues invalidate its role—they simply emphasise the need for *disciplined custodianship.* As with all tools of sovereignty, the freedom gold offers must be matched by the responsibility of securing and deploying it intelligently.

The deeper reason gold still matters, however, may be psychological rather than financial. In times of chaos, people do not seek yield—they seek *certainty.* Gold offers a fixed reference point, both materially and symbolically. It answers an ancient human need: the need to hold something *that does not change when everything else does.* That need is not going away. If anything, it is intensifying.

To believe gold is obsolete is to believe history has ended. It hasn't. The crises of the past are not relics; they are templates. And in each of them, gold re-emerged not as a speculative trade, but as a form of truth. Silent. Weighty. Unyielding.

Gold still matters because it never asked for your belief in the first place. It only asked for your recognition. That, more than anything, explains its 5,000-year record—and why, despite the siren call of ever-more-abstract instruments, it continues to deserve a foundational place in the architecture of personal and sovereign resilience.

Gold in a Digital Age

Quiet Value in a Tracked World

It is an irony worth examining: the more digitised our financial lives become, the more compelling gold becomes—not merely as an asset, but as an idea. In a time when surveillance capitalism extends from our search history to our spending habits, when "frictionless" banking often comes at the cost of visibility and control, gold stands out not as a relic, but as a resistance. It doesn't ask for permission. It doesn't leave a data trail. It simply is. That static, analog permanence is no longer archaic—it's insurgent.

To understand why gold is regaining relevance, one must first acknowledge the tectonic shift in financial infrastructure. In less than two decades, most of the world's commerce has migrated onto rails governed by code, intermediated by platforms, and monitored in ways that defy historical precedent. Cash has receded in favour of contactless cards, QR codes, and app-based wallets—all of which leave exhaust: who you paid, when, where, and often why. This isn't a dystopian warning; it's an operational reality, from London to Lagos. What's sold as convenience is also custody—by someone else.

This doesn't mean the modernisation of money is inherently malign. But it does mean that the risk profile of our personal finances has changed. Whereas theft once involved physical breaking and entering, today it may arrive through a compromised password or a frozen account triggered by an algorithmic flag. We live not just in a digital economy, but a programmable one—where access to your money is contingent on systems, institutions, and rule sets over which you often have no say. In this context, gold's simplicity becomes its strength. It can't be hacked, frozen, or sanctioned. It doesn't go offline when servers crash. It offers continuity without connectivity.

The resurgence of interest in gold is therefore not just about inflation hedging or macroeconomic anxieties—it is, at root, a philosophical shift. As people awaken to the structural fragility embedded in fully digitised systems, the appetite for assets that resist centralisation grows. This is why gold appeals not only to conservative investors or legacy wealth managers, but increasingly to technologists, decentralisation advocates, and even crypto natives. Bitcoin maximalists and bullion purists may argue, but they share a common instinct: *get out of the system before the system locks you in.*

Consider the emergence of Central Bank Digital Currencies (CBDCs). Promoted as efficient upgrades to physical cash, they also introduce programmable features that allow unprecedented control over individual spending. In pilot programmes across China, Nigeria, and soon the EU, authorities have explored features such as expiration dates on money, location-restricted purchases, and even income-based interest rates. While the benefits may be real, the trade-off is unavoidable: *surveillance by design.* For those who understand that financial freedom is not just about having money, but about choosing how and when to use it, gold provides a clean break—a bearer instrument immune to behavioural conditioning.

This shift isn't theoretical. In countries facing authoritarian regimes, capital controls, or sudden demonetisations, physical gold has proven not just valuable but liberating. When Indian policymakers invalidated over 80% of cash in circulation overnight in 2016, long lines formed at banks—but gold traders stayed open. When Turkish citizens watched the lira collapse, many turned to gold jewellery as a culturally acceptable, wearable form of wealth. In Venezuela, where hyperinflation rendered local currency almost useless, scrap gold became a medium of exchange in border towns. These are not exceptions; they are signals. *Gold functions best where trust collapses most.*

In affluent Western nations, the reflex to dismiss gold as a survivalist fringe instrument is beginning to wane. The erosion of institutional trust has reached a level where even established investors are revisiting the logic of allocation. But the appeal goes deeper than numbers. There is a psychological effect to owning something that does not blink or buffer. Unlike equities that refresh with every market cycle or cryptocurrencies that oscillate by the minute, gold just sits. It doesn't promise explosive growth—but neither does it expose you to real-time panic. For many, that constancy is not boring—it's *reassuring.*

This anchoring effect is especially important in times of financial instability. Neurologically, humans are wired to panic in the face of loss or uncertainty. Gold acts as a counterweight—not just in portfolios, but in perception. When markets tumble or digital accounts become inaccessible, a sovereign coin in the drawer or a gold bar in a vault offers a tangible sense of security. You can see it. You can touch it. No password required.

Yet this raises a practical tension: how should one own gold in a digital age? The spectrum ranges from paper proxies like ETFs (exchange-traded funds) to tokenised gold on blockchains, all the way to physical bullion stored at home or in private vaults. Each format carries trade-offs between accessibility, auditability, and autonomy. An ETF is liquid and easy to manage but exists within the traditional financial system—subject to trading halts, custodian risks, and systemic spillovers. Tokenised gold brings some innovation, allowing for fractional ownership and blockchain transparency, but is still dependent on the trustworthiness of its issuer. Physical gold, by contrast, offers true sovereignty—but requires secure storage, insurance, and possibly cross-border mobility if used as an escape hatch.

That decision—how to hold—reveals another truth about gold in a digital age: *it is only useful to the degree that it aligns with your broader strategy of resilience.* For some, a modest holding provides psychological ballast. For others, it's part of a parallel economy—used not for yield, but for exit. For still others, it is the intergenerational anchor: a store of wealth not for selling, but for passing on.

Critics often argue that gold is "unproductive" because it generates no yield. That is true. But neither does insurance—until you need it. Gold's value is not in its cash flow, but in its counterparty independence. It requires no CEO performance, no shareholder report, no regulatory compliance. It simply exists, outside the system. That alone gives it power, especially in a world where *systems increasingly serve their own logic before yours.*

Importantly, this does not mean one should abandon modern tools of wealth-building. A diversified strategy may well include equities, real estate, crypto, and even fiat currency. But gold reminds us that some value should remain *off-grid*—uncorrelated, untethered, and uncaptured. In that sense, it plays not just a financial role but a philosophical one. It whispers: *not everything should be digitised. Not everything should be shared.*

We are entering a period of accelerating convergence between money, identity, and control. In such an environment, owning gold becomes less about tradition and more about choice. It is the right to hold wealth without justification, movement without trace, and value without compromise. For those who see the road ahead and choose not merely to adapt, but to prepare, gold is not nostalgia—it is foresight.

And in a world increasingly defined by what can be seen, tracked, and taxed, the quietest assets may be the most powerful of all.

Owning Gold Without Owning a Safe – A Practical and Philosophical Breakdown of ETFs, Vault Storage, and Physical Possession

The notion of owning gold once conjured images of secret compartments, armed guards, and fortified basements. Today, the landscape is far more nuanced—and more democratised. In a world defined by digital interfaces and geopolitical fragility, the ancient metal remains a cornerstone of enduring value. But for the modern investor, the question is no longer *whether* to own gold. It is *how*. The answer is not simply a logistical one. It's philosophical. Each method of gold ownership—be it direct possession, allocated vault storage, or paper proxies like ETFs—carries embedded assumptions about trust, control, privacy, and systemic risk. This subchapter offers a deeper examination of these trade-offs, not to prescribe a universal solution, but to equip the reader to make a self-aware, context-sensitive decision.

Let us begin with the most tactile—and psychologically resonant—form: physical possession. Owning gold in the form of bars, coins, or jewellery appeals to those seeking a form of value that exists outside the permissioned world. There is no third-party counterparty, no digital ledger, no intermediary to approve or deny access. The gold is yours in the most literal sense. This immediacy is not merely symbolic; it confers genuine autonomy. But autonomy has costs. Security becomes a private obligation, not a public guarantee. Fire, theft, loss, and even human error introduce risk vectors that must be managed with vigilance. Storage solutions range from inconspicuous hiding spots to insured private vaults, but each introduces a tension between privacy and practical accessibility. Moreover, liquidity—especially in crisis moments—can be unpredictable. Selling physical gold quickly, especially at a fair price, requires preparation and trusted networks.

Then there is the layered world of *allocated vault storage.* In this model, your gold is held in your name, often in a professional, audited vault—perhaps in Zurich, Singapore, or Toronto. The allure here is the blend of physicality and convenience. You maintain title to real gold, often serial-numbered and segregated, without the logistical burden of custody. Reputable services may allow inspection visits, delivery on demand, or even third-party audits. However, this approach is not without dependencies. You must trust the vaulting institution, the regulatory environment in which it operates, and the legal enforceability of your ownership—particularly in times of systemic stress. Consider Cyprus in 2013 or Argentina's long history of capital controls; even the safest jurisdictions are subject to political drift. Ownership on paper, even when legally robust, can become fragile under duress. Here, we confront a recurring philosophical theme: *custodianship is never neutral.* It imposes assumptions—about who enforces contracts, how sovereignty is defined, and which emergencies justify exception.

The most accessible—but least autonomous—form of gold exposure comes via *Exchange-Traded Funds (ETFs).* Products like SPDR Gold Shares (GLD) or iShares Gold Trust (IAU) are designed to mirror the price of gold while offering the liquidity and convenience of stocks. For portfolio balancing, tax efficiency, and ease of trade, they serve a legitimate role. But they are not gold. They are synthetic instruments, structured as claims upon third-party custodians, whose internal mechanics are opaque to most retail investors. Ownership here is not of metal, but of financial exposure. If the goal is tactical asset allocation, this may suffice. If the goal is sovereignty, it falls short. ETFs are ensnared in the same ecosystem—clearinghouses, custodians, regulators—that one might be seeking to hedge against. The irony is subtle but significant: many who turn to gold for insulation from financial architecture unwittingly re-enter it through ETFs.

A more granular risk is counterparty concentration. Most gold ETFs are backed by metal held in large bank vaults—often JP Morgan or HSBC—raising questions of systemic entanglement. Can a claim truly be decentralised if all roads lead back to the same financial citadels? This is not a conspiracy theory; it is a structural design critique. The very institutions whose stability gold is meant to hedge against become gatekeepers of that hedge.

Then there is a class of hybrid solutions: digital gold certificates, blockchain gold tokens, and app-based gold aggregators. Companies like Paxos, Kinesis, and Goldmoney promise frictionless access to allocated gold, often with the transparency of blockchain verification. At face value, these tools offer a bridge between the analog solidity of metal and the fluidity of digital finance. Yet their reliance on infrastructure, technology providers, and jurisdictional compliance demands discernment. These systems are only as trustworthy as their weakest institutional link. Moreover, they remain abstract to most users—functionally indistinguishable from fiat money with a gold veneer.

What emerges from this comparative analysis is a deeper insight: *methods of ownership encode philosophies of risk*. Physical possession leans towards radical independence, but demands high personal responsibility. Vault storage offers a middle path—balancing trust with tangible backing—at the cost of jurisdictional exposure. ETFs prioritise liquidity and integration, but depend heavily on the very systems many investors are trying to opt out of. No model is inherently superior. Each reflects trade-offs between security, autonomy, transparency, and access.

Yet what's striking is how few investors reflect on these philosophical premises. Gold is often approached tactically: what price did I pay, how much did it appreciate, what percentage does it constitute in my portfolio? These are fair questions—but insufficient. They overlook gold's historical role as *a form of political dissent.* In regimes where currency has collapsed, savings confiscated, or capital restricted, gold has operated not just as a store of value but as a silent form of agency. Its usefulness in such scenarios is not determined solely by market price, but by *form and format.* A one-kilo bar in a foreign vault may be inaccessible in crisis. A few sovereigns sewn into clothing may be life-saving. It is here that practical planning intersects with moral philosophy.

Ownership is not only a technical condition; it is a relational stance. To own something fully is to accept responsibility for its security, its use, and the consequences of its failure. In this light, gold becomes a litmus test of investor maturity. Are you owning it as a line item, or as a shield? Do you understand the implications of where, how, and through whom your gold is held? Have you mapped the operational chain of control—from acquisition to access to liquidation—under both normal and abnormal conditions?

Perhaps the most overlooked risk in gold ownership is psychological. Many turn to gold as an emotional salve during times of financial instability. It represents permanence, tangibility, and detachment from political manipulation. These are valid instincts. But they can also lead to magical thinking—treating gold as an invincible panacea rather than a specialised tool. Owning gold without understanding *how* you own it, or *why* that method aligns with your principles and scenarios, is not sovereignty. It's ornamental.

What, then, is the prudent approach? Start not with the market, but with the mirror. Ask: what am I optimising for? Privacy? Liquidity? Resilience? Then choose an ownership model that matches those priorities, not just under today's conditions, but under conditions where the financial system may fray, data surveillance may spike, or cross-border mobility may be restricted. Gold's relevance is not timeless; it is conditional. But those conditions—erosion of trust, expansion of digital control, and inflationary drift—are precisely what make its logic durable once again.

In the end, the method of ownership is a strategic declaration. It reveals whether you view gold as a speculative asset, a systemic hedge, a sovereign anchor, or a philosophical stance. A safe is not merely a container. An ETF is not merely a ticker. And vault storage is not merely outsourcing. Each is a worldview—quietly shaping how your wealth behaves in the future you haven't yet imagined.

Gold and the Psychology of Permanence

Gold's role in anchoring the mind during financial chaos—why it feels safe, and how to use that mental effect wisely.

When the scaffolding of modern finance begins to tremble—when interest rates spike, currencies wobble, or banks quietly limit withdrawals—people often turn not to algorithms, forecasts, or policies, but to a lustrous yellow metal pulled from the earth. This is not mere nostalgia. It is a deeply psychological reflex, reinforced by millennia of lived experience: *gold feels permanent.* But why? And more importantly, how should a modern individual interpret and utilise that feeling without falling into superstition, stagnation, or false certainty?

This chapter unpacks gold not merely as a commodity, store of value, or hedge, but as a *mental anchor*—a psychological tool shaped by historical memory, cognitive bias, and existential instinct. Understanding this mental dimension of gold is critical, especially in a world where speed, abstraction, and digital volatility define most financial assets. Amidst all this change, gold offers a powerful constant. And with constants come cognitive comforts—and risks.

The Cognitive Comfort of the Immutable

At a neurological level, the human brain is predisposed to favour what appears stable, tangible, and time-tested. In conditions of uncertainty, we crave what Daniel Kahneman calls "cognitive ease": stimuli or ideas that feel familiar and require less mental effort to process. Gold fits that category perfectly. It looks the same in every age. It does not tarnish. It does not rely on the solvency of an institution or the uptime of a server. There is no login, no password reset, no dependency on third-party APIs. *It just is.*

This simplicity is deceptive in its power. Behavioural finance research has shown that during financial crises, individuals overwhelmingly move toward "perceived safety" assets—often defined not by logical analysis, but by emotional resonance. Gold consistently appears near the top of that list. And for good reason: gold's value is not purely derived from utility, nor purely from speculation. It is derived from *continuity.* Across cultures, regimes, and collapses, gold has preserved purchasing power with a consistency no fiat currency can match.

But the real insight lies beneath the surface: gold functions as a psychological *anchor point*—a mental benchmark that calms the fear of total loss. It's not just about hedging against inflation or deflation. It's about hedging against *institutional betrayal, systemic opacity, and the terror of the unknowable.*

Gold as a Temporal Bridge

To understand the allure of gold in today's digitised financial landscape, it is helpful to recognise that gold is not just a monetary tool—it is a *temporal object.* That is, it connects generations across time. It outlasts banks. It outlasts policy regimes. It outlasts nation-states. The gold coin a Roman senator held, the same weight and purity, might be passed to a Renaissance merchant, and then centuries later to a modern-day investor. No update required.

This continuity has profound implications for how humans psychologically interpret time and legacy. Financial systems based on fiat or code tend to think in quarters or cycles. Gold encourages thinking in *centuries.* It expands the investor's psychological horizon, promoting intergenerational thinking at a time when most wealth planning struggles to see past retirement.

That long horizon can ground behaviour. It can moderate impulsivity. And in the hands of a thoughtful individual, it can lead to remarkably durable decisions. But—*and this is critical—the very permanence that makes gold a powerful psychological tool can also seduce the mind into rigidity.*

The Risk of Romanticising Stability

The danger is not in gold itself, but in what people project onto it. When societies feel betrayed by governments or shaken by rapid change, gold becomes a kind of financial mythology—a talisman against modernity. This is where discernment is needed. Gold is not an oracle. It does not generate yield. It does not protect against every contingency. And its emotional resonance can distort clear decision-making if not properly contextualised.

History is littered with periods where gold became more than a financial asset: it became an *ideological symbol.* In the 1930s United States, fear of capital flight led the government to ban private gold ownership. In Weimar Germany, it became one of the only trusted means of preserving purchasing power. In post-2008 America, it became a cultural line in the sand between those who trusted the Fed and those who didn't. Today, gold straddles similar lines—between digital transparency and analogue privacy, between faith in systems and autonomy from them.

If we are not careful, gold can become a *proxy for moral certainty* in an otherwise uncertain world. This, ironically, undermines the flexibility that true financial resilience demands.

Anchoring the Mind Without Paralysing It

So how does one use gold *wisely*—not just materially, but *psychologically*?

First, recognise gold's role not as a core growth asset but as an *emotional counterweight.* In the face of financial chaos, it allows an individual to hold a portion of their wealth outside the reach of institutions, regulators, and code. This alone can reduce panic and promote clearer thinking when everything else feels like it's in motion.

Second, *treat gold as a strategic boundary, not a sacred doctrine.* Allocate with intent. For some, 5–10% of a portfolio may be enough to invoke the psychological benefits of permanence without crowding out more productive, forward-looking assets. For others in more volatile jurisdictions, or with heightened privacy concerns, higher allocations may be justified.

Third, *revisit the gold allocation periodically*. The irony of "permanence" is that the world around it changes constantly. Gold must be held with *awareness*, not just stored and forgotten. Otherwise, what begins as psychological ballast can become a psychological trap—a reason to disengage from adaptive planning.

Gold in the Age of Digital Surveillance

The resurgence of interest in gold in the 2020s is not random—it is a response to the growing realisation that most digital assets, including money, are increasingly traceable, programmable, and, in many cases, censorable. Gold's appeal lies in its resistance to that trend. It is *value without metadata.*

While this may seem quaint or niche, it is in fact becoming strategically relevant. Central Bank Digital Currencies (CBDCs), the rise of algorithmic taxation, and the proliferation of financial surveillance technologies mean that the right to *opt out*—quietly and legally—is becoming both more valuable and more difficult.

Gold offers one of the few avenues for that option. Not because it is subversive, but because it is pre-modern—designed in a time before the idea of surveillance was even imaginable. In this way, gold is not just old—it is *out of system.* That psychological distinction is not merely symbolic; it is functional. It provides a credible Plan B without requiring a total rejection of Plan A.

Conclusion Without Saying "Conclusion"

To understand gold merely as a hedge is to miss the point. To understand it as a psychological *anchor*—a tool for reducing fear, broadening time horizons, and moderating behaviour—is to unlock its deeper function. In this light, gold is not a superstition of the past. It is a *lens* through which we can think more clearly about the future.

Used with humility and clarity, gold protects not just purchasing power—but perspective. It reminds the investor that amidst noise, there is still signal; amidst velocity, there is still gravity. And amidst all the abstractions of digital finance, there remains something with *mass.*

Gold is not the answer to everything. But when used intelligently, it can be the *answer to panic.* And in a financial world where panic can be more dangerous than poverty, that may be the most valuable role of all.

Chapter 5
Real Estate – Shelter, Strategy, and Soil

6+ asset class. But it is more than a mere financial instrument. Real estate occupies a unique place in the human psyche: it's refuge, it's symbolism, it's proof of one's existence within society's visible grid. For centuries, to own land has meant more than just wealth—it has signified protection, legitimacy, even power. Yet beneath this deep-seated cultural resonance lies a more unsettled truth. Real estate, though grounded in physicality, is anything but fixed in meaning or function. It can be stabilising, yes—but also precarious. It can empower, but under certain conditions, expose. In the right hands, it serves not just as shelter, but as insulation—against risk, against overreach, against the creeping erosion of autonomy.

This chapter isn't concerned with floorplans or price charts. Nor is it about property speculation or aesthetic charm. Its purpose is more elemental: to view real estate through the lens of individual resilience in a world increasingly defined by legal ambiguity, political flux, and jurisdictional instability. The question is no longer, "Where should I buy?" but rather, "How should I structure my presence on the land—and under which legal canopy should I seek protection?"

Our entry point is a shift in perception: the most transformative real estate trend of our time may not be the price boom, but the awakening—an expanding awareness that owning land is no longer synonymous with control, and that geography, by itself, tells you surprisingly little. In a mobile, hyper-digitised, and heavily monitored world, property boundaries don't always align with notions of security or sovereignty. Those who manage wealth, or simply value self-determination, must start to think differently.

Real Estate as Jurisdictional Leverage

Let's start by dismantling a persistent illusion: that real estate is intrinsically local. While the soil underfoot doesn't move, the ownership scaffolding around it—contracts, legal trusts, foreign holding companies—can stretch across continents. What used to be the domain of wealthy families and offshore lawyers is now part of a more democratised toolkit. Leaseholds in Southeast Asia, land-owning trusts domiciled in Jersey, titles digitised on registries halfway across the world and accessed via encrypted VPN—these are no longer exotic outliers. They're options, and increasingly, necessities.

The savvier property investors—those with an eye not just on returns, but on resilience—aren't fixated on postal codes alone. They interrogate the regulatory strata laid atop the land. Who sets planning policy, and with what predictability? How easily can rent controls be introduced? Is the local currency sufficiently stable to preserve the real value of rental income? Will proceeds from a sale be subject to capital controls, or find themselves ensnared in a banking crisis?

These are no longer the abstract worries of magnates and their legal retinues. They are becoming practical concerns for any globally minded individual with assets in more than one country, dual citizenship, or even the quiet desire to not be wholly at the mercy of a single legal regime. In this light, the property isn't the only thing being acquired—it's the legal envelope in which it sits, and the flexibility that envelope offers.

The notion of legal arbitrage—selecting jurisdictions not just for their climate or tax incentives, but for how they structure ownership, dispute resolution, and exit—is becoming embedded in the mindset of a new class of autonomy-seeking individuals. The romantic ideal of real estate as a permanent homestead is giving way to a colder, more strategic interpretation. Land, seen from this angle, is no longer a final destination—it's a position. One that can be re-evaluated, exited, or expanded depending on geopolitical tides.

In this sense, real estate morphs into a geopolitical option—an open-ended claim not only on physical shelter, but on lifestyle fluidity, capital defence, and sometimes, plain escape. Not because one expects collapse, but because one understands that systems shift. And when they do, the wrong deed in the wrong legal environment can turn from sanctuary to trap with astonishing speed.

The Illusion of Local Stability

The second assumption we dismantle is the myth of domestic real estate as the bedrock of safety. Home is where the tax raid happens. Home is where zoning boards stall development for decades. Home is where a populist politician can promise rent freezes and retroactive wealth taxes—policies unthinkable until suddenly enacted. The idea that one's local property market is inherently safer than a foreign jurisdiction is not supported by either history or contemporary policy volatility.

Consider the cases of Argentina, India, or even parts of Western Europe—regions where property taxes have changed abruptly, or where capital controls have prevented homeowners from selling and exiting on their own terms. Even in so-called "rule of law" countries, property rights are more malleable than advertised. The UK's recent policies on second-home taxation, or New York's retroactive rent control expansions, demonstrate how fragile that safety can be when governments face fiscal stress.

This is not a call for paranoia. It is a call for planning. Recognising that no jurisdiction is bulletproof encourages diversification—not just across cities, but across legal regimes. Property ownership, when concentrated in a single legal system, becomes a point of failure. The antidote is not retreat, but structure.

Control Without Exposure

This leads to our third foundational insight: that modern real estate strategy is not about how many deeds your name appears on, but about how much control you retain without undue exposure. Ownership, in many cases, is a liability—an easily targetable signal of wealth, jurisdictional presence, and financial immobility. Control, by contrast, can be designed more flexibly: through trusts, leases, SPVs, and other legal wrappers that offer access without full vulnerability.

Here, we unpack the real meaning of asset resilience: not just hard walls or passive income, but the ability to shelter wealth *from hostile scrutiny, illiquidity, or confiscation.* A trust in Singapore may offer more effective permanence than a freehold in a politically wobbly district. A 99-year lease in Thailand may carry fewer regulatory burdens than a freehold flat in a tax-heavy European capital. And a co-ownership structure in a planned community abroad may offer more lifestyle continuity than a crumbling apartment block in one's native city.

Each structure comes with trade-offs—cost, complexity, disclosure. But in a world where the most dangerous risk is often *being visible in the wrong way*, understanding these trade-offs is not an exercise in legalism. It's a necessity for sovereign planning.

From Shelter to Strategy

Ultimately, this chapter reframes real estate from the narrow view of ROI-maximising to the broader frame of *life infrastructure*. Where do you want the legal right to retreat? What flags do you want to plant—not for signalling wealth, but for securing rights? What jurisdictions offer redundancy, not just yield? These are not theoretical questions. They are increasingly existential ones.

A well-designed real estate portfolio does not merely protect capital. It protects *options*. It allows for temporary withdrawal, regulatory flexibility, and cultural diversification. It allows for transitions—between lifestyles, languages, climates, and legal systems. And it does all this while grounding the portfolio in physical reality—something that, paradoxically, becomes more valuable as finance becomes more virtual and abstract.

This chapter walks through the mechanics of making that shift—from location-driven thinking to structure-aware thinking; from asset chasing to jurisdictional mapping; from national loyalty to legal optionality. You'll learn how to spot false signals of safety. You'll be introduced to ways of controlling property without painting a target on your net worth. And most importantly, you'll be guided through the philosophical shift required to treat land not as static pride, but as mobile *strategy*.

Because in the end, real estate is not just where you sleep. It's where you anchor your autonomy—or lose it.

Beyond Appreciation: Real Estate as Power

We often discuss real estate in the language of returns—capital gains, rental yields, development potential. Yet this conventional framing misses something deeper and far more enduring: *land is not merely an appreciating asset; it is a platform for power.* Economic, political, psychological, even nutritional power. Unlike paper assets that can vanish in a policy shift or a database corruption, real estate—when chosen and structured intelligently—endows its holder with something much more than yield: it grants *leverage* over life itself.

This chapter repositions property investment as something more strategic than speculation and more grounded than passive income. It considers real estate not only for its financial metrics but for its capacity to *anchor autonomy*, to *insulate against supply shocks*, to *secure geopolitical options*, and to *preserve legacy* across generations. The idea is not romantic nostalgia for homesteading or feudal privilege. It is a sober analysis of why land still matters—even, and especially, in a digitised world.

Let us begin where most balance sheets end: at *sovereignty*.

Land as Autonomy Infrastructure

In a world increasingly defined by dependence—on centralised utilities, rented digital spaces, algorithmic access to essential services—physical land remains one of the last forms of *unmediated control*. When you own productive land, you control a patch of the Earth's surface outright. You are not simply betting on price; you are buying a perimeter, a set of legal rights, and a zone of potential independence.

This autonomy becomes especially pronounced when the land is functional: a parcel with water access, arable soil, solar potential, or simply distance from regulatory density. Such land is not just valuable—it is *useful.* It enables you to opt out of fragility. You can produce, harvest, shelter, store. When digital platforms suspend your account, when banking systems freeze your funds, when city infrastructure fails, a well-selected piece of land doesn't just retain value. It *retains agency.*

This is not a ruralist fantasy. It is a recognition that ownership in cities often comes with exposure but no autonomy—an expensive square box surrounded by policy risk and utility dependency. The most sovereign real estate is not necessarily urban or glamorous. It is strategic. It gives you *options when systems don't.*

Food Security: The Overlooked Utility

Few investors include food resilience in their risk models. Yet in times of economic or political crisis, the ability to access or produce food—directly or through proximity—becomes a defining differentiator. Land with agricultural potential is often dismissed by urban investors as low-yield or inconvenient. But during inflationary periods, supply chain interruptions, or state-imposed rationing, such land transitions from an underperforming asset to a critical *supply base.*

Food, like energy, is a foundation layer of sovereignty. A hectare of productive soil with a simple irrigation system can provide seasonal self-sufficiency for a household. Scale that with neighbours, and it becomes a community buffer. In such configurations, land is not only a store of wealth but a store of *life continuity.*

This is particularly relevant as climate instability and geopolitical tensions pressure global food systems. Property that enables local production—either directly through farming or indirectly through community-supported agriculture—is not just prudent. It is prescient. Even for investors uninterested in active farming, leasing land to trusted producers creates a win-win structure: long-term land appreciation coupled with community-level food resilience.

Property and Political Leverage

Another strategic function of land, especially internationally, is its power to unlock *legal status*. Numerous countries extend residency, citizenship, or tax status in exchange for real estate investment. These programmes are often marketed under the term "Golden Visas", but their real value is not prestige—it is *optionality*.

The ability to acquire a second residency through property ownership is more than an immigration benefit. It is a political hedge. It gives you an alternative jurisdiction—of tax, travel, and civil rights—independent of your birth passport. In a time when governments are increasingly willing to restrict capital movement, redefine tax obligations retroactively, or weaponise residency rules, having legal and physical footing in multiple territories is not luxurious. It is strategic redundancy.

Critically, the type of property you purchase under these programmes can also define your ongoing obligations. Some countries allow fractional ownership in approved developments; others require direct landholding. Understanding these distinctions can help you avoid pitfalls such as illiquid assets, overpriced developer schemes, or inflated management costs. Smart investors use such programmes not for quick flips but for *jurisdictional diversification*—an arcane but potent form of future-proofing.

Generational Continuity and the Philosophy of Inheritance

In many cultures, the ownership of land is deeply tied to generational continuity. It is what stays when the business fails, the currency hyperinflates, or the family emigrates. Property becomes *the bridge across disruption*—a physical memory of continuity that survives institutional collapse.

But to harness this intergenerational utility, you must think beyond deed titles. You must consider *structures*—trusts, foundations, succession plans—that allow property to outlive individual control without becoming legally entangled or tax-exposed. This is where many affluent families go wrong. They accumulate assets, but fail to *design permanence*.

Well-structured land portfolios—especially those diversified across jurisdictions—can serve as stabilising anchors for families navigating professional mobility, social unrest, or political change. They become teaching tools for stewardship, continuity, and values. A family that holds land learns responsibility. A family that leases land learns leverage. Both models can work, but only if they are designed with *intentionality*.

Control vs Display: A Modern Caution

The final argument for viewing real estate as power—not just capital—is that power, unlike cash, invites scrutiny. That is why the *form* in which you hold land matters. Visibility can attract regulation, surveillance, or expropriation. The wisest landholders today are not those who shout their holdings from the rooftops, but those who *structure for privacy, control, and resilience.*

Consider land held through nominee entities in stable offshore jurisdictions. Or through irrevocable trusts that separate legal ownership from benefit enjoyment. Or co-operative models that grant use rights without headline exposure. These are not evasive tactics; they are defensive ones. *In a world where power is punished before it is admired*, discretion is strategy.

***

To reduce real estate to a line item in your asset mix is to miss its most enduring attributes. Land is not a luxury—it is a launchpad. It enables sovereignty, shelters continuity, anchors food systems, opens legal frontiers, and creates spaces that endure beyond the lifespan of currency or code. If digital assets offer speed and abstraction, land offers gravity and anchorage. You need both.

What you build on it—economically, socially, or psychologically—is yours to design. But to ignore its power is to walk into the future without a foundation.

Let's now explore how that foundation can be intelligently chosen, securely structured, and globally leveraged—not for display, but for defence.

Global Geographies of Opportunity

Why the Smartest Real Estate Investments Today Aren't in Glamour Zones but in Strategy Zones

Ask most people where the real estate "opportunity" lies in a globalised world, and they will likely default to the familiar narratives: booming capitals, luxury beachfronts, or high-rise hubs in emerging markets. These locations may offer headline-grabbing returns or architectural prestige—but they rarely offer *sovereignty*. They rarely offer *resilience*. And they almost never offer *control*.

This chapter is not about location in the traditional sense. It is about jurisdictional leverage. It is about using real estate not for display, but for *defence. Not for speculation, but for structural strategy*. In a time of intensifying surveillance, taxation without recourse, financial censorship, and migratory volatility, where you hold property is no longer just about yield—it's about legal architecture, mobility engineering, and geopolitical foresight.

This is not real estate as a trophy. This is real estate as a *citizenship tool*, a *tax filter*, and a *continuity anchor*. When selected properly, property can do more than grow your net worth—it can change your nationality, your liabilities, your physical access, and even your digital exposure.

Rethinking "Prime" Real Estate

The traditional understanding of "prime" real estate is increasingly irrelevant to strategic wealth holders. A high-rise penthouse in London may yield prestige, but it also attracts the gaze of regulators, a burdensome tax regime, and little flexibility in times of financial scrutiny. The very visibility of "prime" often comes with embedded liabilities.

By contrast, a modest villa in northern Portugal can offer access to EU residency, tax benefits under the non-habitual resident (NHR) regime, and visa-free mobility across the Schengen area. Similarly, agricultural land in Uruguay can provide asset protection through offshore trusts and sovereign food resilience.

In this context, *prime is not about postcode; it is about posture.* The investor of the next decade must look beyond glossy valuation reports and ask sharper questions:

What does this asset unlock jurisdictionally?

What legal protections does the local constitution offer?

How easily can I exit, sell, or restructure this holding?

Does this property entrench me in one regime—or give me mobility to exit it?

When evaluated through this lens, the definition of "opportunity" expands dramatically.

Legal Arbitrage Through Property

One of the most under-discussed utilities of real estate is *legal arbitrage*: the practice of using international variation in property laws to your advantage. While financial arbitrage exploits pricing inefficiencies, legal arbitrage exploits regulatory asymmetry. Property, as a physical and jurisdiction-bound asset, is a perfect vehicle for this.

Consider the distinction between *civil law* and *common law* jurisdictions. In many civil law countries (e.g. Spain, France), property succession is heavily regulated—inheritance must follow strict familial lines, often enforced by courts. In contrast, common law jurisdictions (e.g. England, Belize, Singapore) allow for greater testamentary freedom, trust structures, and asset shielding. Holding property in the latter can significantly improve estate planning outcomes and generational control.

Then there is the question of *title registration*. In countries like Germany and Switzerland, land registries are transparent, decentralised, and legally enforceable. In others—such as parts of Southeast Asia or Latin America—titles are routinely challenged, manipulated, or lack digital reliability. Investing in the former offers legal clarity; investing in the latter demands a very different risk premium.

Smart investors map not just market performance, but *legal infrastructure*. They look for countries where real estate law is predictable, contracts are enforceable, and dispute resolution is efficient. *The rule of law is not abstract—it's a calculable asset multiplier.*

Residency and Citizenship by Investment (CBI)

Real estate is not only a wealth-preservation tool—it is increasingly a *citizenship gateway*. More than a dozen countries offer pathways to residency or citizenship in exchange for property investment. While these programmes are often marketed by agents as lifestyle perks, their true value lies in *jurisdictional redundancy*.

Take the example of Greece's Golden Visa. For an investment of €250,000 in property—lower than the average apartment in Manhattan—a non-EU citizen can gain full residency rights within the Schengen area. Similar schemes exist in Portugal, Spain, and Malta, often with paths to citizenship after five to seven years of residency.

This is not about migration for lifestyle. It's about acquiring a second legal identity—an alternative exit door—without needing to renounce your primary nationality. In a future of increasing capital controls, these alternative legal domiciles can become lifelines. They are not theoretical. They are real, tangible, and increasingly necessary.

Not all CBI or RBI programmes are created equal. Some, like those in Caribbean nations, offer quick paths to passports but weaker global mobility. Others, such as Austria's investor residency, demand more capital but provide deeper integration. The structure of the programme—and the type of real estate you must hold—should be examined with the same rigour as the property itself.

Lifestyle Arbitrage: More Than Sun and Sand

There is another, quieter dimension to global real estate strategy: *lifestyle arbitrage*. This is not about retiring on a beach. It's about living somewhere where your capital goes further, your taxes go lower, and your stress levels recalibrate.

In the post-pandemic era, with remote work normalised and digital entrepreneurship untethered, increasing numbers of high-skilled individuals are relocating not for glamour but for *sovereignty*. Estonia offers e-residency and an ultra-low bureaucracy tax regime. Panama combines territorial taxation with coastal property markets under $150,000. Georgia (the country) has seen a quiet boom in entrepreneurial immigration, thanks to a business-friendly environment and stable property rights.

The key concept here is *jurisdictional decoupling*. Where you earn your income, where you hold your assets, and where you reside physically can—and should—be three different answers. Real estate in favourable jurisdictions allows you to *anchor your legal presence in one country while maintaining economic relationships with others*. This separation of identity streams—legal, economic, and digital—is the hallmark of the modern sovereign individual.

Diversification Is Not Enough—What You Need Is Differentiation

A common mistake even among seasoned investors is geographic diversification without strategic differentiation. Holding apartments in London, Sydney, and New York is not international resilience—it is *concentration under three correlated systems*. All three markets are highly financialised, overregulated, and politically synchronised.

True diversification looks like this:

A tax-advantaged holding in Uruguay or Paraguay (for agricultural exposure and currency insulation)

A city-centre flat in Budapest (for EU access without Western Europe price tags)

A co-invested development in Bali or Chiang Mai (for rental yield and second-residency options)

This approach is not scattershot. It is structured. Each asset serves a different function: tax, access, yield, identity. That is *differentiation.*

Risk Is Jurisdictional Before It Is Economic

No discussion of international property strategy would be complete without addressing *regime risk*. The illusion of safety in "developed" countries has been shattered repeatedly—by capital controls in Cyprus, sudden tax raids in Canada, eviction freezes in California, and expropriation rhetoric in parts of Western Europe.

Meanwhile, so-called "emerging" markets such as Georgia, Mauritius, or Colombia have strengthened investor protections, digitised land registries, and opened doors to global capital. Risk, then, is no longer a function of GDP per capita. It is a function of *policy volatility*, legal trustworthiness, and institutional responsiveness.

When mapping global opportunity, the wise investor asks not just *"Where is growing?"* but *"Where is governing rationally?" "Where are contracts enforced?" "Where are disputes resolved without political interference?"* These are not philosophical questions. They are filters that determine whether your real estate portfolio becomes a source of leverage or a source of liability.

The geography of opportunity today is not defined by glamour, nor even by growth. It is defined by *architecture*: legal, fiscal, logistical. It is defined by how a parcel of land interacts with the structures around it—tax codes, passports, treaties, supply chains.

In a world where capital is increasingly exposed and movement increasingly scrutinised, real estate offers more than just profit. It offers presence. And presence, properly structured, is power.

Let's now explore the illusions of local stability—why even "safe" markets can turn hostile, and how you can design resilience into your property holdings from the ground up.

The Illusion of Local Stability

Why Familiar Zip Codes Are Not Synonymous with Safety—and How to Build Mobility into Your Real Estate Strategy

The most dangerous assumption in real estate investing is not over-optimism about returns, nor underestimation of maintenance costs. It is the quiet, often unexamined belief that the place you know best is the place you can trust most. This idea—that your home country, your city, your legal system is inherently more reliable than others—rests not on data but on proximity bias. And in a world of escalating regime volatility, that bias is increasingly a liability.

Local stability, particularly in developed economies, is often more performative than structural. Political calm masks legislative fragility. High credit ratings conceal legal ambiguity. Mature democracies are not immune to overreach; they are simply more sophisticated in its implementation. What you assume is permanent zoning law, constitutional protection, or tax clarity today may be rewritten by emergency powers, populist pivots, or bureaucratic drift tomorrow.

Understanding this fragility—and building real estate portfolios that anticipate it—is not pessimism. It is *prudence*. The most effective investors of the next decade will not be those who chase yield or glamour but those who master *jurisdictional agility*. They will not ask, "Where is safest?" but "Where can I leave, adapt, or restructure most efficiently when the rules change?"

Zoning as Political Theatre

Take zoning law—an ostensibly boring, highly localised domain. In theory, zoning codes are the most stable and slow-moving regulations in the property world. In practice, they are levers of social policy and political theatre. Rezoning can upend the economic logic of entire investment portfolios, often with minimal warning.

In 2018, the city of Vancouver dramatically rewrote its zoning landscape to combat perceived inequality and housing shortages. Multi-unit residential zones were downzoned, development rights were suspended, and speculative foreign buyers were retroactively penalised. What was marketed as progressive housing policy amounted to a government-mandated destruction of previously legal investment theses. The losers were not predatory developers. They were ordinary asset holders who had assumed local continuity.

In Melbourne, the imposition of "growth boundaries" revalued farmland overnight, creating winners and losers based solely on geographic accident—not market insight. In Berlin, rent control measures effectively paralysed entire neighbourhoods, creating legal ambiguity that took years to unwind and caused private capital to flee. These are not isolated anecdotes. They are signals.

The lesson is clear: *Zoning is not a technical domain. It is a battlefield of competing visions of society. And the rules can, and do, change.*

Tax Raids in Developed Markets

The illusion of stability often extends to taxation. Investors assume that tax policy in developed countries is governed by predictability, transparency, and rule of law. That assumption is weakening fast.

In 2020, Canada—long seen as a beacon of real estate predictability—introduced a retroactive foreign buyer's tax and a punitive vacancy tax targeting non-resident owners. The measures were politically expedient but economically destructive, particularly to immigrant families who had invested legally and in good faith. In the United Kingdom, successive stamp duty surcharges on foreign buyers and non-residents were introduced with virtually no parliamentary resistance. In both cases, the narrative was the same: property ownership is no longer a neutral act. It is a political signal. And non-citizen owners are soft targets.

In the United States, proposals to tax unrealised capital gains—once considered fringe—are gaining traction. California has floated wealth taxes that would apply even after residents move away. These are not fully enacted policies, but their increasing mainstream support underscores a broader truth: *taxation is no longer a static ledger—it is a dynamic weapon in the hands of governments under fiscal pressure.*

The phrase "tax certainty" should no longer be interpreted as a permanent promise. It is, at best, a short-term truce.

Democratic Regimes Are Not Immune to Expropriation

Many investors mentally associate expropriation or property seizure with unstable autocracies. The historical record tells a different story. Some of the most aggressive property seizures in modern history were enacted by democratic governments under the guise of public interest, wartime emergency, or economic recovery.

Consider Cyprus in 2013, when the government, under direction from the EU and IMF, enacted a "bail-in" of private bank deposits—including those held in accounts used for real estate transactions. The property market collapsed. Confidence evaporated. And yet, Cyprus was—and still is—a member of the European Union.

Or consider the United States Supreme Court's 2005 *Kelo v. City of New London* ruling, which expanded the definition of "public use" in eminent domain seizures to include transfer of property to private developers for economic revitalisation. In practice, this meant that if the government decided a mall would be more beneficial than your family home, it had the legal precedent to take it.

The key insight is this: *the legal right to own property is not the same as the practical ability to retain it during political shifts.* Title deeds are only as secure as the institutional culture and financial health of the regime that backs them.

Mitigation Is Not Local—it's Mobility

So how do you mitigate these risks without falling into paranoia or paralysis?

The first step is psychological: disinvest from the belief that the "known" equals the "safe." This recalibration opens the door to more rational, data-driven analysis of risk across jurisdictions.

The second step is structural: build *mobility* into your real estate strategy. This does not necessarily mean selling your existing property—it means *hedging its exposure.* Consider the following approaches:

Jurisdictional Diversification: Do not anchor all your holdings within a single legal regime. Property in Portugal, Georgia, or Uruguay can offer complementary legal, tax, and political profiles to those in the UK or US.

Ownership Structures: Use international trusts, offshore entities, or multi-layered holding companies to create flexibility in the face of regulatory shifts. Properly structured, these can offer legal distance between your identity and the asset—without compromising control.

Exit Vectors: Invest in properties that are *not only rentable or valuable but sellable*—quickly, to a global market, under different legal conditions. Liquidity under duress is a separate metric from valuation under calm.

Second Residency Planning: Link at least one property holding to a second residency or citizenship programme. This creates legal and physical continuity in the event of future movement restrictions, bank freezes, or capital controls.

These tools are not exotic. They are now essential. The investors who navigate the next decade best will be those who approach real estate as a system of interlocking legal, political, and strategic moves—not just square footage and postcode.

The New Definition of Safe

The traditional markers of "safe" markets—GDP size, political democracy, strong judiciary—must now be weighed against a different matrix: legislative volatility, tax desperation, institutional overload, and regime adaptability.

A small, administratively competent country with limited debt and a constitutional commitment to private property may now offer more stability than a G7 nation under populist economic pressure. A mid-tier city with transparent local governance and low regulatory churn may be more attractive than a superstar capital on the brink of affordability collapse.

Safety is no longer about size. It is about subtlety.

***

What the next wave of serious property investors must internalise is this: *the biggest risk is not collapse—it is confidence erosion.* When trust in legal and political consistency fades, property becomes a liability rather than a pillar. And often, the danger doesn't come from "the market". It comes from the state.

But here's the opportunity: if you can see the illusion for what it is, you're already ahead of 90% of investors. Because what's coming is not chaos. It's *recalibration.* And those who build mobility, structure, and legal diversification into their portfolios will not only survive that recalibration—they will shape it.

Owning vs Controlling Property

Why the Smartest Real Estate Strategy Isn't Always Having Your Name on the Deed

In many cultures, property ownership is treated as the apex of financial accomplishment—a visible, documentable, bank-verified proof of success. Deeds are celebrated, titles framed, land registries trusted as final. But as real estate becomes increasingly politicised, regulated, and exposed to surveillance, the logic of traditional ownership begins to falter. It is not that ownership itself has become dangerous—it is that visibility has. In today's landscape, the most resilient real estate investors are not just owners. They are *architects of control.* And in many cases, they control without owning.

This distinction—between owning an asset and *controlling* it—sits at the heart of sophisticated portfolio design. True resilience is not achieved by collecting properties in your personal name. It is achieved by strategically allocating *control rights* while mitigating exposure. This subchapter dissects that premise. We'll contrast traditional ownership with tools like discretionary trusts, long-term land leases, and fractionalised structures—each enabling access, utility, and control *without the visibility and vulnerability of direct ownership.*

The aim is not to evade responsibility but to *structure intelligently*—to design for longevity, legal distance, and optionality. In a world where property attracts not just attention but intervention, owning everything directly is not a symbol of strength. It's a point of failure.

The Exposure of Direct Ownership

When your name appears on a public land registry, it doesn't simply prove your legal rights. It also broadcasts your economic footprint, your jurisdictional presence, and your vulnerability to taxation, litigation, and political scrutiny. In countries like the United States, the UK, and Canada, property records are public and easily searchable. This openness—lauded as a check on corruption—also functions as a tool of targeting.

Assets held directly are subject to probate, inheritance taxes, creditor claims, divorce settlements, and freezing orders. If you are sued in a civil case, a property in your name can be seized. If the government reclassifies your asset class, it can be retroactively taxed, zoned, or regulated. In short: *ownership is power, but also exposure.* The wealthiest families, sovereign funds, and institutional investors have known this for decades. They seldom own directly. They *control through entities.*

Why, then, do so many individual investors still pursue property in the most exposed, least flexible form?

Because the legal and psychological default is simple: "own it, and it's yours." But as we'll see, that definition of "yours" can be dangerously shallow.

Trusts: Control Without Visibility

A trust is not a loophole. It's a legal structure that separates *ownership* from *benefit.* When a property is placed into a discretionary trust, it is no longer legally owned by the individual—it is owned by the trust, administered by trustees for the benefit of named or future beneficiaries. This creates a crucial layer of protection.

Properly structured, a trust can:

Shield the asset from personal litigation or creditors

Bypass probate and maintain confidentiality after death

Enable multi-generational transfer without triggering repeated tax events

Allow the settlor to retain meaningful control (through protector roles or reserved powers) without direct ownership

For example, a family may hold agricultural land in New Zealand through a local trust, with income distributed to heirs, governance delegated to an independent trustee, and succession secured without a single personal name on the land registry. In jurisdictions with stable trust law (e.g. Singapore, the Channel Islands, New Zealand), this structure offers a highly effective form of private control that is both lawful and enduring.

But this approach is not without complexity. Trusts must be drafted carefully, respecting both the letter and spirit of tax transparency rules. Attempting to disguise control while exercising it absolutely may violate anti-avoidance laws. The point is not deception. It is *separation of form from function*—owning less, but controlling more securely.

Land Leases: Use Without Exposure

Long-term land leases offer another overlooked pathway to real estate control. In many jurisdictions—Thailand, the Philippines, parts of Africa and Latin America—foreigners are restricted or prohibited from owning land outright. But 30–99 year leases are often fully legal, renewable, and enforceable. Properly structured, these leases grant almost all the practical rights of ownership: building, renting, farming, even resale of the lease.

In risk-averse jurisdictions, even domestic investors are beginning to prefer leasehold structures—particularly when layered through corporate entities. Why? Because leaseholds can reduce capital requirements, limit upfront taxation, and provide strategic flexibility if laws or governments change.

The critical insight is this: *control of a physical asset does not require perpetual legal title.* What matters more is the enforceability of use rights—and the ability to renew or exit under favourable terms.

A sophisticated example might involve a holding company based in Dubai leasing real estate in Sri Lanka, governed under English common law, and subletting to digital nomads. Here, ownership is fragmented, yet utility and cash flow remain fully in the investor's hands—without geographic entrapment or reputational exposure.

Fractional and Tokenised Ownership: Access Without Concentration

Another innovative frontier is *fractional ownership.* This model breaks up the equity of a property into shares, allowing multiple investors to participate in ownership or returns. The concept is not new—REITs and property syndicates have operated on this logic for decades—but recent technology has enabled more agile, direct-to-consumer versions.

Platforms now allow buyers to hold fractions of properties across continents, often secured by blockchain smart contracts and governed under special purpose vehicles (SPVs). This model offers several advantages:

Reduced capital risk per asset

Jurisdictional diversification without needing full property management

Exposure to high-value markets otherwise inaccessible

Liquidity, in some cases, through peer-to-peer resale mechanisms

However, fractional ownership is not control. The trade-off is clear: *you gain access, but relinquish strategic autonomy.* You cannot dictate repairs, repurpose the property, or restructure debt without consent. This makes it unsuitable for those seeking hands-on control, but ideal for those prioritising diversification and reduced regulatory exposure.

Used intelligently, fractional models complement more centralised, personally controlled holdings—offering a blended strategy of access, yield, and optionality.

Strategic Implications: Designing for Resilience

Owning property in your own name offers simplicity and pride. But simplicity is not strategy. And pride is not protection. The true metric of success in property investing—particularly at the sovereign level—is not *how much you own*, but *how intelligently you control.*

Ask:

Can your assets be frozen, taxed, or seized by one political event?

Can they be transferred to heirs without legal battles or public disclosure?

Can you restructure, exit, or relocate those assets without triggering punitive costs?

If the answer is no, then you may be wealthy—but not secure.

A resilient portfolio is designed like a chessboard, not a spreadsheet. Each piece serves a purpose. Some should be visible and liquid. Others should be shielded and stable. Some should yield income. Others should yield continuity.

The most strategic investors today are not accumulating titles. They are orchestrating *layers of control*: visible use rights, invisible benefit rights, and flexible governance mechanisms—all built across jurisdictions.

They understand that in the coming decades, *the most dangerous thing to own may be ownership itself*—and the most powerful thing to hold may be *unseen authority*.

Chapter 6
Crypto – The Fire Escape from the System

If gold serves as the memory of money and real estate its tangible form, then cryptocurrency is money's sharp-edged reimagining—less evolution, more rebellion. It is not merely a digitised asset class or an intriguing tech experiment. Crypto has taken on the role of a cultural accelerant, a philosophical irritant, and—depending on your vantage point—a blueprint for financial emancipation. It challenges not just how value is stored or exchanged, but who gets to define value in the first place. For those feeling hemmed in by financial systems that appear increasingly opaque, politicised, or structurally fragile, crypto offers something closer to an exit than an investment.

We do not begin this chapter in the weeds of whitepapers or smart contracts. We begin with something older: context. This is not a paean to Bitcoin maximalism, nor a speculative ride through this week's altcoin gossip. Rather, our focus is on the architecture—the undercurrents shaping why crypto, for all its noise and novelty, has become essential to conversations about personal sovereignty, systemic resilience, and institutional distrust. Crypto should not be approached as a monolith, and certainly not as a miracle. What it demands is close reading. There are strata here—technological, ideological, operational—and unpacking them allows the reader to engage deliberately: to discern what to hold, why it matters, and how it might fit within a broader defence of autonomy.

To appreciate crypto's significance in this age of fractured trust and institutional fatigue, one must trace its story—not merely as a new form of money, but as a movement. Born out of the financial wreckage of 2008, Bitcoin did not emerge to optimise speed or yield; it emerged to challenge premise. Over time, what began as a decentralised alternative to fiat has unfurled into a full-blown ecosystem: DeFi protocols reimagining lending without banks, NFTs bending the boundaries of ownership and culture, DAOs experimenting with governance models, privacy coins wrestling with surveillance itself. Each node in this ecosystem expresses something deeper than code: a worldview, sometimes messy, often contradictory, but consistently animated by a desire to reduce dependence on intermediaries who have long enjoyed unearned trust.

Engaging with this culture—yes, culture, not just codebase—is not optional. It's not window dressing. It's the substrate. Crypto's technological scaffolding is embedded with values: transparency, permissionlessness, resilience through redundancy. To ignore the subculture is to misunderstand the product. To invest in the asset without reckoning with the ethic is to miss the point.

And yet, this is no utopia. Crypto carries its own frictions: volatility, complexity, grift dressed up as innovation. But perhaps that's what makes it so distinctly human—its promise and its peril bound together, neither fully knowable in advance. In this sense, crypto isn't a destination. It's a tool, a response, a provocation. And like any good provocation, it forces us to ask: not just what is money—but who decides?

This chapter, then, is an attempt to equip—not to convince. It is written not for zealots nor sceptics, but for those with eyes open and minds unclosed. For those willing to explore the possibility that money, like power, is undergoing decentralisation. That perhaps the most important feature of crypto isn't its price, but its permissionlessness. And that even if one never holds a single satoshi, understanding this shift is no longer optional for anyone serious about the future of wealth, control, and freedom.

From Currency to Culture: The Reframing of Ownership

The original whitepaper for Bitcoin made a simple claim: that it was possible to transfer money directly from one person to another without an intermediary. What began as a peer-to-peer cash system has evolved into something far larger: a global contest over who defines money, who governs its use, and who gets to opt out.

Crypto today is not just about transacting—it is about *participating* in a system that was built outside the rules of state finance. It offers the possibility—not the guarantee—of ownership that is *self-custodied*, transferable across borders, and not dependent on banks, governments, or corporate platforms. It is a system in which *you are your own bank*, and every transaction is a form of speech.

This autonomy comes at a cost: cognitive overhead, security risks, and a steep learning curve. But that cost is often worth paying for those who feel traditional finance has abandoned its neutrality. For activists in authoritarian countries, crypto is a lifeline. For investors in hyperinflationary economies, it is survival. For builders and technologists, it is a playground for reinventing identity, value, and community—all outside of legacy rails.

To understand crypto's promise, one must first understand its *psychological shift*: it moves the locus of trust from institutions to algorithms, from paper contracts to code, from external authority to internal vigilance.

Cold Storage, Hot Minds: Operational Security as a Mindset

Crypto requires a new kind of financial literacy—one where memorising a seed phrase is as important as reading a balance sheet, and where the user is responsible not only for the asset, but for the environment in which it is held. In the fiat world, one forgets a password and clicks "reset." In crypto, forgetting a private key can mean irreversible loss. There is no helpdesk. There is no appeal. There is only *ownership or absence.*

This reality introduces a shift in mindset: from *transactional convenience* to *operational vigilance.* Cold wallets—hardware devices that store private keys offline—are not just tools; they are symbols of personal accountability. Using them correctly demands a different rhythm of thinking: one that anticipates attack vectors, respects encryption, and embraces delay as a feature, not a flaw.

Learning to store crypto securely is not a checklist exercise. It is a cultural initiation. It introduces the holder to a world of *threat modelling, jurisdictional awareness, and digital minimalism*. It teaches you not only how to hold assets, but how to think adversarially—an increasingly necessary skill in a world of rising surveillance, centralised data harvesting, and political overreach.

In this chapter, we will demystify these tools—not just by explaining how to use them, but by showing why they matter. We will unpack the layers of self-custody: seed phrase management, multisignature wallets, air-gapped devices, and recovery protocols. But more importantly, we will examine the psychological maturity that these tools demand, and how that maturity mirrors the broader ethos of financial sovereignty.

Digital Gold vs Digital Liquidity: Designing Purposeful Crypto Portfolios

Crypto is not one thing. It is many things. Bitcoin, with its fixed supply and slow throughput, functions as *digital gold*—a long-term store of value that prizes predictability over programmability. Stablecoins, by contrast, offer *digital liquidity*—tethered to fiat currencies but operating in a frictionless, programmable environment. Then there are smart contract platforms like Ethereum, enabling an ecosystem of decentralised finance (DeFi) applications that mirror—and in some cases, outperform—traditional financial products.

Each category has a different risk profile, use case, and strategic function. Bitcoin is not useful for day-to-day payments. DeFi tokens are not ideal for long-term preservation. Stablecoins may be pegged to the dollar, but they carry counterparty risk. Treating these assets interchangeably is like treating gold, stocks, and cash as identical simply because they all appear on a portfolio statement.

We will walk readers through a classification framework for crypto assets based not on hype cycles, but on *function.* What assets preserve value? What assets generate yield? What assets provide access to tools, governance, or digital jurisdictions? What assets correlate with fiat liquidity, and which resist it entirely?

We will also explore the interplay between centralised exchanges and decentralised protocols—the trade-offs between convenience and control, between ease and exposure. We'll examine regulatory chokepoints, censorship risk, and on/off ramp design. Because owning crypto is only the beginning. Moving it, securing it, and *spending it under stress* is where strategic clarity is tested.

Crypto as Exit Technology, Not Escape Fantasy

It is tempting to treat crypto as a utopian promise—a world where all intermediaries disappear and perfect markets emerge. That view is not only naïve; it is dangerous. Crypto is powerful not because it erases problems, but because it *changes the terrain on which those problems are solved.* It is not a replacement for discipline, governance, or trust. It is a reconfiguration of how those elements interact.

Used intelligently, crypto is not an escape *from* systems—it is an *exit option within* them. It allows holders to create parallel infrastructures: for value transfer, for identification, for collective coordination. These infrastructures are not flawless. They are often fragile, experimental, and difficult to navigate. But they are *outside the reach* of most centralised coercive tools—and that fact alone makes them invaluable in the modern resilience toolkit.

Bitcoin is not a religion. Ethereum is not a government. DAOs are not a panacea. But all of them represent *cracks in the monopoly of legacy finance*, and each offers different ways to move, save, transact, and build outside the control layers of traditional power.

This chapter invites the reader not to become a crypto evangelist, but to become *crypto-capable.* Not to speculate blindly, but to design purposefully. To see the blockchain not as a tech fad, but as a toolset for financial autonomy.

Designing Your Fire Escape

A good fire escape is not used in daily life. But when needed, it must be accessible, unobstructed, and known in advance. Crypto, for many, will never be a primary residence. But it may one day be the difference between access and isolation—between coerced compliance and financial dignity.

To build a resilient Backup Plan Portfolio, one must learn to treat crypto not only as an investment but as *infrastructure.* This chapter will guide readers through the practical, technical, and psychological architecture required to make that infrastructure usable—before it's urgent.

You'll learn:

How to think in crypto-native terms: keys, protocols, consensus

How to structure holdings to match risk appetite and purpose

How to self-custody assets with discipline, not drama

How to use crypto to extend—not just digitise—your financial autonomy

Because when legacy institutions falter, freeze, or fade, it is not enough to have opinions. You must have exits. And crypto, properly understood, offers one of the few exits that doesn't ask for permission.

Decoding Decentralisation

Beyond Hype, Beyond Bitcoin—Why Blockchain Is a Framework for Individual Power

The term "decentralisation" has been so thoroughly absorbed into tech marketing that its original meaning is now often buried beneath jargon, tribalism, and blind speculation. To some, it's a meme. To others, it's a manifesto. To most, it's still misunderstood—equated with cryptocurrency prices, NFT drops, or the latest DeFi protocol promising triple-digit yields. But at its core, decentralisation is not a financial product. It is a *design principle for power distribution*—a structural response to concentrated control.

This subchapter makes a deliberately sober claim: that decentralisation, when understood properly, is not about utopian idealism or insider terminology. It is about *empowering individuals through architecture*—not by offering them more trust in systems, but by reducing the need for trust in the first place. It is a logic. It is a constraint. And, when well-executed, it is a toolset for *radical independence* in a world increasingly defined by opaque authority.

To decode decentralisation is to understand *how systems can be built to resist coercion, adapt under duress, and function without permission*. This requires moving beyond the spectacle of token markets and toward the engineering of freedom itself.

Why Centralisation Fails the Sovereign Individual

Most systems today—banking, social media, payment networks, identification platforms—are highly centralised. That is, they rely on a single point of control to mediate access, enforce rules, and resolve disputes. Centralisation is not inherently evil; in many contexts, it is efficient and stabilising. But it comes with systemic fragilities.

When central authorities fail—through corruption, incompetence, censorship, or capture—the entire system becomes unreliable. If your bank freezes your account, your assets become unreachable. If your government deplatforms you, your digital identity becomes inert. If your payment processor flags your business, your income stream evaporates overnight. These are not theoretical risks. They are lived realities for individuals across jurisdictions—activists, dissidents, journalists, but increasingly also entrepreneurs, freelancers, and anyone who falls outside the narrow bounds of financial orthodoxy.

Decentralisation does not guarantee safety. But it does something equally valuable: *it removes the need for permission.* A properly decentralised protocol cannot discriminate. It cannot freeze. It cannot forget. It cannot be bribed, pressured, or nationalised. It simply runs—mathematically, predictably, and openly—regardless of who you are or where you live.

This is what blockchain technology—at its best—enables: systems where trust is shifted from intermediaries to code, from institutions to consensus.

The Blockchain as an Institutional Primitive

A blockchain is not a database. It is a time-stamped, append-only ledger that is *replicated across a network of independent nodes*, each verifying and agreeing upon changes through a pre-defined consensus mechanism. This structure means no single party can alter the record retroactively or unilaterally. It is transparent, auditable, and censorship-resistant.

But its true power is architectural. Blockchain allows us to build what the economist Glen Weyl calls "institutional primitives"—core building blocks like contracts, markets, identity systems, and governance frameworks that are not just digital, but *decentralised by design.* They cannot be revoked, suspended, or modified by decree. Their logic is encoded, visible, and enforceable without appeal to a centralised authority.

Consider the simple act of sending money. Through a traditional bank, this requires intermediaries, regulators, and settlement systems. Through a decentralised protocol, it requires only a private key and a network connection. The result? *Disintermediation at scale.* You are no longer subject to gatekeepers. You are operating on an open, permissionless infrastructure.

But decentralisation doesn't stop at payments. Today, we have decentralised alternatives to lending, trading, file storage, domain registration, insurance, and even governance. These systems are still young, often clunky, and not without risk. But they represent the first serious challenge to the default assumption that institutional power must be centralised to be legitimate.

Control Without Custody: A Paradigm Shift in Asset Ownership

Traditional assets—stocks, bonds, property—are controlled via intermediaries: brokers, registrars, banks. Even when you "own" something, it is usually recorded on a central server, subject to the policies of the platform you use. That is not sovereignty. It is delegated access.

In the decentralised world, control is redefined. If you own a crypto asset, and you hold the private keys to the wallet where it resides, *you alone can move it.* No one can restrict your access. No one can reverse your transactions. No one can unilaterally alter your balance. This is not speculative hype. It is a fundamental shift in how custody and control are architected.

Of course, this comes with new responsibilities. There is no password reset. No customer support. The system will not protect you from yourself. But for those willing to learn, decentralised ownership offers something traditional finance cannot: *absolute, uncensorable, portable control.*

This matters because, in times of political upheaval or financial crisis, assets held through centralised intermediaries can become bottlenecks, not buffers. Decentralised assets, when properly stored and understood, can move across borders, survive capital controls, and operate independently of failing institutions.

Decentralisation Is a Spectrum, Not a Binary

It is easy to talk about "centralised" versus "decentralised" as if these were fixed categories. In practice, every system lies on a spectrum. Bitcoin, for example, is decentralised in its network structure and issuance policy, but still faces concentration risk in mining pools and node infrastructure. Ethereum has a decentralised base layer, but many of its applications are still run by centralised front-ends.

Understanding this nuance is crucial. *Not all decentralisation is created equal.* Some blockchains are decentralised in name only—governed by insiders, controlled through backdoors, or vulnerable to state pressure. Others offer radical transparency but lack scalability or usability.

Your task as a sovereign investor or strategist is not to idealise decentralisation, but to evaluate it *functionally.* Ask: What is being decentralised? Who controls the protocol's upgrades? How resistant is it to coercion or censorship? Is the community broad-based, or is power concentrated?

These questions are not technical distractions. They are indicators of whether a system can serve you *when it matters most*—under duress, not just during bull markets.

The Real Use Case: Coordinating Without Permission

At its most powerful, decentralisation is not just about assets. It is about *coordination.* DAOs—Decentralised Autonomous Organisations—are one early example. They allow groups of people to pool funds, vote on decisions, and execute actions through smart contracts—all without legal incorporation or hierarchical management. The early implementations have been flawed, chaotic, even absurd. But the concept is profound: human coordination governed by code, not charisma.

This opens possibilities far beyond finance: decentralised philanthropy, disaster response, protocol governance, censorship-resistant journalism. The common thread is the ability to *act collectively without asking for approval.*

In an increasingly fragmented, polarised, and gatekept world, this capacity is not utopian. It is urgent.

Decentralisation is not a buzzword. It is not a lifestyle brand. It is an *architectural response* to the failures of concentrated power. It is slow, complex, and often misunderstood. But it is real. And it is available.

When central institutions falter, decentralised systems offer not guarantees—but options. They allow you to hold assets that cannot be frozen, coordinate actions that cannot be blocked, and build systems that cannot be hijacked from above.

To engage with decentralisation is to take on new responsibility—but also to regain *a measure of control that legacy systems have quietly stripped away*. This is not about escaping the rules. It's about *choosing the rules you live under—and having a say in how they evolve.*

What follows will equip you with the frameworks to evaluate, engage, and apply decentralised tools—intelligently, critically, and on your own terms.

Let's get technical—without losing sight of the purpose.

From Currency to Culture

How Crypto Redefines Ownership, Identity, and Economic Participation

When people first encounter cryptocurrency, the conversation tends to begin with price: how much is Bitcoin worth, which altcoin is surging, what token is "the next big thing." This fixation is understandable. For many, crypto enters their life through the lens of speculation—an asset class that moves too fast to ignore, too volatile to trust. But to stop at market dynamics is to miss the point entirely. Because crypto, at its core, is not just about *currency*. It is about *culture*—a radical reimagining of how humans coordinate, identify, and own.

This subchapter explores what cryptocurrency has become beyond its market cap: *a decentralised cultural movement that challenges inherited assumptions about trust, authority, and value.* To understand crypto only as a financial instrument is to mistake the plane for the propulsion system. What we are witnessing is not just the emergence of a new form of money, but the construction of *parallel economies*—complete with their own values, governance mechanisms, and social contracts.

It is no longer sufficient to ask what crypto is *worth.* The more relevant question is: *what is it changing?*

Ownership Without Permission

In traditional economic systems, ownership is validated by institutions. Your house is recorded by a land registry. Your bank account is insured by a central authority. Your identity is managed by the state. This architecture functions—until it doesn't. When banks freeze assets, when governments revoke licenses, when platforms deplatform, the fragility of institutional trust is laid bare.

Crypto introduces a different logic: *ownership without permission.* If you hold the private keys to your wallet, no institution can confiscate your funds, censor your transactions, or modify your balance. It is not just that crypto resists control—it redefines what it means to *control* something. For the first time in history, we can possess digital property that is *native*, *sovereign*, and *global*, without relying on third parties.

This shift is not just technical. It is philosophical. It rewires the psychological experience of possession. Owning a digital token is not like owning shares in a brokerage account. It is more akin to holding physical gold—except it's portable, programmable, and borderless. The implications go beyond finance. They touch on self-conception, autonomy, and power.

Identity as a Public-Private Construct

Crypto also challenges our assumptions about identity. In the traditional web, identity is fragmented, platform-bound, and commercially harvested. You are one person on Facebook, another on your banking app, and a third in the government's database. These identities are interoperable only in surveillance systems—not in ways that serve the user.

By contrast, decentralised identity systems—built on public-key infrastructure, verifiable credentials, and on-chain attestations—enable individuals to construct reputations that are portable, privacy-preserving, and composable. You can prove your history, your qualifications, your trustworthiness—*without exposing your personal data.* This is not theory. Protocols like ENS (Ethereum Name Service), Proof of Humanity, and decentralized identifiers (DIDs) are actively prototyping identity outside of state control.

In this emerging paradigm, identity becomes a *public-private construct* you can curate, not a fixed credential issued by authority. Your reputation is no longer owned by a platform. It is built through participation, validated by peers, and anchored cryptographically on chains that no single actor can manipulate.

The stakes are enormous. In an age of increasing surveillance and data monopolisation, decentralised identity is not just a technical feature. It is a civilisational countermeasure.

Crypto as Economic Citizenship

What distinguishes the crypto movement is not only its technology but its *participant logic.* In the traditional economy, you are a consumer, a taxpayer, a borrower, an employee. Your role is largely passive, or at best, procedural. You do not vote on monetary policy. You cannot fork your jurisdiction. You are bound to systems you did not design and cannot directly influence.

In crypto, participation is often *active*, *voluntary*, and *governed by code.* When you interact with a decentralised protocol, you are not just a user. You are a stakeholder. You might contribute code, propose changes, vote on upgrades, or delegate governance. You might help govern a treasury, moderate a DAO, or create a new token economy from scratch.

This is *economic citizenship*, not consumption. And while the tools are still maturing, the principle is profound: that individuals can design, iterate, and migrate between economic systems *without permission from the old ones.*

Case in point: during the Canadian trucker protests in 2022, crowdfunding platforms froze donations. In response, activists raised funds in Bitcoin, routing them directly to recipients through multisignature wallets. The government retaliated by freezing bank accounts, but crypto transfers persisted. This was not just about money. It was about *coordination in a hostile legal environment.* It was a form of economic assembly, enabled by decentralised rails.

Such episodes are often dismissed as fringe. But they are the early signals of a shift from *platform dependence* to *protocol choice*—from being *subjects of systems* to *co-creators of them.*

Crypto as Counterculture

Culturally, crypto attracts those disillusioned with centralisation, opacity, and coercion. It is no coincidence that many in the space are engineers, artists, activists, and misfits. Crypto culture is defined by *intellectual diversity*, *scepticism of authority*, and *an obsession with building things that don't need permission to run.*

This ethos can manifest as techno-utopianism or adversarial arrogance. But beneath the noise lies a shared intuition: that the institutions of the 20th century—banks, nation-states, rating agencies, publishers—are no longer able to fulfil their mandates with trust, neutrality, or adaptability. Crypto is not a clean replacement. It is a *challenge function.* It exposes what breaks when individuals demand control.

You can see this in how Web3 communities form: pseudonymous, global, economically aligned through tokens, coordinated via Discord, governed through smart contracts. There is a rawness to it—chaotic, sometimes reckless—but also a resilience. The culture rewards experimentation. It penalises complacency. And it defaults to openness.

In that sense, crypto is not a product. It is a *protest movement masquerading as a software stack.*

The Future of Economic Participation

To participate in crypto today is not merely to hold tokens. It is to *interact with a new economic model.* One where you can be a liquidity provider on an exchange, a lender in a peer-to-peer market, a governor of a treasury, a builder of a product, and a stakeholder in a protocol—all from a browser, and often with no intermediary.

This changes how value is created, shared, and owned. Traditional businesses concentrate ownership and distribute revenue. Crypto protocols often do the reverse: distribute ownership widely and let the community generate value collectively. This leads to new incentive models, new legal structures, and new forms of cooperation that blur the lines between company, community, and platform.

Critics argue that the space is overrun by scams and speculation. And they are not wrong. The signal-to-noise ratio is low. But to dismiss the space on that basis is to miss the signal entirely. Every frontier is noisy. The relevant question is not "Are there bad actors?" but "What new agency does this technology enable?"

The answer is: *a lot.*

Crypto is not merely an asset class. It is a toolkit for rethinking how value, trust, and power are distributed in a digitised world. It challenges the assumptions of nation-states, corporations, and intermediaries—not by lobbying, but by *building alternatives.*

To ignore crypto is not just to ignore a technology. It is to ignore a cultural shift—a rising expectation that individuals should be able to move value, prove identity, coordinate resources, and own assets *without being monitored, profiled, or censored.* That expectation is not going away. It is growing. And the systems that satisfy it will define the next generation of digital infrastructure.

To engage with crypto seriously is not to gamble on tokens. It is to explore *a new architecture of freedom*—messy, unfinished, but full of possibility.

And those possibilities will not wait for institutional approval.

Cold Storage, Hot Minds

Why Crypto Security Begins with Your Thinking, Not Your Wallet

Most discussions around cryptocurrency security begin with the mechanics: hardware wallets, seed phrases, multisig protocols, encryption standards. This technical focus is understandable—after all, crypto assets are digital, and securing them requires more than a padlock or a safe. But this emphasis, while necessary, is also incomplete. What's often missing is the far more consequential layer: *how to think securely*. In crypto, tools matter—but mindset is paramount.

Cold storage is not just a method of offline storage. It is a signal of intent: that the holder is taking operational responsibility for assets that, by design, have no central authority. To store crypto securely is to *internalise sovereignty*. And that means developing a mindset capable of handling risk, ambiguity, and responsibility in ways few financial systems have ever demanded from the individual.

This chapter does not simply teach storage techniques. It teaches *operational security as a discipline*—a way of thinking about your behaviour, environment, and threat surface that matches the stakes of holding assets in a permissionless, irreversible, decentralised system.

Security Is Not a Product—It's a Posture

Let's begin with a difficult truth: there is no perfect tool. No wallet, device, or app can make you invulnerable to loss or theft. And yet many newcomers are lured into a false sense of security by slick interfaces and brand reputation. They buy a hardware wallet, generate a seed phrase, and assume they're safe—without asking who has access to the backup, how recoverable the wallet is, what metadata is exposed in the setup process, or how social engineering might compromise their system.

Security does not come from having the right device. It comes from *the questions you know to ask*. What happens if my house burns down? Who has plausible access to my seed phrase? Have I written it down in more than one place? Do I understand what a supply chain attack is? Can I spot a phishing email that imitates a firmware update?

These questions are not technical trivia. They are markers of maturity. They separate those who have merely *bought crypto* from those who *understand custody*.

A cold wallet in your drawer is not a security solution. It is an invitation to build one. And that process begins in the mind.

Threat Modelling: Thinking Like an Adversary

One of the most useful mental shifts for crypto holders is learning to *think adversarially*. Not because the world is full of enemies, but because crypto, by design, *removes trusted third parties*. This means that all the guarantees—fraud protection, account recovery, user support—are replaced by *your operational competence*.

Threat modelling is a framework borrowed from cybersecurity that asks: who might want to access your funds, how might they do it, and what are the consequences if they succeed? The answers vary widely depending on context. A high-profile public figure with millions in assets will face different risks than a developer quietly holding tokens for long-term investment. But *everyone has a threat surface*—the sum total of vectors through which they can be compromised.

It is not enough to have a wallet. You must understand *where you are exposed*. Have you ever shared your seed phrase over an insecure channel? Do you use the same email across crypto and non-crypto accounts? Do you log into exchanges from unsecured devices or public networks? These sound like basic questions. But many breaches occur not through cryptographic flaws, but *human shortcuts*.

Understanding threat modelling doesn't mean living in paranoia. It means being honest about your attack surface, and adjusting your behaviour accordingly.

Seed Phrases: The Weakest Strong Link

The seed phrase—a 12- or 24-word mnemonic that can regenerate your private keys—is simultaneously the most powerful and vulnerable component of crypto custody. Whoever holds the phrase holds the funds. Period. No backdoor. No retrieval. No appeal.

This radical irreversibility is both liberating and dangerous. Most people are used to a safety net: password resets, support tickets, fraud departments. Crypto offers none. The phrase is everything.

And yet, people treat seed phrases with casual disregard. They store them in plaintext on cloud services. They photograph them. They email them to themselves. They tattoo them. These are not theoretical lapses. They are common behaviours documented across hundreds of loss reports.

The secure storage of a seed phrase requires more than secrecy. It requires *redundancy without exposure*. If your phrase is in only one place, you risk total loss through fire, flood, or forgetfulness. If it's in too many places, you invite compromise. The solution lies in careful distribution: splitting the phrase using Shamir's Secret Sharing, storing parts in different jurisdictions, using metal backups for durability.

But even this is not enough if the person managing the process is careless. That's why the key upgrade is not the wallet. It is *the operator*.

Multisignature and the Power of Shared Custody

Multisignature wallets—also known as multisig—require multiple private keys to approve a transaction. For example, a 2-of-3 multisig wallet might require two out of three designated signers to authorise any transfer. This adds *resilience* and *defence-in-depth* to crypto custody.

Multisig solves two fundamental problems: *single-point failure* and *delegated trust*. If you lose one key, you can still recover funds. If one key is compromised, it's not enough to move assets. This model is particularly useful for families, companies, or long-term storage strategies where survivability and governance matter as much as access.

But again, the strength of a multisig setup depends on *how it's implemented*. If all keys are stored on the same device, or in the same house, the risk remains. If signers are not trusted or trained, the scheme becomes a liability. The sophistication of the tool must match the discipline of the user.

Used wisely, multisig becomes not just a security model but a *philosophical upgrade*: a way to encode shared responsibility, decentralised control, and robust inheritance mechanisms—without relying on courts or banks.

Operational Security as Culture

Perhaps the most underappreciated aspect of crypto custody is that it creates a *culture of vigilance*. Unlike traditional finance, where responsibility is outsourced to institutions, crypto demands personal discipline. This fosters a mindset—sometimes called "opsec"—that is transferable far beyond digital assets.

Opsec is not paranoia. It is awareness. It is the practice of minimising exposure, managing credentials, securing devices, compartmentalising identities, and anticipating failure modes. In the fiat world, this mindset is rare. In crypto, it is survival.

This mindset shows up in everyday habits: using hardware wallets, disabling browser autofill, verifying URLs manually, separating hot and cold devices, updating firmware securely, using passphrases and second factors, questioning every link, and never assuming safety by default.

Those who succeed in crypto custody are not the most technically gifted. They are the most *disciplined*. They understand that the most likely attack vector is *themselves*—their carelessness, their assumptions, their habits.

And so they build habits that reflect the stakes.

Custody Is the Real Killer App

The mainstream often asks when crypto will produce a "killer app." In many ways, it already has: *sovereign custody*. The ability to store and transfer meaningful amounts of value without institutional permission is not just an innovation. It is a civilisational milestone.

But it only matters if you do it well.

This chapter is not a checklist. It is an invitation: to upgrade not just your storage tools, but your operational mentality. To become the kind of person who can *safeguard freedom*, not just speculate on it.

Because when systems fail, currencies devalue, or accounts are frozen, it won't matter what the market price was. It will matter *what you control*—and how well you've prepared to keep it that way.

Digital Gold vs Digital Liquidity

Designing Crypto Holdings Based on Function, Not Fandom

There's a persistent mistake among casual crypto investors: they treat all digital assets as if they play on the same field, governed by the same logic, with the same objectives. But Bitcoin is not Ethereum. Ethereum is not USDC. And a stablecoin is not a decentralised lending protocol, no matter how convincing its branding. Conflating them is like confusing land title with grain futures—they may both involve value, but they exist for profoundly different strategic ends.

To design an intelligent, future-resilient crypto portfolio, one must disaggregate hype from utility. *We need to distinguish between store-of-value assets (digital gold), transactional instruments (digital cash), and programmable finance (digital liquidity).* Each serves a different psychological, strategic, and economic purpose. The goal is not to "diversify into crypto" as a category—it is to allocate across the correct functions of crypto, with clear intention and technical discernment.

Let's begin with the cornerstone.

Bitcoin: Cryptographic Scarcity as Sovereign Store of Value

Bitcoin did not emerge from financial speculation. It was born of political dissent. In the aftermath of the 2008 crisis, the Bitcoin whitepaper arrived as both a technical solution and a philosophical rebuke—a system with hardcoded scarcity, independent of central banks, and free from counterparty risk.

Unlike fiat currency or even most altcoins, Bitcoin is not governed by a mutable monetary policy. There will never be more than 21 million coins. This predictability is not a trivial engineering detail; it's the moral premise behind Bitcoin's identity. It is *digital gold* not merely because it's scarce, but because it holds value in systems where trust has collapsed.

During the 2022 collapse of centralised exchanges like FTX, Bitcoin retained its narrative coherence. Even when prices dropped, its protocol remained stable, censorship-resistant, and self-custodied. This is what gold-like assets do—they offer refuge, not returns. And that is often misunderstood by short-term thinkers.

Owning Bitcoin is not about capital gain. It is about *exit.* Exit from inflationary policy. Exit from banking jurisdictions. Exit from dependency on permissioned infrastructure. For the thoughtful portfolio builder, Bitcoin should be viewed less as a speculative instrument and more as a geopolitical hedge—insurance against the failure of fiat systems and a bet on technological sovereignty.

But Bitcoin is not agile. It doesn't yield. It doesn't integrate seamlessly into DeFi (by design). It isn't optimised for experimentation. That space belongs elsewhere.

Ethereum and DeFi: Digital Liquidity and the Programmable Economy

Where Bitcoin is digital gold, Ethereum is a financial operating system. The difference is architectural and philosophical. Ethereum's strength is not in being scarce—it is in being *flexible.* Smart contracts allow developers to build entire decentralised applications on top of its network—exchanges, lending markets, DAOs, tokenised assets. These are the mechanisms through which *digital liquidity* is made possible.

If Bitcoin is a vault, Ethereum is a marketplace.

The introduction of protocols like Uniswap, Aave, and Compound demonstrated that financial functions—previously the exclusive domain of banks—could be reimagined without intermediaries. This isn't merely an investment story; it's a civilisational one. With DeFi, capital no longer needs permission to flow. It is composable, autonomous, and global. But with that freedom comes risk.

Liquidity is not permanence. DeFi's very fluidity can lead to structural fragility. Protocols can be hacked. Smart contracts can have bugs. Governance can be hijacked. And unlike a vault of Bitcoin or bar of gold, you cannot audit it visually. The psychological toll this takes on the investor is significant—navigating DeFi requires constant attention, fluency in evolving protocols, and a tolerance for ambiguity. Digital liquidity is an asset class that *rewards knowledge and punishes complacency.*

To hold Ethereum or interact with DeFi is not just to invest—it is to participate. And participation carries complexity.

Stablecoins: The Tactical Utility Layer

Some of the most misunderstood assets in the crypto ecosystem are stablecoins—tokens like USDC, USDT, or DAI that are pegged to the US dollar or other fiat currencies. Critics call them redundant; after all, if you want dollars, why not use dollars?

But this misses the point. Stablecoins are not a currency alternative. They are *a rails alternative.* They allow dollar-denominated transactions to move across borders, settle instantly, and be programmed into smart contracts. They turn money into *code*, making it interoperable with decentralised platforms and exempt from legacy banking bottlenecks.

For crypto portfolio design, stablecoins function less as investments and more as tactical instruments. They provide liquidity without volatility. They offer exit velocity in and out of positions. And when held in decentralised protocols, they can even yield interest without traditional banks. That said, they are not without compromise. Most stablecoins rely on custodial backers. Some are vulnerable to regulatory overreach or blacklisting. The collapse of algorithmic stablecoins like Terra's UST in 2022 was a vivid lesson in how *not all stability is stable.*

Stablecoins are useful, not safe by default. They belong in a portfolio not as a hedge against collapse but as a bridge during rebalancing, cashflow strategy, or cross-border execution.

Purpose-Driven Allocation: Designing Across Functions

The real test of crypto maturity is not how early someone bought Bitcoin. It's whether they can articulate *why* they hold each asset and what function it serves. Let's simplify with a guiding frame:

Hold **Bitcoin** if you want uncorrelated, sovereign, long-term security. Treat it like digital land—hard to move, slow to yield, but enduring.

Hold **Ethereum and DeFi tokens** if you want exposure to programmable capital, decentralised innovation, and economic optionality. Use them as growth assets—but accept their volatility.

Hold **Stablecoins** if you need agility, liquidity, or crypto-native cash without exposing yourself to the volatility of other assets.

Do not confuse popularity with principle. Just because a token is trending does not mean it plays a durable or credible role in a balanced portfolio. Likewise, just because something is technically decentralised does not mean it is economically sound or legally robust.

A mature portfolio treats crypto not as a monolith, but as an ecosystem with distinct layers—each with its own logic, risks, and reward profiles. *That is the difference between gambling and strategy.*

Psychological Anchoring in a Volatile Space

There is also a mental discipline to proper allocation. In traditional finance, asset classes are clearly delineated. In crypto, the lines blur. Tokens wear costumes. Communities project ideologies. Hype cycles distort reality. The investor who lacks psychological anchoring will find themselves overexposed, overwhelmed, and reactionary.

The antidote is clarity of purpose. *What job is this asset performing in your system?* If you can't answer in a sentence, you likely don't need it. The "hodl everything" mentality is not strategy—it's inertia. A well-constructed crypto allocation, like a well-built portfolio in any domain, should reflect your goals, your risk model, and your escape vectors.

Crypto's magic lies in its multiplicity. But multiplicity without intentionality is chaos. To navigate that chaos well, you must not only know what you own—but *why*.

Chapter 7
The War on Wealth – Confiscation, Taxation, and Control

Across the sweep of history, the rules governing wealth have never rested solely in spreadsheets or stock tickers—they've shifted shape through statutes, court rulings, and the veiled manoeuvrings of political authority. The traditional instruments of accumulation—capital, land, discretion—are now met, increasingly and often insidiously, with mechanisms of restraint: surveillance, taxation, regulatory creep. This chapter invites a clearer view of a largely unspoken conflict—the quiet but potent war on wealth. Not a war marked by noise or spectacle, but one unfolding through legal nuance, administrative reach, and policy agendas cloaked in the language of fairness or reform. This isn't a call to panic. It is, unapologetically, a call to lucidity. To help you identify where your assets are genuinely protected, where your independence is most defensible, and how to hold not only value, but volition, in an age where even ownership itself is up for debate.

There is comfort—false comfort—in the assumption that a deed or contract guarantees dominion. Particularly in democratic nations, where property rights are treated as moral bedrock, this belief can go largely untested. Yet the seasoned investor, expatriate, or legal strategist knows better: legal title does not equate to control. Take Cyprus in 2013, when depositors found their bank balances partially commandeered under a state-sanctioned "bail-in" scheme. These were legally held assets, expropriated under legal authority. Or consider the United States' civil asset forfeiture regime, which has quietly claimed billions without the burden of a criminal charge. These events are not flukes. They are signals—indicators of a world in which capital is increasingly interpreted not as private right but as potential public resource.

Seen through this lens, wealth ceases to be a passive by-product of effort or prudence. It becomes a theatre of power, one where governments play an increasingly assertive role—redefining, limiting, and sometimes undermining the rights of the holder. In this climate, jurisdictional arbitrage shifts from the margins of strategy to its very centre. Once the purview of billionaire family offices, the practice of splitting financial presence across legal territories has become a survival skill for anyone serious about financial resilience. It is not about evading tax—it is about mitigating legal monoculture. When one nation veers into unpredictability, another may offer anchorage. When disclosure norms tighten in one jurisdiction, another may still honour discretion. At its core, this is not a numbers game; it is a defence against unilateral dependency. The financial map is political terrain long before it is economic calculation.

Yet despite growing awareness, financial privacy remains stubbornly misread—often conflated with secrecy, or worse, wrongdoing. In reality, the erosion of privacy has come not with fanfare, but quietly, through digitisation and the slow bleed of once-personal data into corporate and governmental control. The decline of cash, the rise of traceable transactions, the normalisation of account aggregation—each has made discretion more rare, and more suspect. Increasingly, to want privacy is to be seen as hiding something. But this is a distortion. Privacy is not evasion; it is choice. It is the ability to decide how and where one's financial life intersects with institutions. Reclaiming that space—lawfully, deliberately, and structurally—may soon prove essential to preserving not just wealth, but dignity itself.

To move forward, certain assumptions must be set aside. That tax codes are immovable. That legal frameworks are impartial. That financial institutions serve merely as custodians. These were tenable ideas when systems were localised, and their reach modest. But the current environment calls for a sharper framework—one that blends legal design, geographic separation, and operational foresight. Net worth, while still a metric, no longer tells the whole story. Exposure now matters just as much. Where are your accounts held? Under what legal systems do your financial relationships operate? Who, precisely, has the final word when disputes arise or crises unfold?

This chapter offers not comfort, but tools. It opens by dismantling the prevailing fiction—that conventional financial assets, located in conventional places, offer conventional security. We then delve into the strategic imperatives of jurisdictional diversification, not as a loophole, but as a buffer. And finally, we confront the thornier issue:

privacy—not as a vice, but as an architecture of control in an increasingly watched and interpreted world. This is not an ode to secrecy, nor a cynical retreat from institutions. It is a case for cultivated independence: the freedom to act within your financial life without overexposure to any single state or system.

There is, to be sure, no universal model for resilience. A tech founder in Tallinn faces different risks than a retiree in Tuscany or a grain exporter in the Pampas. Yet one idea binds all serious wealth strategies today: true stability is no longer inherited. It must be built—carefully, often quietly, and with no small measure of foresight.

As you proceed, let this chapter act both as a map and a mirror. A map, charting the legal and jurisdictional tides reshaping capital's security; a mirror, reflecting the blind spots and dependencies that may lurk, unexamined, within your own financial habits. It is one thing to think you're in control. It is quite another to ensure that control holds when pressure arrives.

Ownership is claimed. Control is constructed. And in a world where title is easy to assert but difficult to defend, clarity may be your most durable form of wealth.

How Governments Weaponise Policy

In modern economies, confiscation seldom arrives under a banner of seizure. It comes cloaked in policy—disguised as prudence, framed as fairness, often passed quietly while headlines fixate elsewhere. This is not a matter of conspiracy but of incentive. Governments in fiscal distress have few politically tolerable options. Raising direct taxes risks backlash. Cutting spending risks unrest. But eroding capital quietly—through currency debasement, surprise taxation, or enforced illiquidity—achieves extraction without spectacle. It's a technique honed over centuries, and yet largely misunderstood by the public. This subchapter aims to lift that veil, exposing the mechanics and logic of economic statecraft when governments begin to see citizen capital as collateral.

To understand how governments weaponise policy, we must first discard the illusion that legal does not mean predatory. A measure passed by parliament is not inherently just—it is merely enforceable. The line between governance and confiscation lies not in legality but in proportionality, transparency, and due process. When these are absent or obscured, economic policy becomes a vehicle for covert wealth transfers, often from the financially literate to the politically dominant.

Consider capital controls—a term that evokes emergency stabilisation but often signals structural desperation. In 2001, Argentina froze bank accounts and limited cash withdrawals in a bid to stem a banking collapse. The public's savings were effectively locked. Depositors had no access to their funds, and when access resumed months later, it was to pesos that had halved in value against the dollar. Legal, yes. But also a devaluation masquerading as a policy tool. In effect, the state used time and inflation to tax savings without parliamentary debate.

Or take the 2013 Cypriot "bail-in." In a coordinated move between the Cypriot government and the EU, uninsured depositors—primarily foreign nationals—found up to 47.5% of their balances above €100,000 forcibly converted into bank equity. No prior notice. No opt-out. The justification was systemic risk. But the reality was simpler: private funds were repurposed to recapitalise failing institutions. This wasn't a policy failure; it was the policy.

These examples are not outliers. They are symptoms of a global trend where the traditional tools of monetary policy have reached their limits. Central banks, having suppressed interest rates for over a decade and expanded their balance sheets beyond historical precedent, now operate with a narrower arsenal. When inflation rises or confidence falters, governments seek alternative levers—not to grow the economy, but to control capital. And when those levers are pulled, the outcomes are rarely evenly distributed.

Currency debasement remains the most politically palatable form of quiet confiscation. Unlike taxation, which is visible and numerically precise, inflation is opaque. It is a theft of purchasing power masked as market fluctuation. When central banks expand the money supply disproportionately to productivity growth, the value of existing savings erodes. But while inflation is often blamed on exogenous shocks—pandemics, wars, or supply chains—the decision to dilute currency is endogenous. It is a political choice dressed as macroeconomic necessity.

In Turkey, persistent inflation combined with authoritarian financial controls has rendered the lira nearly unusable for savings. Citizens have turned to gold, U.S. dollars, or cryptocurrencies—not as speculation, but as survival. The Turkish case illustrates a broader point: when official policy becomes detached from fiduciary duty, financial migration begins. Not just geographically, but ideologically. Citizens stop trusting institutions and start building parallel systems of value and trust.

Surprise taxation is another mechanism increasingly used to access private capital under the banner of "equity" or "solidarity." France's wealth tax, once deemed a model for redistributive justice, led to a sustained exodus of high-net-worth individuals, draining the tax base and reducing net collections. South Africa's emergency tax levies during COVID, framed as temporary, now appear likely to persist. And in the United States, legislative proposals to tax unrealised capital gains—profits never cashed out—signal a willingness to redefine income itself to meet fiscal targets.

These manoeuvres rest on a foundational shift: from taxing flow (income, sales) to taxing stock (assets, potential, even location). And while they are often framed as "making the wealthy pay their fair share," their operational complexity tends to ensnare the financially responsible more than the fabulously rich, who have already relocated or restructured. The middle-high, rather than the ultra-wealthy, bear the brunt—those with enough to be noticed, but not enough to be exempt.

Why does this matter to a globally minded investor or saver? Because *policy is path-dependent.* When a nation begins to see private capital as a buffer for political risk, its appetite rarely diminishes. More importantly, the *velocity of change*—the time between policy conception and execution—is collapsing. What used to take years of legislative debate can now occur through emergency executive orders, court rulings, or regulatory reinterpretation. The rule of law remains, but its scope narrows. The letter holds, while the spirit retreats.

The ethical tension here cannot be ignored. Is it just to preserve wealth when others are suffering? Is it right to move assets offshore when local systems strain? These are serious questions. But they are not binary. *There is a profound difference between evasion and preservation.* One violates laws; the other reads them attentively. One exploits loopholes; the other diversifies exposure. A citizen can simultaneously support fair taxation and resist arbitrary seizure. The goal is not avoidance but continuity—*ensuring that one's life work is not nullified by a policy pivot.*

What, then, is the defence? Legal structure and jurisdictional diversification. Not just trusts and tax shelters, but clarity: knowing where your assets reside, under which laws they fall, and how rapidly those laws can shift. Treat every bank account, brokerage, deed, and contract not merely as an asset, but as a legal relationship. Who can access it? Freeze it? Revalue it? Restructure it? These are no longer theoretical questions. They are strategic imperatives.

The modern investor must think like a geopolitical analyst and act like a constitutional scholar. Not because they wish to be adversarial, but because they wish to remain free. Not wealthy, necessarily. But uncoerced. That freedom begins with understanding how the system can—and does—turn inward. It continues with preparing structures that absorb rather than absorb shocks.

The war on wealth is rarely declared. It is administered. Through a thousand cuts of compliance, a shifting labyrinth of rules, and a narrative that equates independence with disloyalty. To see this clearly is not cynicism. It is realism. And in realism, there is dignity—*the kind that prepares rather than pleads.*

This chapter does not offer refuge. It offers lucidity. What you do with that clarity—where you move, how you structure, what you own, and how you think about ownership—is up to you. But the stakes are no longer abstract. The playbook has changed. And those who recognise the shift are already adjusting course.

Legal Ownership vs Real Control

At the heart of wealth preservation lies a deceptively simple question: do you truly control what you legally own? The intuitive answer—"yes, of course"—has lulled generations into complacency. Yet the more serious and informed answer is: *not necessarily*. Ownership, in the legal sense, is often a facade—shaped by the architecture of jurisdiction, regulation, and increasingly, political whim. Control, by contrast, is both harder to detect and harder to seize. Understanding the difference is no longer a theoretical luxury. It is a practical necessity.

Asset seizure today rarely wears jackboots. It doesn't kick in doors or hoist flags. It arrives via email from a regulator, a court, or a bank compliance officer. It operates in systems that claim to protect the rule of law, but increasingly reframe ownership as a temporary privilege, revocable under pressure. What we are witnessing is not the dramatic collapse of property rights, but their gradual erosion—through litigation, overreach, taxation without recourse, and geopolitically weaponised finance.

This article explores the subtle but critical distinction between legal ownership and real control. It draws from history, law, finance, and geopolitics to map out the vulnerabilities baked into conventional structures—and the paths available for those seeking more resilient ones.

Ownership may place your name on a deed. Control decides who can use, move, benefit from, or protect that asset when the political weather turns.

The Illusion of Safety in Legal Title

Consider the standard model of asset ownership in most developed economies. A property is registered in your name. Your stocks and bonds reside in a brokerage account linked to your legal identity. Your business operates under a corporate structure domiciled in your home jurisdiction. On paper, this offers clarity and legitimacy. In practice, it creates a single point of failure.

What happens when the state, or its proxies, no longer see your interests as aligned with theirs? Look to Cyprus in 2013, where depositors above a certain threshold had their bank accounts frozen or partially confiscated as part of a "bail-in." These were not criminals or tax evaders. They were ordinary savers—many of whom had structured their affairs entirely within the bounds of law. Or consider India's sudden demonetisation in 2016, where cash held legally was rendered temporarily worthless, forcing millions into queues to prove their financial innocence.

The point is not to stoke paranoia. It is to highlight the *fragility* of legal structures that appear stable, but are deeply exposed to jurisdictional risk. Legal title is a matter of record. Real control, however, lies in the ability to access, move, and shield assets when it matters most.

Trusts, Foundations, and the Architecture of Control

Historically, the wealthiest families have understood this distinction intuitively. Their fortunes are rarely held in their own names. Instead, they are nested inside trusts, foundations, and holding entities—legal vehicles that separate *ownership* from *benefit* and *control.* This is not merely for tax efficiency, though that is a factor. It is for durability.

A well-structured trust can place assets beyond the reach of hostile creditors, family disputes, or political expropriation. Foundations in jurisdictions like Liechtenstein or Panama offer a layer of protection not because they are shady, but because their rules are different. They are designed for continuity, not convenience.

Of course, these structures come with trade-offs. They reduce flexibility. They require expertise. They introduce fiduciary dependencies—trustees, protectors, legal drafters—who must be carefully chosen and periodically assessed. But for those serious about control, this added complexity is not a bug. It is a feature. It insulates the asset from one's own mortality, litigation exposure, and shifting regulatory climates.

If you can access your wealth with a password, so can a government. But if it takes a foreign court order, a specialised trustee, and jurisdictional due process, your asset stands a better chance of surviving long-term volatility.

Financial Institutions: Partners or Gatekeepers?

Modern finance has become a network of chokepoints. Banks, brokerages, and custodians are no longer neutral intermediaries. They are active participants in enforcement regimes—whether for taxes, sanctions, or compliance mandates. In most Western countries, they are required to report suspicious activity, freeze funds upon request, and submit to policy decisions made thousands of miles away.

This creates a dilemma for asset holders. Do you trust the convenience of mainstream institutions, knowing their allegiance is to regulators first and clients second? Or do you seek alternatives—multi-jurisdictional accounts, non-custodial crypto wallets, offshore nominees—that prioritise operational freedom over ease?

Neither path is without risk. But the key insight is this: *relying on institutions you cannot influence is not control—it's delegation.* And delegation, under political duress, quickly turns into dispossession.

Citizenship and Residency: Hidden Levers of Power

Control is not just legal or technical—it is also *sovereign.* Where you are a citizen, where you pay tax, where you reside, and under which passport you travel all shape your financial exposure. Most people inherit their jurisdictional framework by birth. Few revisit it strategically. This is a mistake.

Second citizenships, alternative residencies, and expatriation strategies are not fringe ideas. They are increasingly mainstream among those who understand that jurisdictional diversification is not just a geopolitical hedge. It is an instrument of autonomy. If your government imposes capital controls, where will you move your wealth? If your assets are frozen pending litigation, which country's courts will hear your case? These questions are not academic—they are infrastructural.

Just as a balanced portfolio spans asset classes, a truly resilient portfolio spans legal systems. It places slices of wealth in jurisdictions that compete for your trust and respect your autonomy, rather than assuming your perpetual compliance.

The Psychological Hurdle: Clarity vs Complexity

Many readers will find this analysis intellectually convincing but emotionally off-putting. There is a psychological comfort in seeing your name on a property title, in logging into your online account and checking balances, in receiving statements from a trusted bank. These signals create an illusion of control that is comforting but brittle.

By contrast, true control often looks and feels more complicated. It may require cross-border legal advice, encrypted communications, decentralised platforms, or dealing with trustees in jurisdictions whose laws differ markedly from one's home country. It demands cognitive effort. It involves learning. And, for some, it raises ethical questions.

But complexity is not the enemy. Arbitrary simplicity is. In a world where asset seizures can be executed with a keystroke, the illusion of simplicity is often the prelude to regret.

Final Thought: Control Is the Cornerstone of Sovereignty

We are taught to think of ownership as a binary—do you own something, or not? But in reality, ownership exists on a spectrum. At one end are assets you can access, move, and protect without asking anyone's permission. At the other are assets that exist purely on paper, subject to approval, oversight, or confiscation by others.

To build a resilient portfolio in the 21st century is to understand where on that spectrum your assets lie—and to push more of them toward the side of true control.

Because wealth is not what you own. It is what you can keep.

The Importance of Jurisdictional Arbitrage

Wealth, at its core, is not just a function of assets—it is a function of systems. It exists within laws, currencies, tax codes, and enforcement mechanisms. And while most individuals spend their lives optimising what they hold, few give equal thought to *where* they hold it. This geographic blindness is one of the great vulnerabilities of modern wealth strategy. Jurisdictional arbitrage is the corrective.

The term may sound arcane, but its premise is simple: different places treat the same asset very differently. A company share, a trust deed, a real estate title, or a bank deposit will be respected, taxed, or attacked in radically different ways depending on which government is behind the paperwork. This asymmetry can either destroy or preserve wealth—and understanding it is no longer optional. In a world of rising political volatility, financial overreach, and regulatory convergence, *the resilience of your assets increasingly depends on the legal environment they reside in.*

Jurisdictional arbitrage, then, is not about avoiding taxes or exploiting loopholes. It is about building systemic resilience. It is about choosing—deliberately—which rules you play by, and not simply accepting the rules you were born into. This article examines the intellectual foundation and practical application of jurisdictional arbitrage as a pillar of long-term wealth strategy.

Why Geography Still Matters in a Digitised World

In theory, globalisation has made capital borderless. You can buy US stocks from Dubai, open an Estonian company from Buenos Aires, or hold a Swiss bank account while living in Singapore. But the *legal consequences* of each action are deeply tied to jurisdiction. Ownership may be digital. Rights and risks remain profoundly territorial.

Consider these examples:

A brokerage account held in the US is potentially subject to civil asset forfeiture—laws that allow funds to be frozen without a criminal conviction.

A bank account in Argentina might be denominated in US dollars, but its access can be suddenly restricted by currency controls.

Property held in China is technically leased from the state—meaning there is no true private land ownership under the legal code.

A trust established in the UK may be taxed entirely differently than one domiciled in Jersey, Liechtenstein, or Singapore.

This is not simply a list of curiosities. These are facts that determine whether your wealth is *accessible*, *defensible*, and *transferable.* Ignoring jurisdictional differences means playing chess with half the board invisible.

The Legal Map Is Not the Political Map

Most people think of jurisdictions as countries. But a legal jurisdiction is better understood as a *system*—a specific matrix of tax law, regulatory policy, property rights, and judicial reliability. The United States, for example, is not one jurisdiction—it is fifty, layered under federal authority, each with different implications for trusts, LLCs, and inheritance. Switzerland offers multiple cantons with materially different tax treatments. The Caribbean alone contains over a dozen offshore jurisdictions, each with their own financial frameworks, reputational risks, and bilateral treaties.

The legal world is not flat. It is layered, fragmented, and hierarchical. The smart allocator of wealth does not merely consider "offshore vs onshore," or "emerging market vs developed market." They ask: *What is the legal system's history with expropriation? How predictable are its courts? How independent is its judiciary? What treaties bind it to other jurisdictions?*

The answers to these questions determine whether an asset is resilient—or merely appears to be.

The Myth of Global Harmonisation

A persistent myth in financial commentary is that global coordination—through bodies like the OECD, FATF, or G20—has made jurisdictional arbitrage obsolete. This is profoundly mistaken. While compliance standards have increased—particularly around anti-money laundering (AML) and common reporting (CRS)—the *interpretation*, *implementation*, and *enforcement* of these standards remain highly uneven.

The result is not a level playing field, but a complex maze. Some jurisdictions lean into transparency, others protect discretion. Some enforce beneficial ownership registration with rigour, others allow quiet flexibility. Some offer tax deferrals, others aggressively tax foreign-derived income even if it's never remitted. For example:

The UAE taxes local business profits but offers zero tax on most foreign-source income.

Portugal's NHR regime allows certain foreign retirees to pay minimal tax for ten years.

The US taxes citizens on worldwide income, even if they haven't lived onshore for decades.

These are not accidents. They are sovereign choices—each reflecting the political priorities and economic models of their governments. Jurisdictional arbitrage begins with recognising that you, too, can make sovereign choices—*within the law, across borders.*

Jurisdiction as a Layer of Portfolio Diversification

Asset allocation is a familiar concept. Investors spread risk across equities, bonds, real estate, and alternative assets. But few extend this logic to *jurisdictional allocation.* And yet the logic is identical: diversify exposure to avoid concentration risk.

A truly modern portfolio includes:

Financial assets held in jurisdictions with strong creditor protections.

Real estate in countries with clear property rights and low expropriation risk.

Businesses incorporated in regions with favourable legal and tax regimes.

Bank accounts in politically neutral, well-capitalised banking systems.

Trust structures domiciled in jurisdictions with deep common law traditions and minimal treaty vulnerabilities.

This is not exotic behaviour. It is standard practice among global families, sovereign wealth funds, and multinational corporations. What's shifting is the accessibility of these tools to individual investors and entrepreneurs—thanks to digital platforms, cross-border service providers, and the rise of global citizenship planning.

Risk as a Function of *Where*, Not Just *What*

Most investors evaluate risk based on asset class: bonds are safer than equities; gold hedges inflation; real estate generates income. But geopolitical and legal risk often trumps asset-specific logic.

A rental property in Toronto may seem low-risk—until property taxes double overnight, or new regulations cap rent increases below inflation. A perfectly hedged portfolio held in a brokerage account may seem prudent—until that institution becomes the target of sanctions or court orders. A cash reserve may seem wise—until a government freezes withdrawals or imposes negative interest rates.

Jurisdictional arbitrage acknowledges that *your relationship to your asset is mediated by law*. Change the law—or the place where it is applied—and the nature of your control changes as well.

Practical Barriers and Ethical Considerations

Deploying a jurisdictional arbitrage strategy is not without obstacles. It involves legal complexity, cultural unfamiliarity, and administrative cost. Some countries require declarations of foreign holdings. Others impose exit taxes or citizenship-based taxation. The rise of automatic information sharing (e.g. CRS, FATCA) has reduced anonymity, forcing greater transparency in wealth structuring.

Moreover, ethical lines must be observed. Jurisdictional arbitrage is not a licence for evasion or secrecy. It is a strategy for *resilience within legal bounds*. The goal is not to disappear—but to decentralise risk. To ensure that no single government, however well-meaning or well-intentioned, holds unilateral power over your financial life.

The Sovereign Individual, Revisited

The logic of jurisdictional arbitrage ultimately rests on a philosophical foundation: *you do not belong entirely to the place where you were born.* You are not required to leave your fate to a single government's decisions. Wealth, mobility, and information enable new forms of autonomy. They do not guarantee it—but they make it available.

A sovereign individual in the 21st century is not merely someone who earns well or invests wisely. It is someone who places their capital, their data, their structures, and sometimes even their citizenship, across a matrix of systems that respect rather than threaten their autonomy.

Not because the world is falling apart—but because it is not uniform.

And in a world where systems diverge while appearing harmonised, *jurisdictional arbitrage is not a loophole. It is a lifeline.*

Reclaiming Your Right to Privacy

In the modern financial landscape, privacy is often treated not as a right, but as a red flag. The mere act of seeking discretion in how one holds, transfers, or allocates wealth is increasingly conflated with criminality. Regulators label it suspicious, institutions view it as risky, and media narratives frame it as immoral. What was once regarded as prudent—minding one's own business—is now miscast as potentially illicit. This subtle inversion is one of the least acknowledged but most significant shifts in the global order of financial power.

But beneath the noise, a deeper question remains: *Why was financial privacy criminalised—and is it possible to reclaim it without crossing ethical or legal lines?* The answer is not found in evasion, but in sophistication; not in secrecy, but in *strategic discretion.* This article explores how the concept of financial privacy was reshaped, why that matters profoundly for personal autonomy, and how individuals can ethically reclaim this vital dimension of agency in an age of data harvesting and regulatory overreach.

Privacy as a Pillar of Civilisation

Privacy is not a fringe concern. It is a foundation of freedom. Throughout history, it has served as a buffer between the individual and the state, between the household and the collective, between the citizen and the crowd. The right to a private life—to one's thoughts, associations, and property—is enshrined in constitutions, charters, and philosophical tradition.

John Stuart Mill wrote that "the worth of a state in the long run is the worth of the individuals composing it." That worth is diminished when every private financial decision is made under the gaze of surveillance. *A society that equates privacy with wrongdoing forfeits its capacity for dignity, dissent, and diversity.*

In earlier eras, discretion in finance was not a crime—it was common sense. Swiss banking was prized not because it was opaque, but because it was dependable. Family trusts were not vehicles of concealment, but instruments of stewardship. Cash was not a tool of evasion, but of immediacy and autonomy. These instruments protected individuals from arbitrary confiscation, political instability, and social prejudice. Today, they are increasingly framed as mechanisms of guilt by association.

The Path to Criminalisation

The criminalisation of financial privacy did not arrive overnight. It advanced in stages, typically under the banner of noble goals: fighting terrorism, stopping tax evasion, and cracking down on money laundering. Each justification created new layers of surveillance infrastructure, new compliance mandates, and new expectations of disclosure.

Consider the following milestones:

The USA PATRIOT Act (2001): Under the guise of national security, the United States dramatically expanded the powers of financial intelligence units and institutional reporting requirements.

FATCA (2010): The Foreign Account Tax Compliance Act marked a global turning point. By compelling foreign banks to report on U.S. citizens, it set a precedent for extraterritorial reach and turned institutions into enforcers.

The Common Reporting Standard (CRS): Coordinated by the OECD, CRS created an automatic information exchange system, now covering over 100 countries. Data flows globally by default, regardless of context, intent, or due process.

These regimes redefined the default. Once, governments had to prove wrongdoing to access your financial data. Now, you must prove innocence *continuously* to preserve even a modicum of discretion. Compliance costs have soared, not only in monetary terms, but in human dignity and institutional trust.

The Ethical Misframing of Privacy

A dangerous sleight of hand has taken place in public discourse: privacy has been rhetorically collapsed into secrecy, and secrecy into guilt. The result is a moral inversion where those who protect their privacy are viewed as suspect, and those who relinquish it are celebrated as transparent.

But the real question is not whether financial privacy can be abused. Of course it can—just as free speech can be abused. The question is whether the abuse of a right justifies its erasure. *If every mechanism that can be misused must be outlawed, then liberty itself becomes criminal by default.*

There is a difference between privacy and opacity. Ethical privacy is selective transparency. It is about choosing what is visible, to whom, and under what conditions. It is not a rejection of law, but a demand for proportionality and boundaries. It says: I am willing to comply, but not to be perpetually inspected. I am willing to be accountable, but not indefinitely exposed.

Designing for Privacy Without Breaking the Law

The path to reclaiming privacy does not lie in offshore gimmicks, opaque shell structures, or encrypted obscurity. It lies in careful architecture: designing a life, a business, and a portfolio that respects the law but retains control over visibility.

There are several legitimate strategies:

Multiple jurisdictions: Holding assets across jurisdictions with robust legal protections dilutes the power of any single authority to unilaterally interfere. This is not about hiding—it's about hedging systemic risk.

Trusts and foundations: Properly constructed legal entities can offer privacy of administration and asset protection, while fully complying with reporting laws. The key is transparency with the beneficiary, not with the entire world.

Private banking and custody arrangements: Certain financial institutions—especially in Switzerland, Liechtenstein, and Singapore—offer enhanced confidentiality without breaching reporting standards. Choosing the right institution is critical.

Cash equivalents and decentralised assets: Holding small percentages of wealth in physical gold, crypto with cold storage, or bearer instruments can provide last-resort autonomy if access to mainstream systems is blocked.

Minimal viable disclosure: Comply with reporting rules, but design structures and portfolios in a way that reduces unnecessary exposure. Complexity should serve resilience, not obfuscation.

These strategies are not theoretical. They are deployed by diplomats, executives, and ordinary citizens in jurisdictions with weak rule of law. They are tools of prudence, not rebellion.

The Psychology of the Watched

Continuous surveillance changes behaviour. When individuals know they are being watched—by banks, tax authorities, or algorithms—they begin to self-censor. They take fewer risks. They delay decisions. They stop asking the hard questions.

This "panopticon effect" is not hypothetical. It has been documented in psychology and behavioural economics. It erodes confidence and introduces second-guessing into every major move. *The illusion of transparency does not increase trust. It increases conformity and fear.*

Reclaiming privacy is, in part, about reclaiming the capacity to act without that shadow of judgment. To think creatively. To steward wealth without the presumption of wrongdoing. It is a psychological as much as a legal imperative.

Restoring the Principle of Proportionality

For privacy to be reclaimed ethically, it must be re-anchored in the principle of proportionality. Not all transactions are equal. Not all citizens present risk. Not all wealth is criminally derived. The same rules should not apply to the entrepreneur in Lisbon and the kleptocrat in Kinshasa.

The push toward "total transparency" is not neutral—it is politically and economically loaded. It benefits those with the resources to comply endlessly and penalises those who wish to build quietly. It turns financial institutions into gatekeepers of behaviour and due process into an afterthought.

Proportionality demands that governments prove need before demanding disclosure. That reporting regimes respect thresholds. That access to financial data be limited, logged, and contestable. *Privacy should not require justification. Its violation should.*

Conclusion Without Conclusion

Privacy is not a luxury of the paranoid. It is a precondition of autonomy. And autonomy is a precondition of dignity.

Financial privacy, properly understood, is not a tool of escape but of resilience. It is a firewall against abuse, a boundary for self-determination, and a litmus test for how free a society really is. Those who seek to reclaim it are not evading the system—they are affirming a higher standard.

They are saying: *I will follow the law. But I will not live on a leash.*

Chapter 8
Emotional Resilience and the Investor's Mind

Wealth, at its core, is a psychological endeavour. Not in the superficial sense of self-affirmation or wishful visualisation, but in the stark, often unforgiving reality that markets challenge the mind long before they reward the method. Behind the figures and formulas, beyond the elegant abstractions of asset allocation and portfolio theory, lies a messier truth: the first and fiercest contest is waged within. It is not strategy that is tested first—it is sanity.

We're taught, typically, to approach finance with cold logic. Models are revered, metrics dissected. And yet, when the dust of volatility settles, it is rarely the cleverest algorithm that emerges intact. It is the person who kept their nerve. Market cycles are not merely mechanical—they are human dramas, pulsing with emotion, memory, projection. They swing, sometimes violently, between fear and euphoria, between the grip of history and the pull of what might be. In such an arena, the portfolio that looks pristine in a vacuum may prove entirely unfit for its owner. One wrong move under duress, and that elegant design becomes combustible.

A technically flawless strategy means nothing if its owner cannot inhabit it with discipline. Imagine a structure, mathematically sound, but placed in an earthquake zone. That is what an ill-fitting financial plan becomes when psychological turbulence arrives. The cracks don't begin in the data—they begin in the decision-making.

This chapter steps into the territory often skirted in highbrow financial discourse: the emotional metabolism of the investor. How we interpret stress. How we respond to uncertainty. How we metabolise loss or ambiguity. These aren't peripheral issues—they are the pillars upon which wealth either stands or crumbles.

Investing, at its most honest, is not merely about managing capital. It is about managing the self. Those who prevail in the long arc of wealth preservation are not always the most technically sophisticated. They are, more often, those who've learned to remain steady when the world around them grows erratic. It is that rare pairing—emotional precision married to intellectual rigour—that forms the true backbone of financial resilience.

The Myth of the Perfect Investment

Every generation is seduced by the illusion that *one right decision*—the right stock, the right coin, the right country, the right time—will redeem all others. This myth is potent because it is emotionally efficient: it promises liberation from uncertainty. It whispers that discipline can be replaced by insight, that a singular move will grant permanent advantage.

But investing is not a game of singular heroism. It is not chess, with a known board and clear rules. It is more like weather navigation—patterned, but not predictable. There is no perfect investment. There is only *resilience through layers*.

Rather than betting on omniscience, the serious investor learns to design portfolios like ecosystems: diversified not just across asset classes, but across failure modes, time horizons, and *psychological pressure points*. The best portfolios are those you can live with—emotionally, not just mathematically—when things go sideways. This means embracing redundancy not as inefficiency, but as insurance against the blind spots of intellect and the biases of the mind.

Perfection is fragile. Redundancy is durable.

The Investor Identity Crisis

A quiet tragedy in finance is how many people build investment strategies for the person they *wish* they were. The cool, collected, Warren Buffett-like version of themselves who always holds, never panics, and rebalances calmly with the detachment of a machine. But that version rarely shows up when the pressure mounts.

There is often a painful dissonance between an investor's stated risk tolerance and their actual behaviour under duress. This is not a moral failing; it is a diagnostic opportunity. The question is not "What portfolio maximises returns?" but "What portfolio is *survivable* for who you are *right now*?"

Understanding one's investor identity involves more than filling out a risk questionnaire. It requires a candid audit of temperament: how you react to loss, to social pressure, to ambiguity. It means tracking not just returns, but reactions. Did you sell too early in 2020? Did you freeze during the crypto drawdown? Did envy override logic during the bull run?

This chapter will help readers map the terrain of their own investor psychology—not to reinforce limitations, but to work intelligently within them. Temperament is not fixed, but it is real. And *the most successful investors do not fight their nature—they design around it.*

Decision-Making Under Stress

In high-stakes environments, the human brain shortcuts. It narrows focus, discards nuance, and clings to narratives. In markets, this often means liquidating too early, doubling down too late, or anchoring to irrelevant information. When our biology is primed for survival, our logic often becomes a casualty.

That's why the best investors develop not just systems, but *internal models*—ways of thinking that override panic. These include reframing techniques from psychology, decision trees from military strategy, and mental models from behavioural economics.

One such model is the "pre-mortem": rather than asking what could go right, one imagines everything that could go wrong *and prepares accordingly*. Another is "inverse thinking": asking not how to win, but how not to lose. These approaches shift the mind from hope to *design*. They reduce reliance on willpower and increase reliance on frameworks.

This chapter introduces these tools, not as abstractions, but as battle-tested lenses for navigating chaos. Whether you're a solo crypto trader or a portfolio manager stewarding generational wealth, *your decisions under stress will define your long-term success far more than your IQ or initial strategy.*

The Meta-Thesis: Emotional Resilience as Edge

In a marketplace where data is abundant and strategies are increasingly commoditised, the real edge is not hidden in some obscure spreadsheet—it's in *emotional durability.* The ability to think clearly when others cannot. To avoid self-sabotage when rewards are near. To hold the line when liquidity dries up, narratives invert, or regulators shift the goalposts.

Markets do not reward the smartest investors. They reward the most consistent ones. And consistency under pressure is not a function of genius, but of structure—internal and external. This chapter is about building both.

We'll explore:

Why the "perfect trade" fantasy is a psychological trap

How to diagnose and respect your personal risk blueprint

Tools for cognitive clarity during volatile periods

What elite decision-makers do differently under pressure

How to build a portfolio *you can actually live with*—through every phase of the cycle

By the end, readers will not only understand *what* to invest in, but *how to stay invested.* Because in the real world, staying in the game is the hardest and most valuable skill of all.

Welcome to the mind beneath the markets.

Fear, Hope, and Cognitive Bias

There is no such thing as a purely rational investor. The idea persists—taught in textbooks, embedded in economic models—that humans make financial decisions based on logical appraisal of risk and reward. But in practice, money is never just a number. It is memory, status, security, fear, hope, shame, and aspiration—all compressed into decisions made under pressure. The real challenge in asset planning is not beating the market. It is *not being beaten by your own mind.*

We tend to believe we think in facts, but most of the time, we think in feelings disguised as facts. Especially under financial stress—market downturns, career volatility, geopolitical unrest—the cognitive brain hands over the wheel to older, more primitive drivers. Investors retreat into the twin distortions of *fear* and *hope.* Fear makes us overreact. Hope makes us underprepare. And both make us unreliable narrators of our own financial lives.

The work of successful investing is less about predictive brilliance than it is about *internal regulation.* Learning to sit with ambiguity. Learning to delay reaction. Learning to resist narrative closure. These are not emotional soft skills; they are strategic imperatives. Because when your mind runs off-course, your portfolio follows.

This chapter is an excavation. We'll strip away the surface stories people tell themselves—"I just got unlucky," "The market turned," "This was a black swan"—and look at the deeper machinery: how emotional distortions quietly sabotage sound planning, and how to build an architecture of internal calm that outlasts external storms.

The Mirage of Rationality: Why Brains Betray Us

The human brain is not optimised for investing. It is optimised for survival in environments very different from the abstract landscapes of finance. Our ancestors navigated threats that were visible and immediate: predators, storms, famine. Modern investors navigate threats that are probabilistic, long-term, and emotionally charged in far subtler ways. The amygdala, however, doesn't know the difference between a market crash and a tiger.

Behavioural finance, as pioneered by scholars like Daniel Kahneman and Amos Tversky, has shown how these inherited mental shortcuts—heuristics and biases—undermine rational action. We anchor to irrelevant past prices. We chase recent trends, assuming they will continue. We loss-avert to a pathological degree, preferring not to lose £10 over gaining £20. Our decisions are riddled with cognitive distortion, and we rarely notice until after the damage is done.

Fear exaggerates loss. Hope distorts gain. Together, they short-circuit discipline.

The result is a chronic pattern among even experienced investors: buying high, selling low, regretting in hindsight. The illusion of control masks a deep vulnerability to chaos.

The Anatomy of Fear in Asset Planning

Fear is not always visible as panic. More often, it appears as *hesitation*, *overanalysis*, or *defensive conservatism.* People freeze on cash when they should be dollar-cost averaging. They hold onto underperforming assets for fear of realising losses. They avoid rebalancing because any action feels too risky to contemplate.

Fear is particularly insidious because it disguises itself as caution. It feels prudent. But caution is strategic; fear is reactive. Fear doesn't assess risk—it amplifies it. It doesn't question assumptions—it narrows vision.

During the 2008 financial crisis, countless retail investors sold at the bottom not because they didn't understand long-term investing, but because *they couldn't tolerate the emotional weight of uncertainty.* The same dynamic repeated during the COVID-19 market shock in early 2020, and will repeat again in different guises.

The lesson is not to eliminate fear—this is biologically unrealistic—but to *interrogate it.* What exactly are you afraid of? Is it the loss itself, or what it means about your identity? Is it the volatility of markets, or your lack of trust in your own plan? Specificity dismantles general fear. Vague panic destroys plans.

The Lure of Hope: How Optimism Backfires

Hope is more socially acceptable than fear, but no less dangerous. Hope is what fuels the speculative bubble. It is what convinces us that this time will be different. It leads to overexposure, overconcentration, and blind faith in narratives that confirm what we want to believe.

Crypto bubbles. Meme stocks. Real estate manias. They all run on emotional fuel disguised as conviction. Hope says, "I know it looks irrational, but…" It dresses itself in community, enthusiasm, and innovation. But underneath it often lies *avoidance of discomfort.* Hope in this context becomes an evasion of sober thought, not an expression of faith.

Hope becomes toxic when it prevents portfolio adjustment. When it keeps you holding the bag because admitting failure feels worse than staying the course. When it's easier to believe in future redemption than present accountability.

This is not an argument against optimism, but for *informed optimism*—grounded in reality, aware of limits, and balanced by structural risk mitigation.

Building Internal Calm: The Missing Asset Class

Every investor manages three portfolios: the actual assets, the decision framework, and the internal state. The third is the most neglected, yet the most powerful. Your internal environment—mental habits, emotional reflexes, and worldview—colours every financial choice you make.

Building internal calm is not passive. It requires practice. Just as elite athletes train for high-pressure performance, so too must serious investors train for clarity under volatility. This means:

Pre-committing to decisions under calm conditions—e.g. setting automatic rebalancing rules or exit points in advance

Creating distance between trigger and action—such as requiring a 24-hour pause before any major asset move

Cultivating non-market sources of emotional stability—a strong personal life, meditative practice, or meaningful hobbies that dilute the existential weight placed on money

It also means interrogating the stories you tell yourself about wealth: What does it represent? Safety? Status? Control? Freedom? These stories—often unconscious—shape your reaction to gain and loss far more than spreadsheets.

The calmer the internal system, the more adaptive the external response.

Strategic Application: From Awareness to Architecture

Understanding fear and hope is not enough. Insight must be converted into *structure*. The role of emotional intelligence in asset planning is not just self-awareness, but the ability to encode that awareness into strategy.

If you are prone to overreaction, reduce your optionality. Automate. Delegate. Use checklists. If you tend to underreact—delaying hard decisions—schedule portfolio reviews with accountability mechanisms. If you swing between panic and euphoria, build portfolios with hard exposure limits, stress-tested under multiple conditions.

This is where the emotional overlaps with the architectural. You design not only what you *own*, but how you *interact* with what you own. The best financial plans are not only logical—they are *livable*. They work with your emotional bandwidth, not against it.

Final Reflection: The Inner Investor

The greatest risk in investing is not drawdown—it's *misalignment.* Misalignment between strategy and temperament. Between goals and actions. Between facts and feelings. Closing that gap requires more than better information. It requires *better integration.*

Fear and hope will always be part of the investor's life. The goal is not to eradicate them, but to *contain their influence.* To design systems that are robust not only to external shocks, but to *internal volatility.* Because in the end, markets will do what markets do. The only question is whether *you* will still be thinking clearly when they do.

Emotional resilience is not an abstract virtue. It is an operational edge. And in a financial world increasingly shaped by noise, narrative, and behavioural contagion, it may be the only edge that truly endures.

The Myth of the Perfect Investment

The search for the perfect investment is not a financial strategy. It is a psychological trap. It seduces investors with the illusion that a single, decisive move can insulate them from uncertainty, volatility, and regret. But no such move exists. There is no asset immune to systemic shocks, no market free from manipulation, no strategy exempt from time. And yet, this myth—of the one trade, the perfect property, the bulletproof portfolio—persists in both novice and experienced investors alike.

Why? Because it offers something deeper than return: it offers *relief.* Relief from ambiguity, from the burden of ongoing judgement, from the unsettling reality that even the most educated guess remains, at best, a probability. But believing in the perfect investment is like believing in a map without scale. It flattens complexity. It invites fragility.

Instead, a mature investment philosophy begins with the opposite premise: *there is no single right move—only layered resilience.* In other words, the goal is not perfection but *redundancy*—a structural tolerance for error, bias, and surprise. That shift—from optimisation to adaptability—is the mark of an intelligent investor in a chaotic world.

The Lure of Finality

At the core of the perfect investment myth is a psychological desire for finality. The notion that, after years of saving or studying or struggling, one can make a single move that locks in safety or wealth. This narrative is reinforced by media stories that spotlight extreme outcomes: the early Bitcoin adopters who became billionaires, the venture capital bet that returned 100x, the distressed property that turned into a luxury development.

These stories, while real, are the product of extreme survivorship bias. For every investor who struck gold, there are thousands who went broke panning for it. But the human mind is poorly calibrated for this asymmetry. We latch onto what is memorable, not what is representative.

This distorts risk perception. It fosters impatience. It encourages a style of investing that is less about *systematic strategy* and more about *strategic hope.* And hope, while emotionally gratifying, is not repeatable.

There is no final move. There is only the next good decision.

Perfection as a Liability

Ironically, the pursuit of the perfect investment often leads to worse outcomes than a diversified, imperfect strategy. Investors delay action, waiting for clearer signals. Or they concentrate risk excessively, convinced they've found a sure thing. Or they hold too long, refusing to adapt when conditions change.

In each case, the error stems not from ignorance but from *overconfidence*—a belief that one can outsmart uncertainty by sheer cleverness or conviction. This is not strategy. It is ego in disguise.

Consider the tech-heavy portfolios that soared during the post-2010 bull run. Many investors, extrapolating the trend, went all in. Then came 2022—a correction not just of prices but of assumptions. Concentration turned to contagion. The lesson wasn't that tech was bad. It was that no asset class can carry all of your future.

Overoptimised systems break under pressure. Redundant systems adapt.

Layered Redundancy: A Framework for Reality

So what replaces the fantasy of perfection? A layered approach. Redundancy in investing does not mean inefficiency. It means building resilience into the system from multiple angles. This involves:

Asset class diversification: Not just across sectors (equities, bonds, real estate) but across *functional roles*—cashflow generation, capital preservation, inflation hedging, asymmetric upside.

Jurisdictional spread: Wealth held in multiple legal systems, each with its own rules and protections, reduces the risk of total capture by any one political regime.

Time horizon layering: Short-term liquidity needs, medium-term growth goals, and long-term legacy planning require different instruments and behaviours.

Psychological buffers: Holding some cash—not for yield, but for *sleep*—can reduce emotional decision-making and improve long-term discipline.

Each layer provides not just financial insulation but *behavioural space.* You're not forced to act rashly in crisis because your system has slack.

Redundancy is not laziness. It is wisdom in structural form.

Case Study: The Fallacy of Total Real Estate Allocation

During periods of inflation or low interest rates, many investors shift heavily into real estate, lured by tangible assets and predictable rents.

In theory, it feels "safe." But over-allocation can quickly become a trap.

In countries like Argentina or Turkey, aggressive property investment was seen as a hedge against currency devaluation. But changes in tax regimes, rent controls, or capital flow restrictions quickly turned those assets into liabilities. Owners faced frozen rents, forced sales, or outright confiscation.

A redundant approach would have spread that exposure—perhaps with REITs in more stable jurisdictions, a mix of hard and soft assets, and liquid reserves to handle policy shock. The investor may have sacrificed maximum short-term yield. But they gained *durability*—the most undervalued form of return.

Psychological Benefits of Imperfect Systems

Perfect plans are brittle not only financially but emotionally. They increase the cost of deviation. When things go wrong—and they *will*—the fallout is not just monetary, but existential. The investor feels betrayed: "I did everything right. Why didn't it work?" That psychological breach leads to overcorrection: abandoning long-term strategy for short-term damage control.

Redundant systems, by contrast, *expect deviation.* They are designed for the real world, not the whiteboard. This builds a kind of confidence that is deeper than optimism: *quiet faith in structure, not forecast.* You are less likely to panic, because you have multiple ways to respond.

And perhaps most importantly, you are more likely to *act.* Investors paralysed by the pressure to be perfect often delay critical decisions. Redundant frameworks lower the stakes of any one move. They make participation emotionally sustainable.

Replacing the Hero Narrative

At the cultural level, the myth of the perfect investment reflects a broader fantasy: that wealth is the result of singular genius, not disciplined systems. We idolise the lone trader, the contrarian founder, the visionary allocator. But actual financial independence is almost always built through repetition, constraint, and *uncelebrated structure.*

We must replace the hero narrative with the *architect's mindset.* The investor is not a gambler seeking jackpot outcomes. They are a planner, designing a system that absorbs error, learns over time, and performs well enough—even when the world doesn't.

That shift is subtle but radical. It reframes investing not as a quest for brilliance, but as a practice of humility and rigour. The investor's job is not to outguess the world. It is to build a personal system that is *indifferent to being guessed wrong* now and then.

Final Perspective: Good Enough, Repeated Forever

In a world flooded with data, predictions, and opinion, the temptation to optimise is endless. But mastery lies not in selecting the best asset. It lies in building a system that *doesn't require constant perfection.* That system can be reviewed, adapted, and evolved—but never depends on clairvoyance.

The goal is not to make the best move once. It is to make good enough moves *consistently*, with as few unforced errors as possible. The perfect investment does not exist. But layered redundancy—the ability to survive imperfect outcomes and still progress—*does.* And that, ultimately, is what separates the investor who thrives from the one who merely hopes.

Perfection is a mirage. Resilience is a map. Choose accordingly.

Investor Identity Crisis

The most dangerous investor is not the one who lacks knowledge. It's the one who lacks *self-knowledge.* Markets are not rigged against intelligence—they are rigged against delusion, particularly the kind that confuses who we are with who we want to be. Nowhere is this more evident than in the quiet but persistent gap between our *idealised investor identity* and our *actual investor behaviour*. It's the gap between what we say we value and what we tolerate in practice; between the risk appetite we claim and the anxiety we experience when things fall apart. And bridging that gap is not just a psychological exercise—it is a financial imperative.

Investors rarely begin with a clear mirror. Instead, they inherit identities from influencers, family narratives, business cultures, or the fantasy lives of others. A man reads about Ray Dalio and decides he's a macro investor. A young woman listens to friends getting rich on leverage and adopts the persona of a high-conviction speculator. A retiree reads Buffett's letters and insists on value investing—even when they panic at 20% drawdowns. The performance doesn't fail because of strategy alone. It fails because the strategy doesn't fit the *person*. A poorly fitted portfolio is not just uncomfortable; it's unstable. So the question becomes: how do we invest in line with *who we really are*, not who we're trying to impress?

The Danger of Misaligned Identity

Misalignment between personality and portfolio is more than emotional friction. It results in real financial damage. It shows up in overtrading during panic, under-allocation during opportunity, or premature exits that turn potential gains into regrets. But this misalignment is often invisible to the investor themselves. They may believe they're conservative—until a bull run stirs envy. They may swear by long-term compounding—until a market wobble convinces them they're missing out on faster gains.

This identity confusion is exacerbated by the constant marketing of investment lifestyles. Social media and financial journalism don't simply present options—they *assign roles*. If you're not taking massive asymmetric bets, are you even serious? If you're not doing in-depth technical analysis, are you just a lazy indexer? The subtle pressure is not just to choose, but to *become* a certain kind of investor—trader, passive acolyte, value disciple, crypto visionary.

These roles are not inherently flawed. What's flawed is adopting them without assessing your *operating psychology*. Just because a strategy works *in theory* doesn't mean it will work *for you*. As in aviation or surgery, *pilot error*, not the instrument, is what brings the plane down.

Knowing Your Temperament

A productive investment identity begins with a realistic understanding of temperament. This includes:

Volatility tolerance: Not just what you *think* you can handle, but how you *actually* behave in a drawdown. Do you become analytical, frozen, reactive, or opportunistic?

Time discipline: How long can you commit capital without needing liquidity—not just financially, but psychologically?

Information processing style: Do you thrive on noise and newsflow, or prefer quiet rules-based systems?

Decision-making bias: Do you favour intuition, data, narrative, or consensus? Each bias has its advantages—and blind spots.

These traits form a kind of emotional risk profile, distinct from numerical risk metrics like beta or standard deviation. Two people with identical financial profiles may require radically different portfolios simply because one can sleep through a 40% drawdown and the other cannot stomach a 10% dip.

An optimal portfolio is not the one with the highest Sharpe ratio—it's the one you won't abandon during a storm.

The Trap of Aspiration

There is no shame in being a low-volatility, low-return investor. There is danger, however, in pretending not to be. Much like in personal health, where fitness is determined not just by ideal goals but consistent behaviour, investor success depends on system adherence more than system optimisation. A plan followed imperfectly but consistently will outperform the ideal plan you can't stick to.

Aspiration becomes a trap when it overrides design. An investor may want to "be the kind of person" who understands options, leverages yield farming, or times the market with precision. But if the behavioural costs are too high, the system breaks. Resentment builds. Anxiety mounts. And eventually, the structure collapses under the weight of its own pretense.

Authenticity, in investing, is not a buzzword. It is a stability mechanism. It keeps the strategy connected to its executor. It replaces fantasy with function.

Building to Fit, Not to Impress

To align identity and investment strategy, begin not with market views but with behavioural constraints. Ask:

What level of drawdown will trigger second-guessing?

What level of complexity can I realistically manage?

How frequently do I want to engage with this portfolio?

What beliefs am I holding because they sound smart—not because I've tested them?

Then reverse-engineer the structure. A 70% stock allocation may be appropriate for long-term growth. But if you're going to constantly tinker with it during volatility, it's functionally a liability. Similarly, allocating 5% to crypto because you're told it's the "new frontier" might not make sense if you fundamentally don't believe in decentralisation or hate managing keys.

Build a portfolio you can live with—not one you'll constantly want to escape.

Case Study: The Aggressive Investor with a Fragile Ego

Consider a corporate executive in his 40s, accustomed to winning. He decides to "get serious" about investing and immerses himself in high-yield crypto protocols. He reads whitepapers, joins Discords, and pours in capital. For six months, everything compounds. Then a protocol gets hacked. Another faces a regulatory freeze. His portfolio drops by 50%. He holds, then sells, then re-enters higher. By year-end, he's down 70%. The loss isn't just financial—it's personal. He feels embarrassed, violated, disillusioned.

What happened wasn't a failure of intellect. It was a failure of identity misfit. He assumed that his confidence and intellect would translate into crypto resilience. But what he lacked wasn't technical skill. It was emotional architecture—an ability to separate *portfolio risk* from *personal identity*.

Had he allocated a fraction to learn with, and used the rest in a structure better suited to his actual tolerance, the loss would have been painful but not fatal. He confused enthusiasm for suitability. And the market punished him accordingly.

Identity as a Living Framework

Your investor identity is not fixed. It evolves, refines, matures. But it does not evolve by aspiration alone. It requires honest data: *How did I behave when the market fell 30%? Did I follow my rules during greed cycles? What parts of my portfolio cause disproportionate emotional turbulence?*

This feedback loop allows for organic growth. You may begin as a passive investor and gradually incorporate opportunistic trades. Or you may discover that your curiosity leads to deeper specialisation—but only in areas that energise rather than overwhelm you.

Treat your investor identity as a working diagnosis, not a brand. Be sceptical of grand declarations like "I'm a long-term value investor" or "I believe in innovation above all." These are narratives. The market doesn't reward narratives. It rewards *alignment*—between structure, temperament, and action.

Building a Portfolio that Respects the Investor

A respectful portfolio doesn't coddle the investor, nor does it challenge them for sport. It operates in a zone of competence and comfort—with calibrated stretch. It anticipates friction points and builds buffers accordingly. It allows the investor to act—not react.

This doesn't mean staying static. It means recognising that behaviour is the foundation on which all returns are built. Every asset, every strategy, every rebalance must respect the human behind the system. That respect is not sentimental. It is structural. And it is earned through observation, honesty, and design.

The best investors are not the boldest. They are the best-matched to their own constraints.

Closing Insight: Identity Is the First Allocation

Before you buy a single asset, allocate attention to *who you are when the lights go out.* Not when markets are calm, but when they are cruel. Not when your ego is stroked, but when your confidence is tested. The portfolio that holds through those moments is not the one with the best metrics. It is the one aligned to the deepest truths of its owner.

Investor identity is not a luxury. It is the foundation. Know it—or pay for not knowing it.

Decision-Making Under Stress

The most consequential investment decisions are rarely made under ideal conditions. They are made in rooms thick with fear, inboxes flooded with conflicting headlines, and minds fogged by uncertainty. In those moments—when assets plunge, when narratives fracture, when the stakes feel deeply personal—our ability to think clearly is not a function of intelligence but *structure.* The cognitive scaffolding we build before the storm determines whether we react, freeze, or respond with clarity. This subchapter is not about adding more information to your toolkit. It is about *changing the architecture of how you think*—especially when clarity is most elusive.

It is a popular delusion that high-stakes choices are best met with high-energy responses. Yet stress, particularly financial stress, activates biological mechanisms that narrow focus, shorten time horizons, and amplify loss aversion. The prefrontal cortex—the seat of reasoning—yields to the amygdala. We don't think; we *signal danger.* And what feels like "gut instinct" is often just panic dressed in intuition's clothes. To make sound decisions under pressure, we must *design for it in advance.* The mind must be trained like a system—not treated as an emergency switchboard.

The Physics of Stress: Why Rationality Collapses

Stress is not just emotional discomfort. It is a physiological event with measurable cognitive effects. Under stress, cortisol and adrenaline rewire attention. We become hypersensitive to threats, less tolerant of ambiguity, and increasingly reliant on heuristics—mental shortcuts that prioritise speed over accuracy. In finance, this translates to a few predictable behaviours: exiting positions prematurely, chasing confirmation bias, ignoring base rates, or overweighting recent events. The irony is profound: *The more urgent a decision feels, the less suited we are to make it well.*

This isn't just theory. Studies in behavioural economics, such as those by Daniel Kahneman and Amos Tversky, have shown that under pressure, people consistently choose immediate relief over long-term gain—even when it violates their own stated values. Loss aversion triples. Time preferences collapse. It's not just that we fear losing money—it's that we fear losing *control.* The result? We trade long-term advantage for short-term comfort.

Decision Hygiene: Creating Mental Clean Rooms

To counter this, we must develop what psychologist Gary Klein calls *decision hygiene*—the conditions that promote clean thinking even in dirty environments. Good investors, like good surgeons, don't just react well under pressure. They create cognitive clean rooms: environments where distractions are filtered, biases are surfaced, and logic is pre-installed.

This involves several components:

Pre-mortem analysis: Before initiating a position or strategy, imagine it has failed catastrophically. Ask: *What would have caused this? What signs might we ignore?* This reframes decision-making as a dynamic probability map—not a binary outcome.

Decision journals: Log not just your actions, but your *reasons* for taking them. Over time, this creates a map of how you think—not just what you do—and surfaces recurring biases.

Fixed rules under pressure: Define non-negotiable behaviours before the stress hits. For example, *I do not trade within 24 hours of a 10% portfolio drawdown.* These constraints act as guardrails when cognition falters.

Stress-resilient investors don't avoid emotion—they outdesign it.

Mental Models for Uncertainty

The key to making resilient decisions under pressure is not to eliminate emotion but to *reframe information through robust mental models.* Here are three foundational ones:

Expected Value Thinking: In chaos, we anchor on narratives—"Bitcoin is going to zero" or "the Fed will pivot." Instead, force a shift to expected value: *What are the probabilities of different outcomes, and what's the weighted impact?* This turns drama into data. Even if you can't assign precise numbers, the act of structuring the possibility space distances you from panic.

Second-Order Thinking: Ask not just *what will happen*, but *what will happen after that.* In market crises, the obvious reactions are often priced in. The alpha lies in anticipating the response to the response.

Inversion: Instead of asking "What should I do to succeed?" ask, "What would guarantee failure here?" Then avoid that. Inverting the problem often reveals blind spots masked by emotion.

These models don't eliminate chaos, but they translate it into manageable components. *A good model doesn't predict the future—it preserves rationality when prediction fails.*

The Reframing Toolkit: From Panic to Perspective

Reframing is not positive thinking. It is precision thinking. It is the ability to view the same facts through a lens that restores agency. For example:

Instead of "The market is crashing," try "Volatility is exposing fragility in overleveraged sectors—where is the resilience?"

Instead of "I can't afford to lose more," reframe to "What risk levels allow me to sleep at night and stay solvent without retreating from opportunity?"

Instead of "Everyone is panicking," reframe to "Panic is revealing mispricings. Who is forced to sell, and what assets are becoming irrationally discounted?"

Reframing creates psychological distance. It allows the investor to move from *participant* to *observer*—from prey to strategist.

The Ethics of Calm: Why Serenity Is Not Selfish

In periods of social or market chaos, remaining calm can feel detached—or even unethical. But consider this: *When you lose clarity, you increase fragility not just for yourself, but for those who depend on your decisions.* Families, teams, clients—all suffer when your bandwidth collapses. Calm is not apathy. It is *the ethical obligation of a fiduciary mind.* And it must be cultivated like any discipline.

Calm also has practical benefits. It improves information filtering. It reduces error stacking. And it increases the likelihood of recognising rare but asymmetric opportunities—what Howard Marks calls "second-level thinking," the ability to interpret reality not as it is presented, but as it is misperceived.

A Case in Fracture: 2020 and the Price of Panic

During March 2020, when global markets cratered under pandemic panic, many portfolios were liquidated not because they were unsound—but because their owners could no longer tolerate the emotional strain. Some sold near the bottom, locking in losses. Others hedged poorly and compounded their risks. A small cohort—those who had pre-defined principles, decision models, and calm protocols—preserved or even expanded their capital.

The lesson is not that foresight predicted the pandemic. It's that *stress management was the real alpha.* Those who had already interrogated their pain points—who had practiced staying curious under threat—were able to *act while others froze.*

Designing the Inner Control Room

You cannot control markets, headlines, or global policy. But you *can* control the operating system that processes them. To that end:

Limit exposure to real-time news in volatile periods. Most is noise that paralyses, not informs.

Curate your inputs. During stress, consult pre-trusted sources—not new ones that trigger hyper-reactivity.

Establish time delays for key decisions. The simple act of waiting 24 hours before action can separate reflex from reason.

Decision-making under stress is not an act of bravery. It is an act of design. You are not trying to eliminate discomfort—you are trying to ensure that discomfort does not hijack truth.

The Strategic Investor's Edge

What separates the enduring investor from the episodic one is not IQ, access, or tools. It is *response stability*. In every cycle, the winners are not just those who guessed right—they are those who stayed operational when others folded. They made fewer decisions—but better ones. They knew which lever to pull, and which to leave untouched.

They understood that *the quality of your decisions during panic determines the compound rate of your capital across decades.*

So prepare not just to act, but to *think clearly when it matters most.* Build the models. Design the triggers. Know your defaults. And remember: *Stress is inevitable—but reactive thinking is optional.*

Chapter 9
Income vs Independence – The Wealth Illusion

For all the breathless chatter about financial freedom, one rarely hears what, precisely, people believe they're being freed from. Six-figure paycheques, impressively diversified portfolios, thriving ventures—these are often mistaken for security. Yet beneath the sheen lies an inconvenient truth: much of what passes for wealth today is astonishingly delicate. Interruptible. Entirely beholden to systems that sit far beyond our influence. The lexicon of finance—returns, assets, passive income—has gradually eclipsed the deeper aim: autonomy. Not merely acquiring money, but maintaining control when things go sideways. Not just building, but structuring life so that the vital arteries—housing, food, access, mobility—aren't subject to someone else's switchboard. This chapter confronts the paradox that defines modern affluence: the illusion of power in the absence of sovereignty.

The question that matters now isn't "What's your income?" but "How interruptible is it?" And so enters the Independence Quotient—a concept both pragmatic and quietly subversive. It's not a slogan, but a filter. A pressure test for the real resilience of your financial setup. The question it poses is deceptively simple: if your income vanished tomorrow, what percentage of your life would continue untouched? Not for how long—but how much. Which parts of your existence—your food, your home, your communications, your dignity—are arranged in a way that no employer, regulator, institution, or line of code can easily dismantle?

Let's bring this into sharp relief. Picture a high-earning executive pulling in $400,000 annually. Every cent flows through a single, domestic bank account. Transparent. Taxed. Logged. Their lifestyle? Lavish—but fragile. One flick of a bureaucratic wrist, and the entire edifice could buckle. Now, contrast that with a digital craftsperson earning a modest $60,000, dispersed across crypto, peer-to-peer trades, decentralised yield streams—living in a place where privacy isn't treated as an admission of guilt. To traditional finance, the executive "wins." But if tomorrow ushers in a bank freeze, a cross-border seizure, a platform ban, or a geopolitical hiccup—who's truly insulated? Who can ride the storm without first asking permission?

That's the crux: real wealth isn't what you've accumulated—it's what you can still access when things go wrong.

This shift in perspective upends the old metrics. Income is no longer just a figure; it's an ecosystem. A web of energetic inflows—economic lifelines that sustain your autonomy without constant appeals to gatekeepers. Think beyond the obvious: a mobile consultancy untethered from geography, a subscription base that doesn't require visibility, crypto royalties that survive without headlines. The goal isn't to hoard—it's to become uninterruptible. Not because we're heading for dystopia (though some days it feels that way), but because fragility is now built into the system. Not through malice, but through sheer centralisation.

Confidence in traditional pillars—governments, banks, currencies, media—is not just waning; it's decaying structurally. It's been quietly codified: bank fine print, tax code footnotes, user agreements that nobody reads. Accounts can vanish without trial. Funds can be taxed in retrospect. Inflation eats away at your spending power while headlines assure you it's "transitory." In such a climate, it's not your net worth that matters—it's your fallback systems. Your autonomous redundancies. That's why we'll spend little time here fantasising about passive income. This is about resilience income—money that endures in disruption, that flows without exposure, that keeps your systems alive when the lights flicker.

Now let's confront a truth many avoid: the addiction to more. The finance world is drunk on scale. More properties. More portfolios. More income streams. But true sovereignty isn't about magnitude—it's about sufficiency. The sovereign individual isn't obsessed with expansion; they're obsessed with continuity. What is enough—not to merely subsist, but to live alertly and on one's own terms? This isn't a sermon on minimalism or stoicism. It's about understanding the point where growth becomes fragility. Where the next layer of complexity brings not freedom, but dependence. On accountants. On regulators. On platforms whose policies change overnight.

This chapter asks you to strip it all back. Build a wealth architecture not on prestige, but on clarity. Audit your earnings, yes—but audit your vulnerabilities harder. Where are you exposed? Who has the power to revoke your lifestyle? Map your financial dependencies the way an engineer maps failure points. Because the real question isn't what pays you. It's: who could stop it—and how swiftly?

We'll explore the less-travelled paths. Not for the sake of provocation, but preservation. Anonymous earnings. Cross-border royalties. Skillsets monetised through encrypted networks. This isn't rebellion for its own sake—it's about maintaining optionality when centralisation becomes coercive. And it will. In subtle, bureaucratic ways. Which is why independence, like privacy, must be engineered—not assumed.

Independence also begins at the behavioural level. Financial systems, by design, reward conformity. But wealth that bends too far to please becomes a performance. One that's easily cancelled. Many high earners fall prey to this: lavish lives built on geographic immobility, reputational exposure, over-leveraged visibility. Their affluence is theatre—glossy, conditional, fragile. Real independence lies in quiet insulation. Designing privacy not to conceal wrongdoing, but to prevent your freedom being tied to algorithmic acceptability.

And through it all, the central pivot remains: we must move from measuring success in volume to measuring it in durability. Can your lifestyle persist when the system that enables it fails to show up? Can your identity endure if the market punishes your refusal to conform? These aren't doomsday scenarios—they're architectural ones. The way an engineer plans for weather, stress, or sabotage, you must plan for the legal, digital, and social forces that could one day press against your autonomy.

So consider this a nudge—a challenge to stop measuring your life by dashboards and start evaluating it like a fortress. Where are the weak walls? Who holds the keys? What flows nourish you without oversight?

Because in the years ahead, it won't be the loudest or the wealthiest who hold their ground—it will be those with quiet continuity, decentralised leverage, and the foresight to ask not just "What can I earn?" but "What can no one take?"

Forget the charts. What you need now is fewer veto points on your freedom.

This is the art of stepping beyond income, toward independence. And it begins with dismantling the mirage of wealth we've all been conditioned to chase.

Why High Earners Still Feel Poor

There is a quiet paradox haunting the modern professional class. Individuals earning six or even seven figures—lawyers, executives, consultants, engineers—often feel less financially secure than their grandparents did on modest pensions. They have access to international travel, premium healthcare, and digital conveniences unthinkable two decades ago, yet beneath this abundance lies a gnawing anxiety: *Why doesn't it feel like wealth?* Why does a £250,000 salary, which statistically places someone in the upper echelons of the global income pyramid, so often come with exhaustion, obligation, and a vague sense of insufficiency?

The answer is not simply about poor budgeting, extravagance, or entitlement. It runs deeper—into the architecture of the modern financial ecosystem, the psychological distortions of affluence, and the engineered fragility of income-dependent lifestyles. What masquerades as prosperity is often a finely tuned system of dependency: *on employment, on liquidity, on stable markets, and above all, on narratives of security that no longer map to reality.*

Let us begin with the most misunderstood force of all—*inflation.* Not the statistical fiction of headline consumer price indices, but the lived experience of asset inflation, stealth taxation, and declining purchasing power. A home that cost £400,000 in 2012 might sell for £1.2 million today in major global cities. Salaries, meanwhile, have not tripled. The price of financial entry into urban life—housing, education, childcare, healthcare—has exploded at a pace that traditional wage growth cannot match. This is not simply lifestyle inflation. It is *systemic economic inflation*, where the basic requirements for upper-middle-class identity are being repriced out of reach, *even for those who play by all the rules.*

Moreover, much of what professionals spend is not for survival or joy, but for *signalling*. Private schooling, high-tier insurance, prime property postcodes—these are not just functional purchases. They are currencies of trust in a system where opportunity is rationed by optics. And so begins the phenomenon of *status-consumption-as-defence.* You dress the part, commute the part, live the postcode, pay the fees—not out of vanity, but to remain eligible for the game you're already exhausted from playing. *The lifestyle becomes obligatory*, not optional.

Then there is the creeping force of *lifestyle creep*. Unlike overt consumerism, lifestyle creep masquerades as normal progression. A slightly better car. A more central flat. A few more international holidays. Upgrades that feel rational in isolation but compound into a fragile ecosystem where *income must be uninterrupted.* One bonus missed, one promotion delayed, one regulatory change—and the entire financial stack begins to wobble. This is not wealth. This is *performance tethered to inflow.*

What makes this even more insidious is the absence of *slack*. High earners often run leaner than assumed. They may have investments, yes—but those assets are frequently illiquid, tax-exposed, or legally encumbered. They may own homes—but with large mortgages and inflexible debt servicing. Their cashflow is impressive, but their optionality is minimal. And so, when confronted with volatility—be it market-driven, political, or personal—the only viable option is to *maintain momentum*. Pause is not permitted. Rest is unaffordable. *They are rich in income and poor in exit routes.*

This leads us to the psychological toll: *cognitive load masquerading as productivity*. Many high earners cannot switch off because their security is conditional on uninterrupted performance. Every sabbatical deferred, every burnout absorbed, every boundary crossed is a trade: comfort now in exchange for theoretical freedom later. But later never arrives. *The system is designed to consume resilience as fuel.*

And when the resilience runs out, the identity built upon it often collapses.

Then there's the overlooked issue of *structural vulnerability.* Salary, however high, is still a *single point of failure.* Whether it flows through an employer, a client contract, or a licensure-dependent profession, the income stream remains *externally determined.* That is not independence—it is risk concentration. The illusion of safety that comes from a big paycheque is precisely what discourages contingency planning. *And when disruption comes—through layoffs, legal changes, illness, or algorithmic obsolescence—there is no fallback. Only recalibration at speed, often with diminishing leverage.*

Let us also not ignore taxation—not merely as a financial drain, but as a psychological burden. High earners are easy targets for fiscal policy. They are visible, trackable, and concentrated. From marginal rates that approach confiscatory levels to new regimes of wealth monitoring and digital reporting, their prosperity is not private. It is *auditable on demand.* The result is a strange irony: the higher you earn, the more aggressively you must participate in a system that *treats your productivity as public resource.*

All of this culminates in a startling insight: *modern prosperity is heavily subsidised by emotional exhaustion.* The sense of "feeling poor" is not irrational. It is a rational response to living inside a structure where your ability to stay afloat requires absolute engagement, minimal error tolerance, and relentless upkeep. This is *not a mindset problem.* It is a structural feature of an economic design that rewards performance but punishes disobedience.

So, what can be done? The answer is not to retreat from high earning, but to *build sovereignty into the system.* This means moving from performance income to *persistent value.* It means diversifying not just across assets but across *control layers*—ownership, jurisdiction, privacy, and redundancy. It means distinguishing between *signal spending* and *structural wealth.* And above all, it means designing lifestyles where financial wellbeing is not tethered to visibility, compliance, or constant acceleration.

The high earner who feels poor is not delusional. They are perceptive. They are glimpsing the reality beneath the numbers: that without control, optionality, and continuity, *money does not feel like freedom—it feels like obligation.* And unless addressed with intentional design, that obligation metastasises into anxiety, burnout, and eventual collapse.

True wealth begins not with more money, but with fewer permissions required to keep living well. The goal is not merely income. It is *interruption-resilient independence.* That's not just a financial outcome—it's a philosophical orientation. And it begins by dismantling the false comfort of the paycheque, no matter how large.

The "Independence Quotient" Model: Measuring What Truly Can't Be Interrupted

The idea of financial independence has, for decades, been sold as a static number—often a net worth target, a monthly passive income figure, or a multiple of annual expenses. But such metrics, while simple, are profoundly misleading. They measure *magnitude*, not *resilience.* They calculate *quantity*, not *continuity.* And most critically, they tell you how much you *have*—not how much of your life is protected from *interruption.*

This distinction matters now more than ever. In an economic landscape defined by instability—supply shocks, capital controls, inflationary decay, digital surveillance, and employment precarity—the true measure of independence is not how rich you appear on paper, but how uninterrupted your life remains when the external world becomes volatile. *Enter the Independence Quotient.*

The Independence Quotient is not a number you brag about at dinner parties. It's not a passive income goal, nor a simple retirement calculation. It is a conceptual framework—*a diagnostic lens for assessing how much of your life is structurally insulated from disruption.* It asks the question too often ignored in traditional wealth-building strategies: *Can you sustain your lifestyle, obligations, and values without needing permission from employers, governments, banks, or platforms?*

Let us unpack this.

Redefining Independence: Beyond Income Streams

At its core, financial independence has been conflated with the capacity to "not work." But *not working* is not the same as *not depending*. One may quit a job and still be at the mercy of fiat currency depreciation, geopolitical instability, or institutional compliance. A retiree drawing a comfortable pension is not financially sovereign if that pension is held in a jurisdiction that can freeze it. A landlord is not independent if rent laws change overnight. *An income stream is not a moat if it can be legislated away.*

This is the foundational flaw in many FIRE (Financial Independence, Retire Early) narratives. They tend to model independence on linear asset drawdown or compounding returns, assuming a benign environment. But environments are not benign. They are political. They are adversarial. They change. *True independence is not just about asset growth—it's about operational continuity under duress.*

The Anatomy of Interruption

To measure what's truly uninterruptible, we must identify what types of interruptions exist. These include:

Regulatory interference: When government agencies impose capital controls, freeze bank accounts, or change tax codes retroactively.

Platform dependency: When your livelihood or assets are mediated by centralised digital platforms—think payment processors, cloud services, or even real estate listings.

Liquidity traps: When your wealth is locked into assets that can't be accessed or sold without extreme penalties, or during market stress.

Currency decay: When the value of your income or savings is eroded not by market losses, but by central bank policy.

Jurisdictional risk: When all your holdings—real estate, businesses, pensions—exist within a single legal and tax system, creating a single point of failure.

The Independence Quotient asks: *What percentage of your life remains stable when any of the above occur?*

Layered Redundancy: Designing for Continuity

The purpose of the IQ model is not to promote paranoia, but to encourage intelligent redundancy. Much like cybersecurity professionals speak of "defence in depth," resilient wealth requires *income in depth*, *jurisdictions in depth*, and *control in depth*. A practical Independence Quotient analysis looks at multiple domains:

Income redundancy: Do you have multiple, independent income streams that function across currencies, geographies, and platforms?

Asset custody: Do you truly control your wealth, or do you merely have legal title? Is it held in bank accounts, or cryptographic wallets? In domestic trusts, or offshore foundations?

Liquidity resilience: Can you convert parts of your portfolio into usable capital *without institutional gatekeeping*?

Geopolitical dispersion: Is your economic footprint diversified across jurisdictions that are uncorrelated in terms of political and fiscal risk?

Lifestyle portability: How much of your life can relocate—physically, digitally, or operationally—without starting from zero?

Each of these layers contributes to an individual's Independence Quotient. The more layers that are self-reliant, interoperable, and insulated from system shocks, the higher the score.

Case Study: Two Millionaires, Two Outcomes

Consider two individuals, each with a net worth of £5 million.

The first holds the entirety of their wealth in real estate and equities based in one country, has a corporate job with restricted stock options, and relies on traditional banks for all transactions. They have no secondary passport, no offshore exposure, and all expenses are denominated in one fiat currency. *Their lifestyle depends on stability across multiple institutional layers.*

The second has a diversified basket of real estate in two countries, revenue-generating digital assets, a remote consultancy business paid in multiple currencies, a portion of wealth in cold-stored crypto, legal residency in a neutral jurisdiction, and three months' living expenses in physical cash equivalents. *Their lifestyle is designed to continue across a range of interruptions.*

Though both have the same nominal wealth, the second individual's *Independence Quotient is significantly higher.* One lives in economic weather. The other has built a climate-controlled life.

Beyond Theory: Practical Implementation

Designing for a high IQ score is not an overnight task. It involves strategic trade-offs, long-term planning, and a shift in mindset—from accumulation to architecture. Some principles include:

Invert your thinking: Don't start by asking "What's the best investment?" Ask "What part of my life is most vulnerable to interruption?"

Unbundle dependencies: Identify where single points of failure exist—whether in income, jurisdiction, currency, or access.

Prioritise control over returns: An asset that yields 4% annually but is unseizable and off-grid may be more valuable than one that yields 10% but is surveilled and centralised.

Segment liquidity: Build "rings" of liquidity—immediate, mid-term, and strategic—across different forms of custody and jurisdiction.

Upgrade your identity infrastructure: Second passports, offshore companies, decentralised storage—these are not exotic tools. They are increasingly necessary tools for self-defence.

Psychological Independence: The Invisible Dividend

Finally, the Independence Quotient is not merely structural—it is *psychological*. The dividend of real independence is *calm*. When your life is built to withstand disruption, the quality of your decision-making improves. You can say no to bad deals. You can delay gratification without fear. You can disengage from manipulative narratives because you don't need the system's permission to survive.

This is perhaps the most undervalued benefit of the IQ framework: *peace of mind under pressure*. It is not created by more zeros in your account. It is built by aligning your life with sources of income and sovereignty that cannot be easily revoked, reversed, or reinterpreted.

Conclusion Without Saying "In Conclusion"

The Independence Quotient reframes wealth not as accumulation, but as *continuity without compromise*. It is the capacity to live well without reliance on fragile systems. To earn without permission. To relocate without panic. To choose without coercion. The future belongs not to those with the most assets, but to those whose lives remain least interruptible. That is the new definition of wealth—and the new standard of freedom.

Building Income Streams That Can't Be Frozen

The modern investor is not just seeking return—they are seeking resilience. In a world increasingly defined by algorithmic censorship, regulatory overreach, and digital centralisation, income that can be interrupted is income that can be neutralised. As states grow more powerful and platforms more intrusive, the simple truth emerges: *the ability to earn without permission is no longer a luxury—it is a strategic necessity*. This subchapter addresses a challenge that few financial advisors are prepared to confront: how to build income that not only flows, but *cannot be stopped*.

It begins with a fundamental realignment of how we think about revenue. Traditional frameworks—whether salaries, dividends, or rental income—treat income as something derived from access to systems. A job requires an employer. Rent requires a legal contract. Dividends require intact capital markets. Each of these sits on top of legal, technical, or political infrastructure that can be revoked. In benign times, the risk is abstract. But when states invoke emergency powers, when platforms freeze accounts, or when financial institutions are politicised, these assumptions become liabilities. *What you earn is less important than what you can keep earning when you're no longer welcome.*

The Illusion of Security in Conventional Income

Income is often mistaken for autonomy. A high salary, diversified investments, or profitable businesses may signal strength, but if they are all dependent on domestic infrastructure—banking systems, payment processors, contracts enforceable by the courts of a single jurisdiction—then they are *fragile*. And fragility is not always visible. Many investors operate under a false sense of security because their income flows uninterrupted—until it doesn't. History is littered with examples:

Argentina's capital controls in 2011 made it illegal for citizens to purchase foreign currency, rendering dollar earnings inaccessible.

India's demonetisation in 2016 wiped out the legal tender status of over 80% of the cash in circulation, devastating informal income streams.

Canada's freezing of protestor-affiliated bank accounts in 2022, executed without trial, signalled the state's growing comfort with financial censorship.

Russian citizens with foreign assets have watched their brokerage accounts get severed from global access due to sanctions.

In China, tech entrepreneurs found their businesses deplatformed and income destroyed by shifting party priorities—not criminal convictions.

Each example points to the same truth: *income is not secure if it can be frozen by policy, platform, or proxy.*

Redefining Resilient Income

A resilient income stream possesses three core qualities: *location-independence*, *censorship-resistance*, and *non-reliance on centralised third parties*. These characteristics are not binary, but compositional. The more layers of independence you build in, the higher your income's immunity to disruption.

Let's define them clearly:

Location-independence means your income isn't tied to one physical geography or legal system. It can be earned and accessed from multiple jurisdictions.

Censorship-resistance refers to the difficulty of blocking, reversing, or interfering with the flow of funds—typically requiring cryptographic or peer-to-peer architecture.

Platform-detachment minimises reliance on any single point of failure—whether it's a payment processor, employer, or social media algorithm.

These are not abstract ideals. They are operational criteria for survival in a world where income is as much a function of *permission* as productivity.

Examples of Unfreezable or Difficult-to-Freeze Income

This isn't about abandoning legitimacy. It's about building *resilient legitimacy*. The following models demonstrate how people around the world are creating revenue streams that sit outside conventional freeze-points.

Self-Custodied Digital Products

Creators who sell digital goods—courses, books, templates—through their own websites, and accept crypto directly, operate outside the reach of payment processor censorship. Unlike marketplaces like Amazon or Etsy, direct distribution means the creator controls pricing, delivery, and payment rails. Tools like BTCPay Server and open-source storefronts enable this.

Global Freelancing with Crypto Settlement

Freelancers in design, development, consulting, or writing increasingly invoice clients globally and receive payment in stablecoins (e.g. USDC on Ethereum or Solana) or BTC. Platforms like Deel or remote-first talent markets facilitate introductions, but the payment settlement is increasingly decentralised and peer-to-peer. Crucially, self-custody protects against government freezes or PayPal-style deplatforming.

Remote, Non-KYC Business Models

Operators of SaaS tools, niche community memberships, or knowledge platforms who accept crypto or use privacy-respecting gateways like Monero or Zcash enhance their business model's resilience. The principle: *no intermediary, no gatekeeper.* Revenue is routed directly to wallets controlled only by the entrepreneur.

Decentralised Finance (DeFi) Yield Strategies

Though riskier and requiring technical literacy, DeFi allows users to earn returns through liquidity provision, lending protocols, and token incentives. Because accounts are wallet-based and pseudonymous, access is open, and no central authority can block participation unless protocols themselves are compromised.

Jurisdictional Income Splitting

Some individuals split business structures across countries—billing clients via Estonian e-residency, holding crypto in Swiss vaults, and receiving royalty payments via a Panamanian corporation. The result: no single jurisdiction can unilaterally interfere with the full stack. *This isn't tax evasion; it's resilience design.*

Off-grid Productive Assets

For those in agriculture or craft, income can be made resilient via physical production that is sold locally for hard currency, barter, or informal arrangements. While not digital, it resists platformisation and often slips below the radar of formal control mechanisms. Such models are more common in developing economies but are increasingly relevant elsewhere.

Design Principles for Income Sovereignty

There is no one-size-fits-all model. But resilient income strategies share a philosophical spine: *design for exit, not just access.* Ask yourself:

Could a single government, corporation, or algorithm destroy this income source overnight?

Does earning this income require me to disclose personal information that could be used to deplatform me?

Can I still receive this income if the dominant currency in my country collapses or is restricted?

Does this revenue require a permissioned platform—Amazon, Stripe, Patreon, Google AdSense—to function?

How easily can I reroute this income in an emergency?

These questions illuminate not just income strategy, but *sovereignty strategy.*

Ethics, Legality, and Legibility

It's important to distinguish between hiding and *opting out.* Building unfreezable income is not an act of criminality—it's a form of resilience. But that resilience must be *ethical.* Tax obligations should be fulfilled. Clients and users deserve transparency. What's being sought is not anonymity for evasion, but *autonomy from fragility.*

Many who pursue these paths find themselves walking a line between *legibility and leverage.* Too much legibility, and you become vulnerable to arbitrary control. Too little, and you may invite suspicion or lose the ability to interface with mainstream finance. The sweet spot is visibility *on your own terms*, with clear ethical intent and a diversified footprint.

The Psychological Impact of Sovereign Income

When your income can be paused by an institution, your thinking is shaped by compliance. You self-censor. You hesitate. You optimise for safety over truth. When your income is *yours*—resilient by design, earned through systems that don't require external validation—you think differently. You act differently. You plan long-term.

This is the hidden dividend of unfreezable income: not just freedom from interruption, but *freedom from internalised dependence.*

Final Thought Without a Flourish

Building income that can't be frozen is not a fringe pursuit. It is the rational response to a financial system that has become increasingly politicised, centralised, and brittle. This chapter doesn't suggest abandoning the formal economy—it suggests building *beyond* it. Not as a rejection, but as *insurance.* Because wealth that flows only under favourable conditions isn't wealth—it's risk deferred. And risk deferred, when mismanaged, becomes freedom denied.

Sufficiency vs Accumulation

The defining question for any serious wealth strategy is not "How much can I make?"—it is "How much is enough?" And yet this question is rarely asked in earnest. In financial discourse, sufficiency is often viewed as a psychological cop-out, a consolation prize for those who "didn't make it." But this view betrays a critical misunderstanding: *sufficiency is not the enemy of ambition—it is the architecture of clarity.* Without a personal definition of "enough," accumulation becomes compulsion. The pursuit of more continues not because it serves a strategic purpose, but because there is no internal mechanism to signal completion.

This subchapter challenges the orthodoxy of limitless accumulation. It interrogates the narratives that frame wealth as a scorecard, status signal, or existential insurance policy. And it proposes an alternative: *a calibrated system of wealth design*, rooted not in how much capital you can attract, but in how intelligently you define and protect the life you wish to live.

The Infinite Game and the Unanchored Investor

Modern capitalism rewards scale. Businesses are built to grow. Investors are taught to maximise returns. The wealth management industry thrives on the idea that you should never stop accumulating, because *more* is always safer. This logic is seductive. But it is also incomplete.

What it ignores is that in the absence of self-defined boundaries, financial goals become abstract. They float. And floating goals breed anxiety. You never know whether you're ahead or behind, because the game has no end. This is not strategic behaviour—it is *existential drift* disguised as ambition.

The unanchored investor chases more income, more assets, more influence—not because it serves a concrete life objective, but because they are immersed in a cultural system that defines *worth by volume*. This is how high-net-worth individuals can feel perpetually under threat. Their portfolios are massive, but their systems are hollow. They own much, but *know little about what they actually need.*

The Psychology of "More"

Psychologists have long understood the adaptive—and ultimately corrosive—nature of hedonic adaptation. We become used to what we have. What once felt luxurious becomes baseline. What was once aspirational becomes expected. In this context, accumulation doesn't serve satisfaction. It merely *resets the standard.*

Moreover, as Daniel Kahneman and Amos Tversky's work in behavioural economics has shown, humans are loss-averse. We fear losing more than we enjoy gaining. The result? Even as wealth increases, fear does not subside—it compounds. Each added asset becomes something else that can be taken, taxed, or lost.

Here lies the paradox: *without a defined point of sufficiency, wealth creates as much psychological burden as it does security*. We do not buy peace of mind—we lease it, temporarily, at increasing cost.

From Accumulation to Calibration

A more intelligent framework begins by rejecting accumulation as a goal in itself. Instead, the investor defines a *target lifestyle architecture*—the concrete elements of living that matter most—and works backwards to understand what is needed to make it structurally uninterruptible.

This process includes:

Identifying essential costs (housing, food, healthcare, mobility)

Designing optional but meaningful luxuries (travel, education, philanthropy)

Recognising the psychological threshold at which more adds noise, not value

From here, the focus shifts from building a large portfolio to building a *precise portfolio*—one engineered to match function with purpose. This is what makes sufficiency powerful. It is not anti-wealth. It is wealth with direction.

A Case Study in Redundancy vs Redundancy

Consider two investors:

Investor A has a net worth of $8 million, tied up in equity-heavy assets and a private company. They have no real time freedom, live in a high-cost urban environment, and their monthly burn rate is $35,000. Investor A is "rich" by any external metric—but their financial system is brittle. Their security is dependent on business continuity and market performance.

Investor B has a net worth of $1.2 million, largely in diversified, income-generating assets with minimal correlation. They live abroad, have moderate expenses, multiple citizenship options, and draw on three independent income sources totalling $7,000 per month. Investor B has *less wealth*, but *more optionality*. Their income is difficult to disrupt. Their sufficiency is well-defined and protected.

Who is truly free?

The Role of Constraints in Freedom

Counterintuitively, self-imposed constraints often *enhance* freedom. When you define "enough," you free yourself from the tyranny of endless decision-making. You stop reacting to the market's mood swings. You exit the loop of comparative envy.

This is not minimalist posturing. It is optimisation. A well-defined boundary doesn't limit growth—it filters distraction. And that filtration is essential, because *every additional layer of wealth comes with its own administrative, psychological, and security costs.*

In this light, sufficiency is not a ceiling—it is a *strategic checkpoint.* It allows you to decide, with clarity, whether the next financial move adds value—or merely *adds complexity.*

Sufficiency as a Geopolitical Hedge

Sufficiency also has geopolitical utility. When your financial life is designed to meet your needs with margin—not excess—you can *move faster.* You are less vulnerable to tax policy shifts, inflationary spirals, or asset freezes. You are not forced to chase yield in dangerous jurisdictions. You are not hostage to risk just to sustain an inflated lifestyle.

Put differently: *sufficiency makes resilience more portable.* A modest lifestyle, well-defended, is harder to interrupt than a luxurious one dependent on fragile systems.

Legacy Without Excess

A common objection to sufficiency is legacy. What about providing for children, or creating generational wealth? The answer lies not in discarding legacy, but in *redefining its mechanism.* Legacy is not a function of volume—it is a function of *system design.* The most durable legacy you can leave is *a replicable framework for intelligent wealth stewardship.*

This includes teaching heirs the philosophy of sufficiency, embedding structural diversification, and equipping them with tools to evaluate value beyond accumulation. If wealth is transferred without clarity, it becomes *liability disguised as inheritance.*

Reframing "Enough" as a Strategic Question

"Enough" is not an emotional retreat. It is a data-driven inquiry. What is the capital base required to meet your core obligations indefinitely? What are your real inflation exposures? What risk profile is required to sustain your lifestyle, with margin, over decades?

If you don't know those numbers, you're not investing—you're gambling with optics. You are managing image, not engineering outcomes.

The sufficiency model reframes the central question from *What can I afford to acquire?* to *What can I afford to secure, sustainably, without compromise?* This is not less rigorous than traditional wealth thinking. It is *more rigorous*, because it requires confronting the *true architecture* of your financial life.

Final Note Without Closure

The pursuit of sufficiency is not a denial of aspiration—it is its foundation. It offers something that accumulation alone cannot: *a stopping point, a checkpoint, a reference frame for decision-making.* Without it, every market high is still a worry, every downturn an existential threat. With it, your wealth becomes not a moving target, but a *functional system*, aligned with a life designed on purpose—not one distorted by noise.

Chapter 10
The Nomad's Hedge – Mobility as a Financial Strategy

Most people accept geography as fate. Their passport? A birthright. Their residency? A foregone conclusion. Taxes, regulations, civic duties—all tied to the coordinates where they first drew breath. This kind of passive allegiance—call it geographic fatalism—might have been understandable in the last century. Back then, borders were rigid, choices narrow, and international movement the preserve of either the ultra-privileged or the desperate. But today, such inertia has consequences. In an age of near-frictionless capital and increasingly erratic governance, tying your legal, financial, and cultural identity to a single nation-state isn't just limiting—it's reckless.

Mobility, properly reckoned, is no longer about fleeing one place for another. It's about leverage. The ability to shift—your person, your business, your digital footprint, even your legal obligations—is fast becoming the rarest and most potent form of asymmetrical advantage. Not because it's glamorous, but because it grants room to manoeuvre when systems around you tighten. It's your buffer against political overreach, economic decay, or a sudden algorithmic red flag. In a world where funds can traverse borders in a blink but people are still asked to live like static assets, geographic diversification isn't extravagance. It's prudence. A quietly radical form of self-defence.

This chapter explores what it means to become, in the most literal and least metaphorical sense, a sovereign individual. Not merely someone who holds their wealth, but someone who defines the environment in which that wealth exists. That environment is not abstract. It includes everything from tax codes and court systems to cultural attitudes and physical safety. And when that environment shifts—because of inflation, creeping authoritarianism, unstable currencies, or a slow collapse in public trust—the person who can shift with it holds the upper hand.

Mobility, in this light, becomes a hedge—not against any one catastrophe, but against the hubris of permanence.

The False Security of Fixed Roots

The dominant narrative of modern life still idealises stability: the long mortgage, the pension plan, the rooted identity. Stability is equated with safety, movement with risk. But recent history has inverted that logic. Consider the countless professionals whose savings were wiped out by currency devaluations in Lebanon, Argentina, or Turkey. Consider those caught in China's capital controls, or Canadians whose bank accounts were frozen without trial during political protests. These were not cautionary tales from unstable regions. These were real-time disruptions in supposedly developed systems.

And yet, most people remain jurisdictionally naïve. Their entire financial lives—banking, investment, insurance, business registration—exist within one regulatory environment. *That is not patriotism. It is structural exposure.* A single point of failure, disguised as a national identity.

Second Passports, First Principles

The conversation must begin with legal identity. Citizenship is not just a travel document—it is a contract with a government. That contract determines your tax obligations, your access to courts, your eligibility for protection or persecution. When you hold only one passport, your entire legal existence is a hostage negotiation. You are taxed where you live, governed by rules you didn't choose, and restricted from opportunities you cannot access.

This is where *flag theory* enters the conversation—not as a fringe libertarian fantasy, but as a coherent legal strategy. At its core, flag theory is about decoupling the key aspects of your life—citizenship, residency, business operations, asset storage, and lifestyle—so that no single government holds all the levers. It is the geopolitical equivalent of asset diversification.

Second citizenships can be acquired through ancestry, investment, naturalisation, or specialised programmes. Residency permits, often decoupled from work obligations, can be gained through income thresholds, property ownership, or entrepreneurship. And where you spend your time, *legally and practically*, can determine your tax residency status and, by extension, your entire economic framework.

Mobility as a Business Model

Digital entrepreneurs have long understood this. Remote-first companies, location-independent contractors, and cross-border service providers already operate with mobile income. But too often, their business models outpace their personal strategy. They build international businesses while remaining anchored to one tax regime, one banking system, and one legal identity. *This is a mistake of design, not ambition.*

The smart nomad doesn't just move their work. They move their infrastructure. That means opening offshore business entities in jurisdictions that honour contract law and privacy. It means banking in countries with stable regulatory environments and depositor protections. It means converting volatile fiat into harder assets—gold, Bitcoin, real estate—in places where those assets are legally insulated.

And crucially, it means recognising that *mobility is not about movement—it is about optionality.* The right to leave is the ultimate check on abusive governance. The right to stay *on your own terms* is even more powerful.

Lifestyle Design, Not Escape Fantasies

Skeptics often dismiss geographic arbitrage as escapism. They imagine digital nomads sipping lattes in Bali, disconnected from real responsibilities. But this caricature misses the point. The best mobility strategies are not about evading reality—they are about *curating it.*

Consider the American family that relocates to Portugal, cutting their cost of living in half while gaining access to EU healthcare and education. Or the investor who shifts residency to Singapore or the UAE, legally optimising their tax obligations while maintaining global access. Or the retiree who establishes tax residence in Panama, while drawing income from diversified, cross-border assets.

These are not acts of withdrawal. They are acts of *precision*. They reflect a worldview that treats geography not as destiny, but as design.

Cultural Arbitrage: Values, Not Just Costs

Mobility is often framed in economic terms: lower taxes, cheaper labour, better returns. But its true power lies in *cultural arbitrage*. Different societies value different things. Some elevate conformity, others independence. Some reward speed, others wisdom. When you live in one place your entire life, you assume these values are universal. They are not.

Moving between cultures gives you perspective. It allows you to choose not just your tax rate or climate—but your social contract. Do you want to raise children in a society that values free inquiry? Do you want to operate a business in a place that prioritises speed over bureaucracy? Do you want to retire in a region that reveres elders, rather than sidelines them?

These choices are not abstract. They are *system design decisions*. They affect your emotional well-being, your economic resilience, and your ethical alignment. And they are only available to those who cultivate mobility not as novelty, but as strategy.

The Infrastructure of Invisible Wealth

The final dimension of the nomad's hedge is invisibility—not in the sense of secrecy, but in the sense of non-interruption. The most resilient assets are those that *can't be seen, frozen, or stolen by a single authority*. This includes decentralised digital assets, offshore trusts, foreign real estate, or income streams derived from multiple jurisdictions.

But invisibility also includes the way you design your *life*. A low-profile residency in a calm jurisdiction. A modest but efficient asset footprint. A minimalist lifestyle funded by asymmetric returns. These are not compromises. They are *enhancements*. They allow you to live well without drawing attention. They are the geopolitical equivalent of sleeping with one eye open.

A New Definition of Wealth

Ultimately, this chapter is not about passports or tax codes. It is about redefining wealth. Wealth is not just what you own—it is *how freely you can use it*. It is not how much you make, but how interruptible your life is when systems falter.

In this light, mobility is not the opposite of rootedness—it is *intentional rootedness, across multiple systems*. It is not the abandonment of home, but the creation of *multiple homes*, each with its own kind of safety.

This is not theory. It is practice. It is the new blueprint for sovereignty in an interconnected but unstable world. And for those willing to think globally, act strategically, and design their lives with precision, *the nomad's hedge is not a backup plan. It is the plan.*

Where You Live Is a Financial Decision

Most people choose where to live based on familiarity, family, career convenience, or emotional ties. These are all understandable motivations—but they are also economically myopic. *Geography is one of the most under-acknowledged variables in wealth-building, wealth protection, and personal sovereignty.* Where you live determines how much you keep after taxes, what risks your assets are exposed to, the quality of legal protections around your wealth, and the opportunities you can—or cannot—access. Staying put, for all its comforts, may be the most costly decision you'll ever make.

The myth of geographic neutrality—that one's financial fate is primarily determined by effort and skill, irrespective of location—has been thoroughly debunked by history and economics alike.

Whether you're a salaried worker, entrepreneur, or investor, your address is not just a backdrop. *It is a contract.* And most people sign it blindly.

Taxation Is Not a Constant. It's a Choice—If You Make It One

One of the clearest demonstrations of geography's financial weight lies in tax. Two individuals with the same income and spending habits can have radically different financial outcomes depending on where they reside. A software developer earning £150,000 in London may take home barely half after national insurance, income tax, and VAT. A similar professional based in Dubai, Singapore, or even certain parts of Eastern Europe could retain 80–90% of their earnings, all legally, without reducing their standard of living—*and often improving it.*

Corporate structuring follows the same logic. A tech entrepreneur running a bootstrapped business from California is exposed to one of the most aggressive tax regimes in the world. Reposition that same company through Estonia's e-Residency programme, or structure an entity in Ireland, and suddenly profits are reinvested more efficiently, capital gains are better protected, and regulatory burdens become navigable rather than punitive.

None of this is about evasion. It's about *jurisdictional design.* The tax code is not morality; it is policy. Policies differ across geographies. The tragedy is that many people accept their home country's framework as a fixed reality—*when in fact, it's often the least optimised option available to them.*

Geopolitical Risk Isn't Just for "Risky" Countries

There's a dangerous presumption in many Western societies that risk is something that happens "elsewhere." Currency collapse? That's for Argentina. Capital controls? Venezuela. Arbitrary asset seizure? Zimbabwe. These examples are used not to provoke fear, but to dismantle complacency. Because such measures—soft confiscation through inflation, retrospective taxes, frozen accounts during protests—are increasingly appearing in countries once assumed to be paragons of financial security.

The 2022 freezing of Canadian bank accounts linked to peaceful protest donations. The UK's expanding Unexplained Wealth Orders (UWOs), which can seize assets without criminal conviction. The retroactive tax grabs in Australia. The ECB's open debate about ending cash anonymity. These are not anomalies. They are *trends*. And they all hinge on one key variable: *residency*. Where you live determines what tools the state can use against your wealth—and whether you have recourse.

This isn't paranoia. It's historical pattern recognition. And the antidote is not to panic, but to plan. *Geographic diversification isn't fear-based. It's system-aware.*

Access: The Quiet Privilege of the Right Address

Beyond taxation and risk, geography is also about access—to ideas, capital, communities, and infrastructure. A tech entrepreneur living in Lisbon or Tallinn gains proximity to thriving startup ecosystems, preferential EU funding, and globally mobile talent. A retiree based in Chiang Mai or Medellín accesses world-class healthcare at a fraction of Western costs, without compromising quality of life. A crypto founder in Zug, Switzerland, or Dubai can operate in jurisdictions where innovation is encouraged, not penalised.

Meanwhile, someone clinging to their hometown out of inertia might find themselves shut out of emerging economic sectors, trapped in depreciating real estate markets, or reliant on decaying infrastructure. This is not elitism—it's structural truth. *Your location is a multiplier or divider of your efforts.* Ignoring this is akin to launching a yacht and pretending the direction of the tide doesn't matter.

Lifestyle Arbitrage: Earning in One Currency, Spending in Another

The power of geographic choice also lies in cost efficiency. It's one thing to earn a high income. It's another to make that income stretch.

Those who earn in strong currencies (USD, GBP, EUR) and spend in lower-cost jurisdictions enjoy what can only be described as *purchasing power asymmetry*. This isn't just about spending less. It's about *living better* on the same income—or building faster toward independence.

A British couple earning online can reduce living costs by 60–70% by relocating to Portugal, Georgia, or Thailand, without sacrificing healthcare, education, or connectivity. The net effect over ten years is not just higher savings. It's *freedom acceleration*. You get to the point of "enough" sooner—not by working harder, but by *changing your denominator*.

The Inertia Trap: When Familiarity Becomes Fragility

Why, then, do so many high-functioning people remain fixed in one location—even when the data shows better options? The answer, unsurprisingly, is psychological. The known is safer than the optimal. The pain of change exceeds the discomfort of inefficiency. There's also the cultural myth that "home" is a moral obligation—that leaving is disloyal, rootless, or indulgent.

But let's be honest: the 21st century has already redefined identity. Most people already work for global companies, use multinational apps, consume borderless media, and invest in international assets. Their digital life is post-national. Their physical life is the lagging variable. *Mobility is not betrayal. It is congruence.*

Moreover, the idea that your country of origin deserves blind allegiance ignores the reality that most systems are designed with baked-in trade-offs. If your nation taxes you aggressively while providing little value, or restricts your financial options while demanding compliance, staying isn't loyalty. It's *submission without negotiation*.

The Calculus of Change: When the Cost of Staying Exceeds the Cost of Leaving

Every location has trade-offs. No jurisdiction is perfect. But the goal isn't perfection. It's *fit.* The real question isn't "Should I move?" It's: *Is where I live optimised for the life I want to live?* Does it reward my effort, protect my wealth, honour my values, and support my growth?

When you stop treating your address as accidental and start treating it as *strategic*, everything changes. You begin to see your country not as a home, but as a service provider. And like any provider, it should be judged on merit, not sentiment.

Some readers may never relocate. That's fine—*if the choice is conscious.* But most people never even run the numbers. They don't compare tax regimes, evaluate healthcare systems, or benchmark living costs. They don't ask whether their local regulations support their goals. They live in default mode.

The invitation here is not to move tomorrow. It is to *question the premise* that where you live is neutral. It isn't. *It is one of the most consequential financial variables you control—and one of the least examined.*

Final Thought: Owning Your Coordinates

In finance, leverage is the ability to amplify outcomes. Geography, properly understood, is one of the greatest levers available to the modern individual. But it must be handled with clarity, not wanderlust. The goal isn't movement for its own sake—it's *agency.* You don't have to become a nomad. You don't have to sever ties with your home country. But you do have to stop treating your address as incidental.

Because *where you live is not just where you sleep. It's where your rights are defined, your money is taxed, your freedoms are negotiated, and your future is priced.* That makes it, undeniably, a financial decision. Treat it like one.

Second Passports and Flag Theory

Citizenship is typically viewed as a birthright—an inherited accident of geography. Yet few recognise that this foundational identity also serves as *the primary operating system of your financial life.* Your passport governs your tax obligations, your mobility, your investment options, your exposure to geopolitical risk, and even your access to basic freedoms like banking or encryption. To treat citizenship as static is to accept vulnerability by default. *Second citizenship is not an act of disloyalty. It is an act of design.*

Flag Theory is the practical philosophy that underpins this strategy. Originating in the 1960s among international businessmen and dissidents alike, it proposes a straightforward idea: *plant different parts of your life in different jurisdictions to maximise freedom, security, and prosperity.* While the average person entrusts every element of their identity to a single nation-state, Flag Theory decentralises your personal infrastructure—creating resilience through diversification, not just of assets, but of access.

This is not about tax evasion or escaping obligations. It is about *legal autonomy.* And in an age of increasing financial surveillance, rising authoritarianism, and institutional overreach, it has never been more relevant—or more ethical.

The First Flag: Citizenship as a Choke Point

Your citizenship dictates where and how you pay tax, regardless of where you live. For example, American citizens are subject to global taxation even if they haven't lived in the United States for decades. This extraterritorial tax regime places them in a rare global category alongside Eritrea. It also means that having a second passport—*especially one that allows you to renounce or neutralise the burden of your first*—can be a structural unlock.

But beyond taxation, your citizenship also determines what currencies you can freely use, which countries you can visit without a visa, whether your bank accounts can be frozen for political reasons, and which wars your taxes may fund without your consent.

To rely on a single citizenship is to tether your entire future to one legal and political framework—however flawed, unstable, or declining it may be.

By contrast, a second passport offers not only mobility, but *optionality*. It transforms your relationship to risk—from passive exposure to strategic choice. Whether you're a digital nomad, a legacy-minded investor, or simply someone who values privacy and liberty, citizenship diversification is a tool of empowerment.

The Second Flag: Residency as Regulatory Leverage

Citizenship may be your legal identity, but residency is your day-to-day regulatory habitat. Where you live determines your access to services, your exposure to inflation, and—critically—your tax base. Many countries operate on a residence-based tax system, which means you are taxed only if you spend a certain number of days there per year.

Savvy individuals use this to their advantage by acquiring legal residency in countries with favourable tax codes and stable institutions. For example, Portugal's Non-Habitual Resident (NHR) programme, the UAE's Golden Visa, or Panama's Friendly Nations Visa offer pathways to low-tax or no-tax residency, often with minimal physical presence requirements. These frameworks allow you to live—or at least be *resident*—on your own terms, not under a blanket system that assumes your loyalty is economic servitude.

Residency also facilitates access to healthcare, education, and banking—on your terms. For instance, being a legal resident of Mexico or Thailand unlocks affordable, high-quality medical care without dependency on Western insurance frameworks. In jurisdictions like Singapore or Switzerland, residency connects you to global financial hubs with mature infrastructure and respected rule of law.

The ability to live somewhere should be earned—but the right to choose where to live should be designed.

The Third Flag: Incorporation and Economic Presence

Your business is its own legal entity. So why should it be confined to your personal place of birth? Flag Theory advises separating your economic activity from your physical and national identity. That means incorporating companies, bank accounts, or intellectual property holdings in jurisdictions where the rules are aligned with your goals—not imposed by historical accident.

For example, Estonia's e-Residency programme allows you to register and run a fully legal EU company without setting foot in the country. Entrepreneurs in the blockchain space frequently incorporate in Switzerland, Singapore, or the Cayman Islands to benefit from regulatory clarity. Creatives and consultants often use Irish or Dubai entities to reduce tax drag and reinvest capital more efficiently.

This isn't about secrecy—it's about sovereignty. When your economic engine is housed in a system that values and rewards enterprise, you gain not only tax efficiency but also stability. This is especially critical in an age where businesses are deplatformed, PayPal accounts frozen, or Stripe terminated—often without appeal—simply for expressing controversial ideas. *Where your business "lives" should be a matter of values and logic, not legacy inertia.*

The Fourth Flag: Asset Protection and Legal Arbitrage

Where your money resides matters as much as where it's earned. Holding assets in a single country—especially your country of citizenship—subjects them to local court judgments, political instability, inflation, and devaluation. Even high earners with diversified portfolios are often shocked to realise that all their brokerage accounts, pensions, and property are bound to one jurisdiction's whims.

Flag Theory offers an alternative: custody diversification. That might mean holding gold in a Swiss vault, real estate in Colombia, brokerage accounts in Singapore, or crypto with multi-jurisdictional keys. It's not just about return—it's about *resilience.* A well-diversified portfolio is not only spread across asset classes, but across legal frameworks.

In a world of creeping capital controls, this kind of design is not paranoia. It's prudence. Just ask the Cypriots whose bank accounts were raided in 2013. Or the Argentinians whose USD savings were forcibly converted. Or Canadians who watched their accounts frozen after political donations. *Wealth that's not legally agile is not truly secure.*

The Fifth Flag: Personal Life and Identity Portability

The final frontier of Flag Theory is deeply human: *where and how you live.* Your lifestyle, social connections, healthcare access, and even dating prospects are influenced by geography. But most people never consider the ROI of these factors when making decisions about citizenship or residency.

Living in places where your values are respected—where your privacy is honoured, your choices are tolerated, and your ambitions are supported—is not a luxury. It is a multiplier. From raising children in a culture that values critical thinking, to retiring in a country where cost of living doesn't force dependence, these quality-of-life flags *compound quietly but profoundly.*

For some, this means moving away from unstable democracies or overregulated economies. For others, it's simply the choice to live among likeminded people, in climates and cultures that promote health, creativity, or calm. Mobility, here, is not flight. It's strategy. *You are not a tree. Your roots are portable. And so are your rights—if you design them that way.*

Obstacles and Misconceptions

Critics often dismiss Flag Theory as elitist or evasive. But this misunderstands both its philosophy and its application. The goal is not to abandon responsibility, but to *reclaim consent.* Wealthy individuals and corporations have used these tools for decades. What's changing is the accessibility: from digital nomads with online income, to families exploring second passports for mobility, *this model is democratising.*

Others fear the legal complexity. And yes, navigating cross-border law demands clarity. But the frameworks exist. From CBI (Citizenship by Investment) programmes in the Caribbean to naturalisation paths in Paraguay or Italy, the landscape is increasingly navigable for those who do their homework—or work with experts.

The real obstacle is mental: most people never question the invisible chains their birth country has wrapped around their money, movement, and mind. They confuse compliance with virtue. Stability with safety. Familiarity with freedom.

Conclusion—Without Concluding

Second citizenship is not about fleeing, hiding, or avoiding. It is about *engineering.* Engineering choice. Engineering safety. Engineering alignment between who you are and where you are allowed to be. In a fragile, networked world, optionality is not indulgence. *It is responsibility.*

Flag Theory, properly applied, is not escapism. It is systems thinking for sovereign individuals. And it starts with one question: *What part of your life is more exposed than it needs to be—and where might it flourish instead?*

Portable Wealth, Portable Life

At first glance, the notion of portability sounds like a logistical convenience—a suitcase, a laptop, a cloud account. But underneath it lies a more powerful design principle: *resilience through mobility.* In a world defined by volatility, control over one's location, capital, and access is no longer a luxury reserved for the elite. It is a strategic requirement for anyone seeking autonomy. *To make your wealth and your life portable is to reclaim agency from the systems that presume to manage you.*

The global professional today may earn income in Singapore dollars, hold crypto in multisig wallets secured across continents, run a business incorporated in Estonia, have clients in North America, and live in Portugal. This is not escapism or exoticism. It is structural realism in an age where institutions are fragile, borders are politicised, and local risks increasingly ripple across global systems. When you decouple your earning capacity, legal identity, and intellectual labour from geography, *you begin to operate at a higher tier of strategic freedom.* Portability is not about rootlessness—it is about designing roots that travel.

The Fragility of Fixed Infrastructure

The modern economic system still assumes that most people will anchor their identity and livelihood to a single location. Home ownership is marketed as the ultimate financial milestone. Government IDs tie your legal existence to one jurisdiction. Most banks, tax offices, and bureaucracies expect static residency and permanent employment.

This static model creates exposure. If your income comes from one employer, in one industry, taxed by one government, stored in one currency, and tied to one physical location, you are essentially betting your entire future on a single set of laws, leaders, and institutions staying functional. *That is not security. That is systemic risk in disguise.*

History is littered with examples: Venezuelan engineers whose bolívar salaries became worthless. Ukrainian freelancers who lost banking access when SWIFT restrictions hit. British retirees in Spain blindsided by Brexit bureaucracy. Even affluent professionals in stable economies often find themselves cornered—unable to leave, change, or adapt without dismantling the very scaffolding that supports their lives. *The most dangerous form of captivity is the one disguised as success.*

Rebuilding from First Principles: What Needs to Move With You

Portability begins with rethinking what parts of your life are essential—and which can be designed to move with you. For the modern individual, there are three foundational pillars: identity, business, and wealth.

Identity includes your citizenship, legal name, residency status, and digital persona. Making this portable doesn't mean rejecting formality. It means structuring your legal and digital self so it can function in multiple environments. That may include holding dual citizenships or long-term residencies, using privacy-respecting identity protocols for online verification, or building reputational capital that transcends national borders (e.g. open-source contributions, remote portfolios, blockchain-based credentials).

Business includes how you earn income and serve others. Remote work has expanded dramatically, but true business portability goes further. It means designing a revenue engine that is geographically agnostic—whether it's an online consultancy, a productised service, a licensing model, or even a sovereign media brand. The key is *owning the platform, the audience, or the IP*—not just being employed by someone else's portable system.

Wealth is more than net worth. It is access, optionality, and survivability. Portable wealth resists being frozen, inflated, or regulated into irrelevance. That might include digital assets like Bitcoin or Monero, physical assets like gold or art held in offshore vaults, or cash-flowing real estate in jurisdictions with investor-friendly laws. The point is not secrecy. It is sovereignty. *Your wealth should not require permission to move—or survive.*

Real-World Examples of Portable Living

Consider the case of a Canadian software engineer who moves to Georgia (the country, not the U.S. state). By working remotely for U.S. clients and incorporating through Estonia's e-Residency programme, she earns in dollars, pays tax in Estonia, spends in lari, and gains residency benefits unavailable at home. Her cost of living drops by 60%, her exposure to local economic volatility is reduced, and she gains lifestyle upside—safer streets, better food, slower pace.

Or the American copywriter who splits time between Mexico City and Lisbon, lives off a diversified stream of royalty income, holds cryptocurrency in cold storage, and uses a second passport (acquired through ancestry) to minimise tax risk. He doesn't own property, but he owns leverage—legal, geographic, and psychological.

These are not edge cases. They are prototypes. And they represent a quiet revolution in what "success" looks like. No longer defined by fixed location, prestige employment, or institutional dependence, success is increasingly about *the ability to move, adapt, and endure—without starting over each time.*

Constraints Are Often Psychological, Not Logistical

Many people assume this model is inaccessible. "I have kids." "My job doesn't allow it." "I'm not a tech person." These are valid constraints—but often more negotiable than they seem. Families increasingly take "edventures" or worldschooling sabbaticals, educating children through curated travel and global curricula. Professionals once tethered to offices now thrive as consultants or remote executives. And non-technical individuals monetise everything from voiceovers to coaching to niche writing through platforms that reward expertise over credentials.

The real constraint is not skills or capital. It is imagination. It is the mental model that assumes your life must be lived inside the narrow economic geography of where you were born. Portability requires neither constant travel nor total detachment. It requires design. *Design backed by systems thinking, legal literacy, and clarity of values.*

Design Frameworks for Portability

To make a portable life viable, certain frameworks help. One is the concept of *Minimum Viable Geography*—asking yourself: *What is the smallest number of jurisdictions I need to live legally, work freely, and bank securely?* For some, that might be just two countries. For others, five. The goal is not maximal complexity, but optimal resilience.

Another is *The Sovereign Stack*: a layered architecture of assets, tools, and relationships that function across borders. This might include:

– An offshore company that holds your IP or service contracts
– A second passport or long-term visa
– Multiple bank accounts (including in fintech-friendly jurisdictions)
– Decentralised communication tools (Matrix, Signal, ProtonMail)
– Crypto wallets with multisig governance
– Trusted service providers for tax, legal, and admin help

Each layer adds redundancy. Each is legal. None is optional if you intend to live *by design rather than by default.*

Philosophical Reflections on Rootedness and Freedom

Portability is often misunderstood as disconnection. But the opposite is true. People who design for mobility tend to be more intentional, more values-aligned, and more community-oriented—because they are *choosing* where to be, rather than inheriting it unexamined.

There's also a deeper philosophical point: *true freedom is not the ability to leave, but the capacity to stay by choice.* Portability enhances—not reduces—your commitment to a place, because it removes the coercion. You stay where you are not because you must, but because it serves your goals, values, or sense of belonging.

Portability also forces clarity. What do you actually need? Which of your possessions, obligations, and routines are non-negotiable—and which are baggage? Designing a portable life often reveals that you were carrying far more than necessary—not just physically, but financially, legally, and emotionally.

Risks and Missteps to Avoid

This strategy is not immune to pitfalls. Relying too heavily on emerging tech platforms can expose you to sudden service changes. Operating in opaque jurisdictions may create legal ambiguities.

Assuming every problem can be solved with an internet connection can lead to neglecting local compliance or social integration.

Portability is not the same as invisibility. It is traceable, taxable, and inspectable. What makes it powerful is not secrecy, but structure. A well-designed portable life *withstands scrutiny and interruption.* It is robust precisely because it is not ad hoc.

Closing Perspective—Without Closing

In the industrial era, stability meant fixed address, permanent job, and predictable routines. In the digital era, *stability is optionality.* Your greatest asset is not a postcode. It is the ability to relocate your life's functions—income, access, protection, meaning—across contexts. Not reactively, but intentionally.

To live portably is to live prepared. Prepared not just for crisis, but for opportunity. *Not just to survive disruption, but to make disruption irrelevant.* The person who can move their wealth, re-establish their enterprise, and sustain their identity without panic or dependence—*that person is not fragile. That person is free.*

Cultural Arbitrage and Lifestyle Engineering

There is a quiet revolution taking place among professionals, entrepreneurs, and intellectuals—people who, far from fleeing their home countries out of fear or failure, are choosing to relocate based on *strategic alignment of values, cost-efficiency, and quality of life.* This is not expatriation as escape. It is *cultural arbitrage*—the informed leveraging of geopolitical and cultural differences to construct a lifestyle that is more sane, secure, and sovereign.

At its core, cultural arbitrage is about rejecting the notion that your nation of birth should dictate your cost of living, your access to safety, or the moral temperature of your daily environment. It challenges the inertia that keeps high-functioning individuals shackled to systems that no longer serve them—systems bloated with taxation, social disunity, political theatre, and unsustainable overhead. It says: *if your current context extracts more than it offers, consider changing contexts*. And increasingly, many are.

This movement is not reactionary. It is reasoned. It is rooted in the belief that *culture is infrastructure*—that the daily norms, social incentives, legal expectations, and philosophical undercurrents of a place are not merely background noise, but the invisible architecture that determines whether you thrive or decay. A city's cost of living, its sense of time, its approach to community, its laws on autonomy—these are not trivial footnotes. They are central inputs to human flourishing. And if one culture demands 70-hour work weeks to afford a home in a decaying suburb while another offers safety, health, and autonomy at half the cost, *the choice is not radical—it is rational.*

From Geographic Arbitrage to Cultural Intelligence

Geographic arbitrage—the concept of earning in a strong currency while spending in a weaker one—is well-known among digital nomads and remote entrepreneurs. But that's a shallow version of a deeper, more durable strategy: cultural arbitrage. Here, the value differential is not just monetary, but *philosophical, social, and regulatory.*

Consider a London-based professional earning £100,000 per year, heavily taxed, navigating long commutes, inflationary rent, and increasing surveillance. That same professional might relocate to Lisbon, retain 90% of their client base, halve their tax burden, reduce their rent by 40%, and gain access to a culture where community is prioritised over consumption, and leisure is not a sign of laziness but of wisdom. Or think of a family leaving San Francisco for Montevideo—exchanging urban tension and identity politics for relative calm, excellent public services, and a deeper sense of collective decency.

These moves aren't always permanent, nor should they be. But they demonstrate the power of examining *values, not just visas*. Arbitrage in this context is about optimising for *what matters most*: safety, time, mental clarity, sovereignty, and meaning.

Why Staying Put is Often the Most Expensive Choice

The hidden cost of not moving is rarely calculated. People remain in cities that drain them, economies that inflate away their savings, and cultures that reward exhaustion—because that's what everyone else is doing. But when you add up the full cost—financial, emotional, moral—the "normal" life often reveals itself as the most fragile.

Living in a high-cost city with low-quality infrastructure, divisive politics, and social decay is not just a financial burden—it's a spiritual tax. The myth is that moving is risky. The truth is that *staying put is often a form of slow failure.* The mortgage, the school fees, the health insurance, the emotional bandwidth consumed by navigating dysfunction—it all adds up to a life that may be "secure" on paper, but hollow in practice.

What if moving could buy you *a better society*? Not utopia, but simply a place where politeness is common, food is healthy by default, stress is not a badge of honour, and government interference is the exception—not the rule. This is not fantasy. It is the lived reality of many who have traded hyper-growth cultures for more human ones. And yet, most never even run the numbers.

Engineered Living: Designing a Life You Don't Need to Escape From

Lifestyle engineering is the conscious practice of building a life that aligns with your values, temperament, and long-term goals—*not the implicit blueprint inherited from your peers or parents.* It involves ruthless clarity: what kind of pace energises you? What social norms do you find corrosive or nourishing? What tax burden feels justified? What kind of food, noise, climate, and pace keeps you sane?

This is where culture matters. In Japan, silence is sacred. In Spain, dinner happens at 9pm. In Costa Rica, "pura vida" is more than a slogan—it is a philosophical commitment to present-tense living. These aren't just cultural quirks. They are *software environments* that you inhabit every day. And like software, some are bloated, glitchy, or filled with spam. Others are elegant, light, and designed for coherence.

To engineer your life is to treat these inputs with respect. You would not run your business on buggy software. Why run your soul on a culture that bankrupts your joy, time, or agency?

Real-World Case Studies: Migration as Strategy, Not Reaction

The modern investor, entrepreneur, or creative professional now has access to a range of geographies where tax burdens are lower, social cohesion is higher, and state overreach is comparatively muted. Consider Estonia, which pioneered e-residency—a digital identity allowing individuals to run EU-based businesses without physical presence. This is not just convenience; it is geopolitical leverage for small business owners, enabling them to incorporate and operate in a regulatory framework with low friction, high transparency, and minimal corruption.

Or take the example of Singapore: an authoritarian-lite city-state with a rule-of-law environment that prioritises order, cleanliness, and business-friendliness. While it may not suit every temperament, for certain profiles—particularly those in finance or logistics—it offers a clarity and coherence that can feel like an antidote to the disorder and regulatory sclerosis of Western capitals.

Then there's Portugal, particularly appealing to those in tech, design, or consulting. With its Non-Habitual Resident (NHR) tax regime (until recently), mild climate, and emphasis on community and quality of life, it has become a haven for knowledge workers seeking sanity with sophistication. These aren't random migrations. They are *calculated pivots* toward more sustainable life-design systems.

What unites these cases is not a specific place, but a specific mindset: *sovereign pragmatism.* The willingness to re-evaluate the "default setting" of one's life based on clear-eyed analysis, not inherited assumptions.

The Emotional Intelligence of Migration

Contrary to caricatures, most who engage in lifestyle arbitrage are not fleeing. They are *choosing*. They are not anti-nationalist exiles or rootless profiteers. They are professionals trying to escape the emotional taxation of bureaucratic absurdity, decaying public infrastructure, and socio-political volatility.

That emotional cost is not incidental. It's central. One cannot make coherent decisions about investing, entrepreneurship, or family-building if they are constantly swimming upstream against a cultural current that penalises coherence, rewards distraction, and mistakes conformity for decency.

Cultural arbitrage, then, is a form of emotional intelligence: the recognition that where you live shapes *how you think*, *how you feel*, and *what you allow yourself to imagine*. Changing geography often recalibrates one's baseline assumptions about what is acceptable, desirable, or even possible.

Designing for Peace, Not Just Profit

Too often, the discourse around relocation focuses narrowly on tax arbitrage or financial engineering. This misses the deeper insight: *peace is profit*. A lower-tax jurisdiction is worth little if the infrastructure is broken, corruption is endemic, or safety is compromised. Likewise, a low-cost city that strips you of intellectual stimulation, aesthetic beauty, or future-proofing may ultimately erode more than it preserves.

That's why lifestyle engineering must include not just spreadsheets, but soul-checks. What brings you peace? What reduces your cognitive load? What restores your creative energy without requiring three weeks of "holiday" to recover from your working life?

Answers vary. For some, it's the slow rhythm of a Thai beach town. For others, the disciplined structure of a Swiss alpine village. The point is not to prescribe, but to encourage *deliberate discovery*—to experiment with environments until you find one that doesn't just fit your finances, but your values, your family, and your physiology.

Strategic Questions for Cultural Arbitrage Practitioners

As you evaluate your options, consider these foundational questions—not as checkboxes, but as prompts for deeper clarity:

Does the local legal system offer genuine due process and property protection, or does it operate on informal influence and arbitrary discretion?

Is the cost of living proportionate to the quality of services and infrastructure, or are you funding systemic decay through inflated rents and stealth taxes?

Are the norms of the culture—its views on time, family, privacy, decency—aligned with your own, or are you subtly eroded by misalignment?

Does your business model or income stream benefit from geographic diversification, and if not, *should it?*

Are your children, employees, or future self likely to thrive more in a new cultural context than the current one?

These are not romantic musings. They are strategic imperatives for anyone who recognises that *money is only one variable in the equation of sovereignty.*

Cultural Arbitrage as a Hedge Against Civilisational Decline

There is one final layer: risk mitigation. While mainstream discourse remains tethered to debates over tax brackets or GDP growth, many high-functioning individuals are quietly preparing for a more multipolar, volatile world—one in which capital controls, ideological censorship, and mass psychological instability become more common.

In such a world, *your address becomes a source of risk or resilience.* A passport can become a trap. A property can become a liability. A political climate can turn a neutral citizen into a suspect overnight.

Cultural arbitrage, then, becomes a kind of moral and financial hedge: a way to move toward environments where basic freedoms are less precarious, where the social contract is still intelligible, and where the velocity of crisis is slowed enough to allow for reflection, correction, and dignity.

Conclusion Without Saying "In Conclusion"

To live deliberately today is to acknowledge that geography is not fixed. It is a variable—and one of the most powerful levers for shaping your personal, financial, and psychological future.

Cultural arbitrage and lifestyle engineering are not for the restless. They are for the resolved. For those willing to look at their country of birth not as a prison or privilege, but simply as a starting point. And for those who understand that the greatest luxury in life is not wealth, but *the ability to choose how—and where—you live.*

Chapter 11
Decentralised Legacy – Protecting the Next Generation

A quiet revolution is unfolding—subtle yet profound—in the ways wealth is owned, stored, and ultimately handed down. Not by hedge fund architects or legacy family offices, but by individuals awake to the fact that conventional inheritance frameworks weren't built for a world of cold wallets, sovereign identity, and borderless assets. The tools of old—wills, trusts, probate courts—are showing their cracks. They strain under the weight of decentralised innovation. In their place, a different kind of philosophy is taking root. One that treats legacy not as a legal document to be notarised, but as a portable system—resilient, discreet, and empowering.

This chapter isn't about estate planning in the traditional, polite sense. There are no flowcharts of offshore entities, no glossy tax mitigation brochures. Instead, we delve into the realities of a new kind of succession—where a single misstep can render fortunes inaccessible, and where pseudonymity both protects and complicates everything. It's not simply about leaving something behind—it's about ensuring that what's left can't be seized, corrupted, or rendered obsolete.

In this emerging era, legacy no longer announces itself as a notarised event. It operates as continuity—ongoing, embedded, and often invisible.

And at the centre of this shift sits a rather inconvenient question: How do you pass on value that has no physical form, no official registry, and no recognition from the institutions your parents relied on? More than that—how do you pass on capability? Not just ownership, but the intuition, fluency, and discretion required to preserve and wield it?

We begin with custody—not theoretical, but actual. Think Monero keys, tokenised metals, distributed vaults, multi-signature wallets. These assets are powerful precisely because they evade regulation.

But that same quality renders them brittle. A pension fund can be inherited with paperwork. A passphrase cannot. A land deed invites legal dispute. A decentralised wallet does not care who believes they own it. The absence of intermediaries is what gives these instruments strength. But it also compels us to engineer a new kind of intergenerational relay—one not based on legal authorisation, but on shared operational literacy.

This chapter will walk you through that architecture. We'll begin with the scaffolding—multi-sig protocols, inheritance encryption, fragmented backups, and disaster-resistant key storage. But those are just the mechanics. The real challenge, inevitably, becomes human. Whom do you trust? When do you trust them? And more subtly—how do you sequence their understanding so that it is neither overwhelming nor exploitable?

Which brings us to a deeper, often neglected truth: legacy is not about riches—it's about resilience. Most inheritance systems don't fail because assets vanish. They fail because beneficiaries lack the worldview to wield what they've been given. Especially in the decentralised realm, where a wrong click or forgotten phrase can be fatal, ignorance is not a luxury your successors can afford. There is no customer service for lost sovereignty.

And so, you must shift roles—from benefactor to mentor. From the giver of things to the builder of minds. That involves crafting an educational arc, not just a handover document. Begin early. Start simple. Model decisions, rather than issuing commandments. Frame your teaching in stories, not warnings. Most importantly, cultivate habits of thought that prize both scepticism and curiosity. These are not just values—they are survival traits in a world where freedom is increasingly routed through systems designed to misunderstand it.

This is not estate planning for a legal system. It is continuity planning for a world that may no longer recognise the old rules.

Wills Are Not Enough – Why Traditional Estate Planning Fails in a Digital and Global Wealth Context

If you die with a will, most jurisdictions will declare your affairs "in order." But in the age of decentralised finance, digital assets, pseudonymous wallets, stateless bank accounts, and nomadic lives, that declaration is dangerously out of date. A will is not a vault. It is not a key. It is not an execution plan. At best, it's a declaration of intent. At worst, it is a bureaucratic bottleneck—a stack of paper asking slow-moving courts to untangle your modern financial life with tools better suited to property deeds and family heirlooms.

The core problem is this: legal instructions do not equal functional access.

You can list a crypto wallet in your will, but if your heirs do not have the passphrase, it might as well be a safe with no combination. You can name your children as beneficiaries of an international brokerage account, but without the correct digital authentication, jurisdictional residency, and access devices, that money is frozen in place—sometimes for years. The machinery of traditional estate law assumes a world where wealth is local, visible, and slow-moving. Increasingly, the opposite is true.

This subchapter addresses a hard truth: *wills are obsolete for many of the most valuable—and most vulnerable—assets of the 21st century.* If your legacy depends on decentralised systems, international accounts, or encrypted access, then your estate plan must evolve into something operational, not merely aspirational.

The Legacy Bottleneck: Legal Rights vs Functional Access

A will confers rights. It does not confer capability. This distinction is often overlooked by even the most experienced estate lawyers. You can be legally entitled to an asset and still be functionally incapable of retrieving or managing it. For example:

A beneficiary of a hardware wallet may be entitled to its contents, but unless they know how to use a seed phrase, configure a wallet interface, and navigate gas fees, that asset is *inert.*

A child named in a foreign trust may inherit legal control, but if they cannot speak the language of the jurisdiction, access its platforms, or even locate the intermediary institutions, the trust becomes an opaque abstraction.

A spouse listed on a will as the successor of a digital business may have no login credentials, no operational awareness, and no understanding of customer flows or intellectual property.

In this context, the modern executor must be more than a legal proxy—they must be a systems operator. The "will" is no longer the endpoint of estate planning; it's a single node in a much larger architecture of access, security, education, and continuity.

Digital Assets Are Structurally Immune to Probate

The traditional probate system rests on three assumptions: that assets can be discovered, that their ownership is centralised, and that they can be transferred with legal oversight. Cryptographic assets defy all three.

A decentralised wallet may never be discovered unless the owner has left precise digital breadcrumbs. It does not reside in a bank, institution, or regulated body—it lives across a global, permissionless ledger, accessible only to those with cryptographic keys. And crucially, there is no third-party mechanism to recover access. If the owner dies without distributing this access *before* death, there is no probate judge on Earth who can unlock that wealth.

This isn't a flaw—it's a feature. But it's a feature that demands *an entirely different succession mindset.* If you are holding wealth in a format designed to be seizure-resistant, you cannot expect a system designed for centralised recovery to serve as your fallback. *Custodianship is a living responsibility. It cannot be outsourced to lawyers or solved with paperwork post-mortem.*

International Lives Demand Post-National Solutions

The second structural problem with traditional estate planning is geographic. In a world where families live across borders, assets reside in different legal regimes, and citizenships are layered or fluid, the jurisdictional integrity of a will is often partial at best. Consider these scenarios:

A digital entrepreneur domiciled in Singapore but holding assets in Switzerland, real estate in Portugal, and crypto wallets registered to a Panamanian IBC.

A family trust based in the Cayman Islands, with beneficiaries residing in Canada, Argentina, and Thailand—all subject to different inheritance tax rules, residency disclosures, and foreign asset reporting laws.

Wills, by design, are territorial. They apply within the jurisdiction they are notarised, unless specifically supported by complex treaties or multi-jurisdictional instruments. In practice, this creates vulnerability: *assets may be split, frozen, or delayed* by legal incompatibility, while different courts assert competing claims over the same estate.

What's required is not a better will, but *a different model*—one that treats wealth not as a static pile to be distributed, but as a *living architecture* to be maintained across jurisdictions.

Operational Succession: Designing for Continuity, Not Just Distribution

True resilience comes not from documenting your intentions, but from *designing systems that can survive you.* This is the essence of operational succession. It involves three essential components:

Multi-phase access protocols – Create layered access systems that allow trusted parties to assume limited or increasing control over time. For example, a parent might share one shard of a private key with a spouse, another with an adult child, and a third with a secure dead-man's switch that activates only after non-response over a fixed period.

Succession training and simulation – Just as military units rehearse contingency scenarios, families managing decentralised assets should practise knowledge transfer, password drills, and offsite recovery. If your heir cannot perform a basic recovery simulation while you're alive, they won't succeed when you're gone.

Cross-jurisdictional access structures – Leverage international entities (such as IBCs, foundations, or nominee agreements) to separate beneficial control from operational custody. This allows wealth to move without triggering immediate tax or legal events, and helps ensure *flexibility in the face of geopolitical risk.*

A robust estate plan for global and digital wealth must *look more like a protocol stack than a legal filing.* And like any resilient system, it should be tested, maintained, and periodically reviewed.

The Ethical Dimension: Beyond Money, Toward Stewardship

This shift from legalism to operationalism raises an important ethical question: what does it mean to leave wealth responsibly in an age where control is absolute and privacy is programmable?

When you give someone the passphrase to a cold wallet, you are not merely giving them access to capital—you are conferring *power without oversight.* This makes the question of timing, maturity, and moral conditioning central to the succession conversation. Not every heir is ready. Not every heir should inherit at the same time, or in the same form.

The goal is not equality—it is stewardship.

For many, this means integrating legacy conversations into family culture long before death. It means building what some families call a "continuity council": an intergenerational practice of discussing, rehearsing, and reviewing the principles, responsibilities, and technical realities of managing inherited systems. In a decentralised world, wealth is not merely protected by keys and backups—it is protected by *shared knowledge and shared readiness.*

...stead: A Brief Blueprint for Real-World Action

...ile this chapter is not a substitute for personalised legal or financial advice, the architecture of a decentralised succession system typically includes the following elements:

A decentralised asset inventory, reviewed regularly, with secure, tiered backups.

A knowledge transfer document or protocol guide—encrypted, redundant, and known to key stakeholders.

A recovery mechanism using multi-signature logic or trusted access nodes distributed across people and locations.

Pre-tested execution procedures (with simulations), not just intentions on paper.

A clear educational plan for successors, phased by readiness, not age or hierarchy.

International structures aligned to protect privacy, enable flexibility, and reduce jurisdictional risk.

None of this is found in a boilerplate will. And none of it can be executed posthumously by someone who didn't understand what they were inheriting.

The Future of Legacy is Sovereign and Decentralised

The institutional tools we inherited were designed for an institutional world—banks, nation-states, paper trails, courts. But the frontier of wealth is now borderless, encrypted, and often anonymous. The legacy infrastructure we need must reflect that reality.

Wills are not enough because the world they were built for no longer exists. What's required now is a mindset shift—from distribution to continuity, from law to protocol, from inheritance to stewardship.

If your assets can outlive the institutions that created them, your legacy plan should too.

Custodianship of Crypto and Gold – How to Pass on Decentralised Assets Without Relying on Flawed Legal Infrastructure

The modern holder of wealth faces a paradox: the assets most capable of surviving geopolitical collapse, banking failures, or legal overreach are often the hardest to pass on securely. Crypto and physical gold—the twin pillars of sovereign finance—are resistant by design. Resistant to seizure, resistant to inflation, resistant to censorship. But that same resistance complicates inheritance. They sit outside the traditional estate ecosystem, immune to court orders and probate procedures. *They don't obey legal documents; they obey keys, codes, and physical custody.*

If your wealth is in decentralised form, your legacy cannot rely on centralised tools. A will won't unlock a cold wallet. A trust can't find a hidden vault. A lawyer may have authority, but not access. *To secure continuity, you must become both architect and teacher—you must think not in legal abstractions, but in operational systems.*

This chapter explores how to transmit decentralised wealth—specifically crypto and gold—*securely, privately, and functionally*, without exposing your heirs to technical paralysis or legal bottlenecks. This is not an exercise in tax efficiency. It is a blueprint for *resilient custodianship.*

The Nature of the Assets Dictates the Nature of the Succession

Crypto and gold differ in form—one is digital and cryptographic; the other physical and elemental. But both share core traits that break traditional inheritance tools:

They are bearer assets. Whoever controls them, owns them. No court can "assign" control after the fact without direct access.

They are off-ledger. They do not appear in public registries, estate databases, or third-party account systems. They can easily go undiscovered.

They are seizure-resistant. A judge can order the release of a bank account. He cannot compel a private key, nor can he locate a bar of gold buried on private land.

They require specialised knowledge. A lawyer may know how to execute a will. He likely doesn't know how to use Gnosis Safe, broadcast a transaction, or identify a counterfeit Krugerrand.

This creates a design requirement: the knowledge and access structures for these assets must be built *before death*, and the tools of transmission must be embedded in a living system, not a legal fantasy.

The Failure of Paper-Based Planning

Legal documents assume continuity of institutions. They imagine an executor who can call a bank, show a death certificate, and receive access. With crypto and gold, there is often *no counterparty* to appeal to. This creates a fatal flaw in most estate plans: *they describe intent, but do not engineer execution.*

Example: a man holds 10 BTC in a cold wallet, with the passphrase memorised. He dies unexpectedly. His will lists the wallet address, but no one knows the password. That wealth is functionally destroyed. Or consider a woman with 50 ounces of gold stored in a private vault under a pseudonym, with access granted by biometric scan. Her children are named in the will, but the vault company is in Singapore, and no one knows her alias. The gold is, for all practical purposes, inaccessible.

In both cases, wealth dies with the owner—not because of malice, but because the plan was theoretical, not operational.

Operational Custodianship: A New Mental Model

Wealth transfer in decentralised systems requires a *custodial mindset*, not just a legal one. The custodian's role is not simply to own or protect—it is to prepare for handoff. The following principles underpin a successful system:

Access is not automatic—it must be designed.
If your assets require keys, devices, PINs, locations, or insider knowledge, those dependencies must be mapped and transmitted. Not all at once. Not to everyone. But to *someone*, with logic.

Custodianship must be tiered.
Full access should rarely rest with one individual. Use structures like multi-signature wallets, shared secrets, and distributed recovery systems. Think in layers: immediate access, delayed access, conditional access.

Instruction is a moral duty.
If your heir cannot *use* what they inherit, they don't inherit wealth—they inherit confusion. Functional transfer requires both tools and training.

Fail-safes matter more than wishes.
Redundancy beats intent. A backup passphrase in a dead man's switch is worth more than a beautifully drafted will with no digital scaffolding.

Practical Framework: Crypto Custodianship That Works

Passing on crypto requires an understanding of both the asset and the human. The plan must be *technically robust* and *psychologically realistic.* Consider the following real-world strategies:

Use time-locked smart contracts. Platforms like Ethereum enable contracts that release assets based on verifiable conditions—e.g., if no movement is detected for 12 months. This automates transfer without external authority.

Deploy multisig wallets. Gnosis Safe or Casa allow control to be shared among several parties (e.g., 2 of 3 keys required). This reduces the risk of single-point failure and enables *coordinated access*, not unilateral exposure.

Create a "Crypto Codex." This is a private, encrypted document (or offline printed copy) that explains wallet types, seed phrases, passphrases, addresses, transaction history, and security principles. Ideally stored with a trusted third party or via dead-man-switch protocol.

Educate heirs through simulations. Have them set up dummy wallets. Walk through a token transfer. Introduce them to blockchain explorers. If they cannot conduct a basic transaction now, they won't manage the real one later.

Gold Custodianship: Physical, Private, and Prone to Decay

Gold, unlike crypto, is tangible. This makes it harder to erase—but easier to steal or lose. The two central risks in gold legacy planning are *opacity* and *centralisation.* A bar of gold stored in a private vault may survive a collapse—but if no one knows it exists, or how to access it, it may as well be buried treasure.

Key practices include:

Avoid sole-location dependency. Do not rely on a single vault, jurisdiction, or safe. Use redundancy: home safe + private depository + international storage.

Diversify jurisdictions. Store in politically distinct locales—Switzerland, Singapore, New Zealand—not all in one country vulnerable to asset freezes or seizure.

Maintain private maps. Whether digital or written, create a simple, encrypted guide describing locations, custodians, access codes, insurance documentation, and point-of-contact protocols. Share it selectively with trusted parties.

Verify authenticity regularly. Over time, gold can become mingled, re-allocated, or forged. Annual physical checks, third-party audits, or serial-number scans maintain integrity.

The Human Layer: Trust Without Naivety

Every custodial system must answer a hard question: *who do you trust, and how much?* The default answer in legacy systems is "a lawyer" or "a bank". In decentralised systems, trust must be rebuilt. There is no helpdesk. There is no override.

This doesn't mean full transparency with every heir. It means *strategic, conditional, tiered delegation*—a balance of secrecy, security, and operational clarity. For example:

One person may hold the location of the gold, but not the access code.

Another may know the device, but not the seed phrase.

A third may have the recovery phrase, but not the protocol to initiate retrieval.

Together, they form a distributed, fail-resistant architecture. Alone, they hold nothing of value. *This is how you preserve both control and continuity.*

Ethical Stewardship vs Blind Automation

It's tempting to automate everything: time locks, smart contracts, custodial tools. But automation without human readiness is fragile. A family member who receives access to a seven-figure wallet they don't understand is a danger to themselves—and to the legacy.

The true custodian's role is not to remove friction, but to *curate learning.* To leave not just instructions, but *wisdom.* To engineer a handoff that is not only successful, but *meaningful.*

This means legacy isn't just about wealth. It's about the *transmission of competence.*

Conclusion? No—Continuity

There is no final step in custodianship. Only evolving systems, reviewed periodically, updated as tools and people change. Wills are static; real legacies are dynamic. If your crypto and gold are worth protecting, they're worth operationalising.

The wealth that survives you is not the one you write about in a legal document. It's the one your heirs know how to use before you're gone.

Teaching Resilience, Not Just Riches – Preparing Heirs to Understand and Protect Wealth

A fortune can be transferred with the stroke of a pen. A legacy cannot. The modern world is littered with examples of inherited capital squandered by unprepared hands—trust fund heirs collapsing under the weight of unearned abundance, or second-generation entrepreneurs eroding empires built by their predecessors. The pattern repeats across cultures, currencies, and continents: *wealth outpaces wisdom*, and in doing so, becomes fragile. If the goal is long-term financial continuity, the priority must shift. Instead of merely teaching heirs to *receive* wealth, we must teach them to *defend, interpret, and extend* it. This is the heart of true legacy: resilience, not just riches.

Wealth alone cannot inoculate against financial entropy. It is not an endowment of certainty. Without the inner architecture of strength—discernment, adaptability, situational intelligence—an inheritance becomes a liability, not a safeguard. This subchapter unpacks what it means to prepare the next generation not simply for abundance, but for stewardship. It explores how families can instil antifragility, transmit operational understanding, and create a lineage of *competent custodians*, not passive beneficiaries.

The Limits of Financial Literacy and the Problem of the "Well-Educated Fool"

It is tempting to assume that financial literacy is the solution. Enrol your child in an investing course, teach them how compound interest works, and expect maturity to follow. But literacy is not fluency. Knowing what a balance sheet is does not equate to strategic thought. Teaching budgeting does not prepare someone to navigate capital controls, inheritance tax loopholes, or global macro volatility.

Moreover, traditional financial education is deeply skewed toward *accumulation mechanics*, not resilience-building. It trains students to optimise yield, track markets, or build diversified portfolios—but it rarely teaches when to *pull back*, how to interpret political risk, or how to mentally model *unknown unknowns*. This is why so many heirs become what some private wealth advisors now call "well-educated fools": individuals who can discuss equity risk premium but panic during a liquidity crisis; who can build spreadsheets but cannot detect a predatory advisor.

Resilience is not a technical function. It is a cognitive and philosophical stance toward uncertainty.

Resilience Begins with Exposure, Not Protection

The paradox of preparing heirs is that too much protection creates fragility. If every problem is solved for them—if friction is removed from their path—they learn dependency, not discernment. Contrast two teenagers: one receives a monthly allowance deposited automatically into a trust-linked debit card. The other is asked to earn part of their spending money through freelance work, exposed to real client feedback, late payments, and price negotiation.

The first learns about money as a passive inflow. The second learns that income is earned, contested, variable. These early exposures create durable psychological patterns. Parents and mentors seeking to foster resilience must consider not how to *shield* their children from volatility, but how to *introduce them to it safely*. Exposure therapy, not insulation, is the developmental template.

Introduce heirs to mild forms of financial stress:

Have them manage a small amount of crypto in a hot wallet.

Ask them to compare offshore jurisdictions for a hypothetical residency plan.

Present them with a scenario where inflation erodes 30% of their savings and ask how they'd reallocate.

This is not pedagogy. It is inoculation.

Teach in Questions, Not Answers

One of the most effective tools in legacy education is the *guided dilemma*. Instead of giving definitive advice, offer your heirs conflicting viewpoints and let them wrestle with trade-offs. For example:

"Would you rather own land in Argentina with high yield and political instability, or a low-yield property in Switzerland with maximal security?"

"How would you split an inheritance between three siblings with vastly different worldviews: one a crypto anarchist, one a conservative dividend investor, one living in a commune?"

"If you could only store wealth in one form—gold, Bitcoin, or citizenship in a neutral country—what would you choose and why?"

These scenarios develop a form of *contextual literacy*—not memorisation of rules, but capacity to think through edge cases. *Resilient heirs are not those who know the answers. They are those who know how to interrogate uncertainty.*

The Role of Mentorship Over Management

Wealth continuity requires more than parenting. It requires mentorship—and often from someone *other* than the parent. Heirs tend to reject direct instruction from their benefactors, especially if the family dynamic is fraught. Bringing in a trusted external mentor—a retired entrepreneur, a privacy-focused technologist, or a values-driven investor—can reframe wealth conversations.

This mentor must not be a generic financial advisor. They should represent a philosophy of wealth that aligns with your principles: anti-fragility, integrity, strategic independence. Mentorship is not tutoring. It is proximity to someone who *models lived resilience.*

Invite your heir to observe—not just be told—how a mentor:

Navigates a high-stakes decision.

Deconstructs a news headline.

Responds to a market panic.

Evaluates new technologies or investment classes.

Information is forgettable. Observed philosophy is memorable.

The Emotional Grammar of Inheritance

One of the most overlooked aspects of legacy is emotional calibration. If heirs feel guilt, shame, or confusion about their wealth, they may sabotage it. If they feel entitlement, they may abuse it. If they feel nothing, they may neglect it.

Therefore, teaching resilience includes building *emotional fluency.* Encourage reflective conversations around:

What does it mean to deserve wealth?

How do you distinguish between self-worth and net worth?

What responsibilities come with owning assets others do not?

These aren't theoretical exercises. They are training in *ethical navigation*. Without moral weight, wealth becomes disorienting. And disoriented heirs don't just make poor decisions—they attract predators, con artists, and destructive ideologies.

Wealth without meaning becomes a liability. Wealth with meaning becomes an anchor.

Translating Complexity into Operational Wisdom

The contemporary world of wealth is too complex for static principles. A twenty-year-old heir might one day be forced to choose between keeping capital in a sanctioned bank, moving assets into decentralised protocols, or obtaining a second passport to access capital controls. That decision won't be solved by a spreadsheet. It will require *pattern recognition*, moral clarity, and functional adaptability.

To prepare them, the learning environment must include:

Exposure to *geo-financial variables*—how law, borders, and capital flows interact.

Understanding of *information asymmetry*—how to verify, not just consume.

Strategic patience—learning when *not* to act is as powerful as taking bold moves.

These attributes are not downloaded. They are cultivated, over time, through active, lived frameworks.

From Inheritance to Initiative

The best measure of legacy success is not whether your heirs protect what you built. It's whether they can build something new that reflects what you taught. The goal is not duplication—it is *extension with integrity.*

To get there, you must shift the mental framing:

From assets to *architecture.*

From entitlement to *embodiment.*

From static planning to *dynamic readiness.*

Resilience is not an inheritance. It is a transmission of perspective.

The most powerful tool you can pass on is not a trust fund, a legal structure, or even a well-diversified portfolio. It is an internal compass calibrated to uncertainty, grounded in values, and capable of navigating chaos. That compass, once embedded, cannot be taxed, frozen, or revoked. It becomes sovereign.

And it's the one asset no future generation can afford to lack.

The Family Wealth Council – Wealth Conversations as a Tradition of Empowerment, Secrecy, and Solidarity

Wealth is not preserved by silence. Nor is it advanced by merely drafting documents or writing cheques. Throughout history, families that managed to sustain influence, assets, and cohesion across generations did not rely on legal trusts alone—they relied on *ritualised conversation.* Not casual updates or reactive disputes, but structured, intergenerational dialogue about purpose, power, responsibility, and continuity. What endures is not the portfolio. What endures is the *culture of communication* that surrounds it.

The "Family Wealth Council" is not a financial institution. It is a philosophical practice: an intentional forum where families meet to discuss wealth not merely as capital, but as a multi-dimensional force—one that shapes identity, loyalty, and legacy. In this model, conversation itself becomes an asset. Regular, structured, and secure wealth councils create the space for heirs to grow into stewards, for founders to transmit not just instructions but insight, and for shared values to outlive individual preferences. This chapter explores the framework, mindset, and deep logic behind turning family conversation into a source of resilience, discretion, and cohesion.

The Cost of Secrecy: Silence Breeds Fragility

In many high-net-worth families, secrecy masquerades as strategy. Founders often avoid discussing their wealth in detail—especially with children—out of fear it may weaken their work ethic, invite entitlement, or trigger premature conflict. But the unintended consequence is that wealth becomes *abstract.* Heirs are left to make assumptions, invent stories, or inherit without context. And context, once lost, is rarely recoverable.

The paradox is this: *secrecy meant to protect wealth often destroys it.* Because when financial knowledge is withheld, successors must make decisions in the dark. They cannot anticipate legal risk. They don't understand jurisdictional complexity. They have no emotional map for navigating sudden inheritance. Wealth becomes a stranger in their own house.

The Family Wealth Council counters this by establishing *ritualised disclosure.* It creates a safe, non-performative space for knowledge transfer—not just of amounts and structures, but of *intentions and convictions.* This is not about giving young heirs control. It is about giving them *orientation.*

The Architecture of the Council: Not a Meeting, a Mechanism

A Family Wealth Council is not a single event. It is a recurring, evolving structure. At its core, it blends four dimensions:

Operational Education – Sessions focused on understanding asset classes, legal arrangements, succession pathways, taxation, and risk exposure. This includes walkthroughs of trust instruments, digital asset custody, and sovereign diversification strategies.

Philosophical Dialogue – Conversations on the *why*, not just the *how*. What is the purpose of this wealth? What is it not for? What principles should govern its use—and when do those principles override profit?

Crisis Rehearsals – Scenario planning for stress-testing both financial and familial infrastructure. What if the founder dies suddenly? What if capital controls freeze bank access? What if an heir is targeted in a divorce or lawsuit?

Emotional Calibration – Naming and navigating the psychodynamics of inheritance: guilt, comparison, imposter syndrome, rebellion, fear of irrelevance, or the temptation to escape identity through consumption.

This multi-dimensionality is what distinguishes a Council from a briefing. It does not just share facts—it builds frameworks.

Timing and Exposure: When to Invite the Next Generation

One of the most delicate aspects of family wealth governance is timing. Introduce too early, and children may not grasp the gravity. Introduce too late, and they inherit without compass or conviction. The question is not age—it is *readiness*, and readiness is demonstrated through character, curiosity, and consistency.

Indicators that a family member is ready to join the Council:

They ask not just about *what* assets exist, but *why* those assets were chosen.

They demonstrate a track record of responsibility in smaller financial matters.

They show emotional maturity around status, privacy, and delayed gratification.

Start with *observer status*. Let them witness the cadence and tone of Council dialogue before contributing. Let them absorb the seriousness, the discretion, the intellectual quality of discussion. This is not a classroom. It is a sovereign forum—and the tone must reflect that.

The Power of Secrecy: Confidentiality as Strength, Not Obfuscation

The word "secrecy" has been tainted by PR scandals and shadow banking narratives. But secrecy, in the context of a Family Wealth Council, is not about hiding from scrutiny—it's about *guarding integrity*. Publicly accessible wealth invites litigation, opportunism, and political scrutiny. A council meeting conducted with confidentiality cultivates solidarity without performative signalling.

Confidentiality also allows for brutal honesty. Founders can express their true fears: about geopolitical risk, about a child's spending habits, about their own cognitive decline. Heirs can ask questions without being ridiculed for ignorance. These meetings are not for external advisors, not for in-laws, and certainly not for social media. They are sacred space.

The practice of discretion itself becomes a generational trait. Families who learn to speak openly *within*, while remaining silent *without*, form a fortress of both knowledge and restraint. *This duality is not hypocrisy—it is strategic dignity.*

Embedding Rituals: Continuity Beyond the Founder's Lifetime

Too many succession plans collapse because they are framed around a patriarch or matriarch. Once the central figure dies, the unity collapses. The Council must therefore become *ritualised*, not personalised. Think of it less as a leadership structure and more as a rhythm of shared responsibility.

Examples of ritualisation:

Annual strategy summits hosted in neutral locations with rotating moderators.

Quarterly secure briefings on geopolitical risk, tax code shifts, or asset rebalancing.

A digital vault accessible only by Council members containing key governance documents, educational modules, and scenario plans.

"Silent seat" traditions where younger heirs attend but do not yet vote—until a rite of passage is fulfilled.

By embedding *ritual over personality*, the council survives founders. *It becomes a sovereign operating system for the family.*

Teaching Through Transparency: Use Real Decisions as Case Studies

One of the most underutilised tools in legacy education is the family's own recent history. Instead of abstract lessons, use real events as teaching moments. Why did we exit that investment? Why did we reject that advisor's proposal? Why did we structure our crypto holdings offshore? What happened the last time a relative violated information protocols?

Treat these decisions as *case studies*. Create a narrative thread through family memory—not just of numbers and returns, but of wisdom earned. This transforms financial planning from compliance into culture.

And crucially: let heirs *challenge* the thinking. Let them see your reasoning, contest it, and learn through tension. These debates are the training ground for future leaders. *If you cannot tolerate disagreement, you are raising dependents, not decision-makers.*

Solidarity Over Sentiment: Building a Cohesive Identity

Finally, the Council is not just about protecting assets—it is about building identity. Too often, wealthy families collapse into internal factions because they have no shared purpose. The wealth becomes a mirror for projection, not a platform for solidarity.

The most successful Councils articulate a *unifying philosophy*. Whether it is geopolitical independence, decentralised living, philanthropic conviction, or cultural preservation, that core purpose becomes the gravitational centre. Without it, wealth fragments. With it, wealth compounds across generations—not just financially, but culturally.

Solidarity is not a by-product of family. It is engineered through practice.

Conclusion Without Saying 'In Conclusion'

If you do not have a system for talking about wealth, then wealth will talk for you. It will erupt in misunderstandings, misallocations, and mistrust. The Family Wealth Council is not a trend or luxury. It is a necessity in an age of financial complexity and institutional fragility. By creating a space that is regular, principled, and discreet, families do more than manage assets—they transmit wisdom.

And in the final analysis, *wisdom is the only inheritance that appreciates with use.*

Chapter 12
Tools, Rituals, and Systems for Enduring Wealth

Most imagine wealth as a matter of amassing. More is better, bigger is safer—or so the common story goes. But if you look closer, beneath the surface of long-standing fortunes and resilient financial lives, a quieter truth emerges: enduring wealth is not accumulated so much as it is engineered. Not through lucky breaks or raw brilliance, but through the patient design of systems—quiet, persistent structures that sense disruption early, adapt on cue, and cut through noise with disciplined clarity.

The families who stay wealthy, the individuals who navigate chaos without flinching, the institutions that outlive their founders—all tend to share one unfashionable trait: they ritualise awareness. They've stopped chasing motivation. Instead, they've built mechanisms.

This chapter steps inside that invisible scaffolding—the inner workings that most never think to document. Habits. Dashboards. Thresholds. Triggers. Files you'd never show off at a party, but which quietly hold your financial life together. This is where lofty ideas are tested in the mundane; where principles turn into protocol; where "backup planning" isn't a box to tick but a breathing framework that evolves as you do.

Because the real question isn't "Do you have a plan?" Anyone can cobble together a plan. The real test is subtler: How does your plan remain awake? How does it adjust to your changing context—your health, energy, location, values, and the broader political weather? A plan on autopilot, no matter how elegant at launch, will eventually drift off-course. It will go stale. And when needed most, it may fail you.

Enduring wealth doesn't resist change; it rehearses for it. It is not fixed in form. It renews itself. Quietly. Relentlessly. Not through grand overhauls, but through regular tune-ups—an ongoing choreography of careful recalibration.

The Danger of Inert Wealth

Inertia is seductive. When things are working, when assets are appreciating, when the system appears calm, the instinct is to do nothing. Rebalancing feels unnecessary. Reviewing systems feels tedious. But what's missed is that *risk accumulates silently*. You don't lose wealth because you made no decisions. You lose it because you made no adjustments.

Just as biological systems die without feedback loops, financial systems stagnate without *periodic reassessment*. The most robust portfolios are not those with the most aggressive upside. They are those that respond quickly to stress, reposition early, and discard strategies that no longer serve. This is the paradox of sustainable wealth: the more "set it and forget it" your system feels, the more urgently you must review its assumptions.

One purpose of this chapter is to confront that inertia head-on—with practices that help you notice, reallocate, and respond.

Wealth as a Signal Processing System

Most people view the economy like a weather report: they watch it, comment on it, maybe complain—but they don't have an internalised *signal framework*. They react, rather than recalibrate. But the world is not short on data. It's short on *meaning filters*. Without a system to discern what matters, people get hijacked by headlines and distracted by irrelevant trends. They become paralysed not by fear—but by noise.

This is where the *System of Signals* comes in. Every robust wealth strategy must be embedded in a framework that monitors not just financial metrics, but *contextual health*. That includes:

Economic shifts: inflation breakouts, rate volatility, capital control trends

Legal and geopolitical warning signs: residency rules, regulatory overreach, tax treaties

Psychological shifts: fatigue, obsession, anxiety, loss of interest—internal states that distort decision-making

Social and cultural tremors: polarisation, tribalism, institution breakdowns

Signals don't predict. They *prompt reflection.* A good signal system doesn't forecast exact futures—it tells you when your assumptions need to be audited. That's a crucial distinction. This chapter outlines how to design that system so it fits your worldview, your risk exposure, and your lifestyle pace.

From Planning to Ritual: Why Systems Must Be Rhythmic

Wealth management tools are often episodic. Annual reviews. One-time legal updates. Sporadic family conversations. But endurance isn't built from sporadic intensity—it is built from *structured repetition.* You don't secure wealth by working harder. You secure it by working rhythmically.

That's where the idea of *rituals* becomes central. The most effective systems are those that embed decision-making into a recurring process: monthly reassessment days, quarterly allocation reviews, annual "strategic resets." These rituals remove the emotion and ego from financial decisions. They create space for deliberate calibration—*before* crisis hits.

Rituals also reduce mental overhead. When your system is rhythmically maintained, your attention is free for higher-level strategy. You're not firefighting. You're fine-tuning.

This chapter will show you how to convert theoretical practices into actual calendar-anchored rituals. Not everything should be automated—but everything should be *scheduled.*

The Wealth Compass Document: Condensing Complexity into Clarity

Wealth, once it reaches a certain threshold, becomes cognitively burdensome. You don't just manage money. You manage structures, jurisdictions, passwords, philosophies, preferences, and people. The more diversified and decentralised your life becomes, the harder it is to maintain *cohesion.*

The Wealth Compass Document is designed to solve this. It is a single-page artefact that encapsulates *your strategy, your principles, and your signals.* It is not a portfolio statement. It is a strategic document that answers, at a glance:

What assets do I hold, and why?

What risks am I hedging, and how?

What assumptions underlie this plan—and when do they expire?

What are my personal red lines (what I will never trade, expose, or compromise)?

What shifts would trigger a review or reallocation?

Think of it as your own user manual—a living map of how you protect, grow, and adapt your wealth. Not just for yourself, but for anyone who may need to continue the system if you are incapacitated or absent.

The Compass isn't a replacement for professional advice. It's the *interface between advice and action.* Without it, knowledge fragments. With it, knowledge consolidates—and adapts.

Why Most Systems Fail (and How Yours Can Survive)

Most systems break for one of three reasons:

They are overly complex. When wealth systems rely on multiple intermediaries, exotic structures, or rare expertise, they become fragile. Complexity without clarity invites chaos.

They are personality-dependent. If your entire system relies on *your* attention, *your* knowledge, *your* memory—then it is one unexpected illness away from collapse.

They are event-driven, not signal-driven. Waiting for markets to crash, rules to change, or emergencies to occur before adjusting is a formula for reaction, not resilience.

This chapter offers principles and practices that address each of these failure points. You'll learn how to simplify without diluting, how to decentralise responsibility without losing control, and how to shift from an *event-driven life* to a *signal-responsive one.*

Beyond Resilience: Designing for Optionality

The endgame isn't just protection. It's optionality. The goal of these systems isn't merely to defend what you've built—it's to *expand what you can do without permission.* Optionality is the real currency of independence. It means:

Being able to leave a country within 24 hours—with assets, identity, and mobility intact

Being able to shift from fiat to crypto to metal to barter seamlessly

Being able to live on low overhead when necessary, or scale when opportunity strikes

Being able to pause, rethink, and redesign your life at intervals—because the structure supports change

None of this is theoretical. It has been stress-tested by entrepreneurs under persecution, families under asset seizure, and investors under collapsing markets. This isn't alarmism. It's *structural realism.*

Optionality is not a side effect of good fortune. It is the result of deliberate architecture. And architecture begins with tools, rituals, and systems—designed not for perfection, but for endurance.

The Weekly Portfolio Ritual

In wealth management, it is often assumed that big decisions are what determine financial success. But in practice, the most powerful decisions are small, structured, and repeated. The difference between clarity and confusion, between a portfolio that adapts and one that stagnates, often hinges on one simple habit: *the weekly check-in.* A short, intentional ritual—executed with discipline and reflection—can serve as the nervous system of an enduring financial life. It's not glamorous. It doesn't require spreadsheets. But its compounding impact is profound.

Most investors treat their financial lives episodically. They check in when something breaks, when markets spike, or when fear strikes. But reactive management is fragile management. By the time a portfolio crisis is visible, the decision window has already narrowed. What distinguishes resilient investors is not predictive genius, but *predictable attention.* They don't try to control the future—they watch the present carefully enough that their responses are timely, not panicked.

The weekly portfolio ritual is a deliberately minimalist practice. It's not about day-trading or micromanagement. It's about surfacing signal, reducing friction, and maintaining *continuity of thought*—so that wealth isn't just preserved, but stewarded with coherence.

Attention Is a Form of Asset Protection

There is a quiet cost to not paying attention: *drift.* Asset allocations gradually shift away from intended targets. Fees accumulate. Tax liabilities are triggered unintentionally. Risk exposures morph into vulnerabilities. And worst of all, strategic clarity dissolves into fog.

The weekly ritual interrupts that drift. It does not mean obsessing over every market fluctuation. It means re-establishing a conscious link between one's long-term plan and current positioning. It means asking, each week: *Is my system still aligned with my strategy?* Not because it must change every time—but because *you must remain in dialogue with it.*

A portfolio is not a passive container. It is a living reflection of your worldview, your priorities, and your tolerance. If it is never reviewed, it cannot stay congruent with the rest of your life.

The Ritual Is the Practice

Why weekly? Because daily is too reactive. Monthly is too disconnected. Weekly offers the ideal cadence—*frequent enough to catch friction early, infrequent enough to avoid noise addiction.* It is the rhythm of serious stewardship.

Executed properly, the weekly ritual should take no more than 20–30 minutes. It's not a performance. It's a check-in with the machinery that underpins your freedom. It is best scheduled at the same time each week—first thing Monday morning or Friday afternoon, for instance—anchored like a recurring meeting with your future self.

The content of the ritual can evolve with the complexity of your portfolio, but at minimum, it should address three domains:

Signal recognition – What has changed? What's new in the economic, legal, geopolitical, or personal landscape that might warrant a closer look? Not all signals trigger action—but *you must be aware of them.*

Alignment check – Are your current allocations still aligned with your stated goals, risk appetites, and liquidity timelines? Are you overexposed, under-hedged, or drifting off-policy?

Behavioural hygiene – Are any of your decisions (or temptations) being driven by emotion rather than reason? Have you been influenced by panic, greed, fatigue, or trend-chasing?

By surfacing these questions in a non-emergency context, you build the cognitive muscles that prevent rash action when volatility does strike. *Calm attention today inoculates you against chaos tomorrow.*

The Psychological Benefit of Ritual

Financial decision-making is never purely mathematical. It is psychological, emotional, and sometimes existential. Ritual offers a stabilising force. It *externalises reflection.* It provides structure in the face of complexity. And it turns what could be an abstract burden into a practiced behaviour.

There is a reason high-functioning individuals ritualise everything from exercise to writing to planning: *ritual compresses resistance.* It lowers the activation energy required to think clearly. When you know exactly when and how to engage with your finances each week, you are far less likely to avoid, defer, or forget.

Moreover, ritual desensitises fear. By checking in regularly, you normalise financial data. You see losses, gains, volatility—and gradually, you stop reacting. You start *responding.* And in this shift, your behaviour becomes your edge.

From Visibility to Anticipation

The purpose of the weekly ritual is not just to see what's happening. It's to *anticipate* what's next—not by prediction, but by position. It trains you to think in second-order consequences. For instance:

Interest rate changes → Bond exposure rethink

Capital control rumours → Cross-border liquidity check

Tax rule proposals → Jurisdictional asset relocation prep

None of these require action every week. But when you're in regular contact with your portfolio, you notice when conditions accumulate to require one.

Think of this like a pilot scanning a cockpit—not to fix something every moment, but to ensure all systems are operating within acceptable parameters. When a dial flickers or a pressure rises, the pilot doesn't panic—they adjust early. This is the function of the weekly ritual: not control, but *readiness.*

Integrating Philosophy with Practice

Wealth without awareness is precarious. A portfolio may grow, but if the owner is not engaged—philosophically and practically—it becomes a hollow construct. Eventually, something unexpected will test the coherence of the structure. And if that coherence was never rehearsed, it will crumble.

The weekly ritual is the rehearsal. It embeds the philosophy of sufficiency, decentralisation, and resilience into a tangible, repeatable practice. It makes your financial life *conscious*, not just optimised.

Critically, the ritual also allows for the integration of non-financial insights. A shift in personal health, a change in family obligations, a new priority—all of these must ultimately be expressed in how you manage capital. If there is no weekly interface to surface those shifts, the portfolio becomes disconnected from the person it serves.

What the Weekly Ritual Is Not

It is not a time to over-analyse charts. It is not a justification to tinker. It is not an anxiety ritual disguised as discipline. It is not another productivity hack.

It is a structure for attention. A rhythm for recalibration. A protected space to ensure that wealth is not something that merely exists—it is something you *live into.*

The ritual is also not a solo exercise, necessarily. It can be conducted with a partner, spouse, or advisor. In some cases, families institutionalise it as a micro-version of the *Family Wealth Council*—creating shared vocabulary and transparency without opening the door to constant debate. The ritual becomes a practice in *continuity*, across people and generations.

The Cost of Skipping It

Most financial mistakes are not made in one day. They are made *over many weeks of not paying attention.* A small allocation error becomes a tax event. An overlooked signal becomes a crisis. A forgotten password becomes a lost asset. A misaligned strategy becomes an existential liability.

The weekly ritual costs little. But skipping it eventually costs a lot.

Final Thought: The Ritual as Compass

In the end, the weekly portfolio ritual is a discipline of *orientation.* Not just toward markets, but toward self. It's an exercise in staying connected to your strategy, your values, and your capacity to respond with clarity. Wealth, without stewardship, decays. But stewardship begins with observation—structured, humble, consistent observation.

The ritual is not a burden. It is a privilege. And for those committed to enduring wealth—not just accumulation—it may be the most high-leverage 30 minutes of the week.

System of Signals

The difference between those who adapt early and those who react too late is rarely intelligence—it's *attention.* In a world saturated with noise and governed by complexity, foresight doesn't begin with prediction. It begins with *perception.* And yet, most people manage their financial lives as if they are navigating through fog—without a compass, without a lookout, and without a plan for when the weather turns. The solution is not clairvoyance; it is a disciplined system of signals: a personalised architecture for noticing early warnings before they become irreversible events.

A well-designed signal system is not about chasing headlines or forecasting markets. It is about cultivating *structured awareness.* It recognises that risk accumulates quietly, that opportunity often arrives disguised as discomfort, and that silence is rarely neutral. A system of signals teaches you to ask better questions, to contextualise faster, and to act while others are still frozen by ambiguity.

Most investors only realise they needed an alert system *after* it would have helped. But just as pilots scan for changes in engine pressure or temperature—not because they expect failure, but because early detection is survival—so too must serious wealth stewards build a cockpit of their own. What are the indicators—economic, social, and psychological—that deserve your attention? What patterns precede change? And more critically: *How will you notice the difference between static and signal before it costs you?*

Signal vs Noise: Training the Eye for Pattern

Not all data is information. Not all change is meaningful. The first step in building a signal system is recognising that most of what you see, hear, and read is *designed to distract, not to inform.* Markets, media, and social sentiment bombard us with updates—99% of which are irrelevant to sound decision-making. The goal, then, is *not to consume more—but to observe better.*

This requires the development of what the military calls *situational awareness*—a state of continuous observation where anomalies are not ignored or explained away, but logged and layered into broader context. In wealth terms, this might include things like:

Anomalous policy moves in peripheral jurisdictions

Illiquidity in obscure corners of bond markets

Subtle changes in capital controls or banking behaviours

Increasing tension between tax jurisdictions and crypto exchanges

A spike in cyberattacks on decentralised financial infrastructure

Declines in trust in core social institutions or legal systems

None of these signals alone constitutes an emergency. But together, they may paint a picture of latent fragility or nascent opportunity. The skilled observer connects these fragments—not to panic, but to prepare. *The art is in learning which tremors precede earthquakes, and which are just noise from the street.*

Three Domains of Critical Signal

To be effective, your alert system must draw from *diverse categories of input*. Focusing solely on charts or price action is like trying to read the weather by only looking at the sky. The full picture demands that we monitor at least three domains:

Economic Signals – These include interest rate shifts, inflation trajectories, credit tightening, trade imbalances, central bank posture, shadow banking activity, and asset correlation breakdowns. But more crucially, they include *divergences*—moments when traditional relationships between indicators stop behaving predictably. For example, when gold and bonds move *together* during a downturn, it may indicate distrust in fiat rather than a conventional risk-off rotation.

Social and Political Signals – Cultural fractures, regulatory overreach, migration trends, debt protests, language in political speeches, and behavioural shifts in populations (e.g. surging homeschooling, cash hoarding, or rural flight) can offer profound insight into future risk landscapes. Most asset holders only see the after-effects—those who pay attention to social friction see *precursors.*

Psychological and Behavioural Signals – These are harder to quantify, but just as vital. They include shifts in sentiment, decision fatigue in peers, sudden changes in investor narratives, herd-driven re-allocations, or risk blindness in financial media. The 2008 crisis was preceded not by technical data alone, but by a *collapse in narrative coherence*. When the story no longer made sense, trust evaporated—and with it, liquidity.

Your alert system should be structured to touch each of these categories weekly—briefly, efficiently, and with a focus on *change in pattern*, not raw volume.

Designing a Personal Dashboard

A sophisticated signal system is not built from scratch. It is evolved—*calibrated over time to reflect your priorities, risks, and exposures.* The best systems are simple enough to maintain, yet rich enough to provoke action.

This might take the form of a single-page document updated weekly with five core segments:

Macroeconomic Check – 3–5 key metrics you track consistently (e.g. yield curve steepness, energy price movement, liquidity ratios)

Jurisdictional Risk – Notes on policy developments in the countries where your assets or residencies are concentrated

Sentiment Snapshot – Quick notes on tone shifts in media, peer behaviours, or online forums you trust

Asset-Specific Observations – Any irregularities or pricing disconnects in your specific holdings (e.g. token delistings, bank letters, unexpected costs)

Open Signals – 1–3 trends or curiosities you are watching but don't yet understand. These are potential *weak signals*—often where the next shift begins

The goal is not volume. The goal is *coherence*. This dashboard is your memory, your reference, and your prompt. It should create continuity between weeks, so that trends emerge not through guesswork, but through comparison.

The Psychology of Early Action

One of the most overlooked barriers to effective signal use is *emotional resistance*. It is not always easy to act on information that contradicts comfort. You may sense that a region is becoming politically unstable, but the cost of moving capital—or the social inertia of staying put—leads to rationalisation. You wait. You hope. You explain.

This is why a signal system must be accompanied by *pre-committed thresholds for review*. For example: "If capital controls are proposed in a country where I hold more than 10% of my net worth, I will initiate contingency planning within seven days." Or: "If three of five behavioural indicators in my dashboard show signs of distress, I will rebalance to defensive assets."

These rules protect you from your own delay. They *create permission to act*, backed by forethought—not panic. A signal is only useful if it leads to a response. Otherwise, it's just data you chose to ignore.

Calibrating for Your Exposure

No two signal systems should look alike. An entrepreneur with operations in five countries needs to track different inputs than a retiree with a passive portfolio. A family holding crypto across multiple wallets must monitor different risks than one with land and precious metals.

The beauty of a personalised signal architecture is that it reflects *your unique risk surface*. Where are you most vulnerable? Where are you concentrated—legally, economically, and behaviourally? What would *hurt* the most to lose?

This is where your signal system becomes not just a tool, but a mirror. It teaches you where you've over-committed, where you've neglected diversification, and where your blind spots lie. *It is both a radar and a report card.*

Conclusion: The Privilege of Preparedness

The future will not reward the most credentialled—it will reward the most perceptive. In every domain, those who notice early, respond early. And while luck cannot be engineered, *readiness can be.*

A system of signals is not about control. It's about clarity. It doesn't prevent surprise—but it ensures that surprise doesn't equal paralysis. It is the invisible scaffolding behind confident decision-making. It is the difference between being dragged by change, and *surfing it with intentionality.*

The wise investor does not wait to see the headlines. They are watching the water while others are watching the shore. And when the tide shifts, they are already moving—quietly, decisively, and ahead of the crowd.

The Power of Periodic Reallocation

Wealth is not merely built by choosing good assets; it is preserved—and often multiplied—by knowing when to move between them.

The assumption that once you've created a balanced portfolio you can leave it untouched is a comforting fiction. Reality is more dynamic. Markets change, asset correlations invert, political climates shift, and personal goals evolve. The enemy of financial resilience is not volatility—*it is inertia.* Without deliberate, periodic reallocation, even a thoughtfully constructed portfolio can drift into misalignment, exposing the owner to concentration risk, opportunity cost, or systemic fragility.

Periodic reallocation is not about reacting to every fluctuation or chasing short-term performance. It is about *intentional recalibration.* It treats wealth as a living system—one that must be reviewed, tested, and adjusted in response to both external signals and internal changes. To reallocate well is to acknowledge that no financial configuration is permanent, and no allocation is neutral over time.

The most dangerous phrase in long-term wealth stewardship is: "It's been working so far." That statement is usually uttered just before a correction, a collapse, or a wake-up call. Smart investors understand that success accumulates not from static strategy but from disciplined iteration.

Portfolio Drift: The Silent Saboteur

Most portfolios don't implode—they *wander.* They gradually move away from their intended design through benign neglect. A portfolio that began as a diversified allocation across real estate, commodities, crypto, and cash equivalents may, over the course of 12–18 months, become heavily skewed towards one asset class simply because of differential performance. This is not strategy—it is statistical gravity.

For instance, if your gold holdings double in value while your rental income remains flat and your crypto segment declines, the psychological temptation is to celebrate the growth. But the result may be a portfolio now overexposed to a single asset class, with reduced liquidity and increased political or market vulnerability. Without rebalancing, the portfolio's risk profile has changed—even if no new money was invested.

Periodic reallocation forces visibility into that drift. It reasserts the principle that *allocation reflects intent.* When you rebalance, you are not simply adjusting numbers—you are reaffirming your thesis about what you want your capital to do, under what conditions, and over what timeline.

The Psychology of Rebalancing: Rationality vs Reward

Reallocating intelligently requires more than spreadsheets. It requires the courage to *sell your winners and buy your laggards*—a psychological move that often feels counterintuitive, if not downright irrational. Behavioural finance has repeatedly shown that humans are wired to extrapolate trends, avoid regret, and anchor emotionally to gains. This creates inertia—not from laziness, but from fear of being wrong.

A disciplined reallocation framework protects you from these distortions. It replaces emotion with principle. For example: if your framework dictates that no asset should constitute more than 25% of your net worth, and one surges to 38%, you sell down—not because you distrust the asset, but because *you trust your system more.* You reallocate not to chase returns, but to restore integrity to your design.

This mindset mirrors that of elite athletes or military tacticians. They do not act on impulse—they act on pre-planned protocol. The ability to override immediate gratification in favour of long-term structure is one of the hallmarks of enduring wealth builders.

From Static Allocation to Dynamic Strategy

Traditional financial planning emphasises *target allocations*—fixed percentages assigned to asset categories like equities, bonds, real estate, and alternatives. While useful as a starting point, such models assume a stable world. But the world is not stable. Geopolitical tension, fiscal mismanagement, currency dilution, and technological disruption all demand *adaptive strategy.*

Periodic reallocation turns a static allocation into a *living strategy*. It does this by applying structured review at predetermined intervals (e.g. quarterly, biannually, or annually), and by integrating a broader set of inputs—including macroeconomic shifts, personal risk appetite, jurisdictional developments, and technological innovation.

For instance, a high-net-worth investor based in Europe may decide, after reviewing recent regulatory developments and energy volatility, to reduce exposure to EU-based equities and increase holdings in Asian real assets or decentralised assets like bitcoin or gold. The decision isn't reactive—it's strategic. The reallocation is not simply a numerical tweak, but a *tactical evolution* rooted in observed change.

Case Study: The Defensive Reallocator

Consider the case of an investor who held a well-diversified portfolio in early 2021: 40% equities, 20% bonds, 20% real estate, and 20% crypto. Over the next 18 months, crypto experienced both meteoric rises and sharp contractions. Meanwhile, inflation rates accelerated, interest rates spiked, and the bond market experienced its worst drawdown in decades.

Those who failed to rebalance remained exposed to assets that had become structurally misaligned with the macro reality. But one client—let's call him Thomas—applied a biannual reallocation ritual. In early 2022, he trimmed his tech-heavy equities and reallocated into precious metals and short-term TIPS. He reduced stablecoin exposure in favour of physical gold. He initiated a minor foreign residency process to diversify legal risk.

By the end of 2023, while many of his peers had watched their portfolios whiplash in value, Thomas's net worth had not only held steady—it had become *more liquid, more jurisdictionally agile, and more psychologically stable*. The power of reallocation is not merely in avoiding loss. It is in *staying relevant*—financially and operationally.

Frequency, Not Friction

Some misinterpret reallocation as synonymous with overtrading. It is not. Reallocation should not be continuous—it should be *periodic and principled.* The goal is not to micromanage volatility, but to prevent drift and decay.

Think of it as a form of wealth hygiene: like dental care or physical exercise. Done too often, it becomes neurotic. Done too rarely, it leads to preventable damage. The correct rhythm depends on portfolio complexity, asset liquidity, and external context. A crypto-heavy portfolio in 2024 may warrant quarterly reviews. A conservative land-and-gold allocation might require only annual assessment.

The reallocation rhythm is your feedback loop. It lets you measure not just returns, but *resilience.* It trains you to ask, "What is this capital doing for me today, and is it still optimised for tomorrow?"

Beyond the Numbers: Ethical and Existential Reallocation

At its highest level, periodic reallocation becomes a philosophical discipline. It forces reflection on what your wealth is *for.* Are you accumulating for control, for freedom, for family continuity, or for social contribution? Has that goal changed? Has your context evolved?

Sometimes, the most important reallocation is not from one asset to another—but from one *purpose* to another. Perhaps part of your capital should move from growth vehicles to intergenerational trusts. Perhaps you should reduce exposure to paper assets and increase holdings in tangible, real-world structures that serve your future self. Perhaps it's time to shift from optimisation to simplicity.

Every reallocation is a chance to *redeclare your strategy.* And in a world where capital is increasingly surveilled, politicised, and weaponised, that act of deliberate reassessment is not just practical. It is radical.

Conclusion: Iteration Is Integrity

A wealth plan that does not evolve is not a plan—it is a trap. Periodic reallocation is not about constant change, but about *intentional correction.* It keeps your wealth strategy honest. It disciplines your psychology. It aligns your present exposure with your future priorities.

The difference between those who endure and those who fade is not luck—it is *iteration.* And iteration begins with a question asked regularly, ruthlessly, and without excuse: *Is my current allocation still serving its intended purpose?* Everything else follows from that.

The powerful do not hold still. They reposition. Periodically, patiently, and without sentiment. That is how real wealth survives its owner—and grows stronger in the hands of those who inherit it.

Your Wealth Compass Document

If your entire financial strategy vanished from memory, could you rebuild it with clarity—or would you be left piecing together fragments from spreadsheets, advisors, and fading assumptions? Most people, even the affluent and educated, carry a dangerously scattered understanding of their own wealth architecture. Assets are siloed. Risks are unexamined. Goals are abstract. In a crisis, or even a significant life shift, few could articulate their financial priorities coherently. This is not a technical failure. It is a *strategic absence.*

The solution is disarmingly simple: a one-page Wealth Compass Document. Not a balance sheet. Not a will. Not an investment plan. A *strategic synthesis*—a distilled guide to what you own, why you own it, and what principles govern your next move. This is not a document for your accountant. It is a document for *you*, your future self, and—eventually—those you trust to carry your financial legacy forward. In volatile times, clarity is a form of security. And clarity begins with compression.

Why a Single Page Is So Powerful

In a world of expanding dashboards, apps, trackers, and data feeds, information overload is the default. But strategic insight rarely comes from more data—it comes from *better framing.* A single page forces priorities. It demands synthesis. Just as elite military teams carry mission briefs that fit on one page, and successful founders use one-page business plans to clarify vision, the Wealth Compass strips away clutter to reveal *what matters most.*

A well-designed one-page document does not simplify your thinking—it *sharpens* it. It reveals contradictions. It surfaces assumptions. It demands that you declare your positioning not in spreadsheets, but in *sentences.* When you're forced to write, in plain language, "My number one financial goal is X, and my current allocation supports that by Y," you begin to see where your portfolio supports—or betrays—your intentions.

This exercise is not administrative. It is philosophical. And it is also a test of sovereignty. If you cannot articulate your own financial system, then someone else will—an advisor, an institution, or the market itself.

What a Wealth Compass Is Not

It is not a net worth summary. It is not a tax document. It is not a forecast model. Those have their place, but they do not answer the deeper questions:

What role does each asset play in your life?

What are you optimising for: growth, liquidity, resilience, autonomy?

What risks do you explicitly accept—and which ones are you ignoring?

The Compass document is the strategic core that connects *all* of your assets to a coherent worldview. It replaces jargon with insight. It demands that you label the function of your capital: "This property exists to generate passive income. This crypto wallet exists as an exit valve. This cash reserve exists to buy freedom." Every component is named, every purpose claimed.

The Core Sections of a Wealth Compass

Though the form can be adapted, the structure should follow a logic of clarity and function. A mature Wealth Compass typically includes:

Financial Purpose Statement – Why are you accumulating and protecting wealth? What are the values, principles, or outcomes guiding your system? This is not about vague aspiration. It is a declaration of design: "My wealth is for optionality, privacy, and intergenerational stewardship."

Current Strategic Allocation – A high-level breakdown (by percentage) of your holdings across major asset classes: real estate, cash, equities, gold, crypto, private business, and so forth. This is not granular accounting—it is *strategic positioning.*

Asset Functions – A sentence or two about the *purpose* of each major asset type. "Bitcoin holdings serve as borderless, self-custodied reserve capital." "My apartment in Lisbon exists as both a lifestyle hedge and a residency anchor."

Risk Map – A concise naming of major risks you are exposed to: jurisdictional, counterparty, inflationary, technological. The goal is not exhaustive listing—it is to *acknowledge exposure* and consider counterweights.

Signals & Triggers – A brief outline of your personal alert system: What signs would prompt a shift? For example: "If local inflation exceeds 6% for two consecutive quarters, I increase gold allocation." This trains you to connect *external change to internal action.*

Next-Action Horizon – The 1–3 major portfolio actions or strategic reviews to undertake within the next 90 days. These are not goals—they are *decisions in motion.*

Heir Insight Section – A note or instruction set for a future inheritor, business partner, or trusted advisor. This might include a password vault location, legal contact, or a simple statement: "If I am incapacitated, refer to XYZ custodian with the enclosed authorisation." This is not legal advice—it is *strategic redundancy.*

Strategic Benefits of Having a Compass

The value of the Compass Document is not merely the content. It is the *discipline of synthesis.* Just as a pilot checks their cockpit instruments not because they don't trust their plane, but because flight demands vigilance, the Wealth Compass is your way of *checking the horizon.* It embeds five essential strategic habits:

Self-accountability – No hiding behind complexity or delegation

Narrative clarity – Understanding your own portfolio as a story, not a list

Psychological alignment – Ensuring your assets match your tolerance, philosophy, and life stage

Frictionless communication – A tool you can share with a partner, spouse, or trusted advisor

Crisis readiness – If everything went dark, this document lets someone rebuild what matters

The moment you complete the Compass, you also test the soundness of your system. If you struggle to explain the role of a major investment, or find gaps between goals and strategy, those aren't flaws—they are *insights.* The Compass doesn't judge. It reveals.

Case Example: From Overwhelm to Orientation

Consider Marina, a 43-year-old tech entrepreneur with assets across four countries, a mix of fiat, crypto, and private equity, and a family of four. Her spreadsheets were up to date, her financial planner was competent, and her legal documents were in place—but she still felt disoriented. "I know what I have," she said, "but I don't know what it's *for.*"

When she drafted her first Wealth Compass, it surfaced three major realisations: first, her primary wealth driver was her business—but she had no liquidity plan if it faltered. Second, her crypto assets lacked a succession plan. Third, her lifestyle spending had crept beyond what her asset base could support in a downturn. None of this was news—but now it was *visible.*

With a 30-minute review each quarter, she used the Compass to iterate. Within a year, her confidence had increased not because of performance—but because of *positioning.* She wasn't wealthier. She was *oriented.* That's the real value.

The Compass Is Not a One-Time Exercise

The Wealth Compass must evolve with your life. A 28-year-old digital nomad will need a different set of signals, asset roles, and objectives than a 62-year-old founder preparing a transition. The point is not permanence—it is *periodic recalibration.*

Update it when major shifts occur: a new jurisdiction, a liquidity event, a crisis, or a meaningful change in life priorities. Review it at least once a year, ideally during your quarterly or annual wealth audit. Treat it as a living map, not a static artefact.

In time, the Compass becomes a tradition—something you teach your children or partners, something that creates a *language of stewardship* in your family. Not "how much do we have," but "why do we hold what we do—and how do we protect it?"

Final Thought: Compression Is Sovereignty

True wealth is not about accumulation. It's about coherence. When your strategy is so clear that it fits on a single page, you are no longer just navigating the system—you are *mastering it.* The Wealth Compass Document is not a bureaucratic tool. It is a declaration of intent. It says: *I know what I own. I know why I own it. And I know what I'll do if things change.*

In a noisy, fragile world, that clarity is not just useful. It's essential.

Your Wealth Compass Document

Wealth without direction is not wealth—it is noise. In the fog of complexity, the default posture of most affluent individuals is not confidence, but quiet disorientation. They may have advisors, spreadsheets, vaults, policies, assets scattered across geographies and platforms—but ask them to explain their overall strategy, and what you get is abstraction: "We're diversified." "It's mostly long-term." "We're building for the future." These are not plans. They are evasions. *When there is no synthesis, there is no clarity. When there is no clarity, resilience becomes accidental.*

The antidote is deceptively simple: a single-page Wealth Compass Document. Not a tool for your wealth manager or tax accountant—but for *you.* A living, dynamic statement that captures the essence of your strategy, risk posture, allocation principles, and long-range intentions. It's a document that synthesises—not itemises. It clarifies *why you own what you own*, what your capital is positioned to do, and what shifts would prompt a review. It compresses strategy into language. And it forces you to face, with radical precision, the core architecture of your financial life.

Why Strategic Compression Is Essential

In modern wealth management, detail is abundant—but orientation is rare. We have analytics tools, dashboards, performance metrics, and AI-driven financial planning. But *none of these guarantee coherence.* The more complexity we outsource to interfaces and professionals, the easier it becomes to lose sight of *first principles.* What does this capital serve? What would make me change course? What is my threshold for exposure in each domain?

The Wealth Compass exists to strip away the informational bloat and extract *strategic signal.* It is not about minimalism—it is about mental posture. If you were locked out of your portfolio apps, cut off from advisors, and forced to rely on a single sheet of paper to guide financial decisions for a year, what would that sheet say? That is your Compass.

The Problem of Fragmented Planning

Many individuals—even sophisticated investors—operate with fragmented planning. Their estate plan is with one lawyer. Their investment overview lives in a Google Sheet. Their private assets are remembered through mental notes or buried in contracts. Their crypto seed phrases are saved somewhere "safe." The assumptions driving their choices are often unspoken or outdated. The overall system works—*until it doesn't.*

The deeper risk is not operational loss—it is strategic drift. You continue to accumulate, optimise, protect—but without knowing what the system is optimised *for.* A well-constructed Compass document surfaces this drift early. It reconnects you with *intent.* And it does so without drowning you in mechanics.

The Philosophy of a Wealth Compass

This is not a compliance tool. It is a philosophical artefact. Creating a Compass forces you to confront wealth not as an abstract noun, but as a *functioning system.* That system must serve specific ends—freedom, security, family continuity, optionality, purpose. And it must do so across regimes: inflationary shocks, geopolitical turbulence, health changes, intergenerational handover.

Unlike a will or trust document, the Compass is not bound by legal formalism. It speaks the language of *personal sovereignty.* It captures design choices in plain speech. It names the trade-offs you've accepted. It acknowledges exposure zones without illusion. In short, it tells the truth of your capital—not just what it is, but what it *means.*

Core Components of the Wealth Compass

While format may vary, an effective Compass should include the following seven elements—each expressed in language that is *specific, self-authored, and honest:*

Statement of Financial Purpose

A one- or two-sentence declaration of what your wealth is *for.* Not generic aspiration—but a strategic anchor. For example: "My wealth exists to ensure cross-border mobility, long-term autonomy, and intergenerational trust protection—without dependence on state or institutional systems."

High-Level Allocation Map

A simplified, percentage-based breakdown of asset classes—real estate, cash, digital assets, precious metals, equities, private business. No exhaustive detail. Just the overview, with sufficient signal to understand your risk symmetry.

Asset Function Summary

A line or two for each major asset group explaining *its strategic role.*

"Gold: geopolitical hedge and jurisdictionally portable store of value." "BTC: long-duration capital reserve and digital bearer instrument." "Lisbon property: residency anchor and lifestyle inflation buffer."

Risk Exposure Notation
A concise statement of your top 3–5 accepted risks. These may be jurisdictional (e.g., tax regime dependency), structural (e.g., low liquidity), or philosophical (e.g., high exposure to volatile innovation sectors). Naming risks explicitly reduces the likelihood of being surprised by them.

Signals & Thresholds
Your personal indicators for reevaluation. What would prompt you to change your allocation? Examples might include: "If USD loses 20% purchasing power over 12 months, reallocate 10% from cash to hard assets." These are not predictions. They are *instructions to your future self.*

Next Strategic Moves
A rolling 90-day action field. Not tasks—but high-leverage adjustments or reviews. E.g.: "Evaluate second residency options in a neutral jurisdiction." "Test cold storage transfer protocol for heirs."

Heir Orientation Note
A short, plain-language message to your future executor, spouse, or children—explaining what this document is, where to find supporting assets, and the *principles* behind your system. It is not a legal instruction. It is a human handoff.

Case Study: The Compass in Crisis

Julian, a 55-year-old entrepreneur with operations in South Africa and Portugal, faced an unexpected health crisis that left him temporarily incapacitated. His business interests were diversified. His personal net worth was substantial. But his family had no central reference to understand what the system looked like.

The Compass document he had created six months earlier—a personal project prompted by travel downtime—became the Rosetta Stone. It enabled his spouse to speak fluently with advisors. It clarified which capital pools were long-term versus deployable. It identified safe jurisdictions. Most critically, it outlined *why* certain assets were untouchable. The Compass didn't solve the crisis. It turned it from chaos into choreography.

The Compass Is a Living Document

You don't create it once and shelve it. You update it quarterly, or at minimum biannually. It reflects change. New jurisdictions. Shifts in macro regime. A liquidity event. A health scare. A change in worldview. It is a tool for dynamic alignment. Not a tombstone of past beliefs.

In this sense, it functions more like a *private constitution*—a statement of ongoing governance principles that evolve with context but remain anchored in a core ethos. And because it is short, it invites revisiting. It avoids the trap of unread binders and forgotten plans. It is designed for *recurrence.*

Transferring the Compass Culture

One of the least discussed, yet most critical, elements of long-term wealth resilience is *intellectual inheritance.* Families that fail to transmit principles alongside assets eventually watch those assets erode. The Compass, when shared selectively and intentionally, becomes a template for transmission.

You can teach your children or heirs *how* to build theirs. You can walk them through what each section means. You can use your own document not as dogma—but as invitation: "This is how I think about wealth. Let me show you how you might begin to think about yours."

In elite families, this becomes a generational ritual—not a document, but a *discipline.* A quarterly review. A holiday conversation. A rite of initiation into responsibility.

Creating One Is a Test of Coherence

If you struggle to fill out any section—especially the purpose, asset functions, or risk posture—then you have identified an area of strategic blindness. That is the point. The Compass *reveals what you haven't been seeing.* It is an intelligence test for your own system, built not in metrics, but in meaning.

It also unearths contradictions. When your purpose statement says "privacy and agility," but your asset list is jurisdictionally exposed and custodian-reliant, the Compass holds up a mirror. This isn't failure. It's design feedback. The Compass doesn't just track your strategy—it *sharpens* it.

A Single Page to Reassert Sovereignty

There will be a day when the noise is overwhelming. When markets freeze. When headlines scream. When access is denied. And on that day, you won't ask, "What's the yield on my portfolio?" You will ask: *What was I trying to do? Where is my control? Who else can understand this system if I cannot?*

That's when the Compass becomes more than a tool. It becomes a declaration: *I am not lost in my own architecture. I have thought this through. And if I need to, I can rebuild it.* On one page.

That is not minimalism. That is mastery.

CONCLUSION
A Fortress You Can Carry

The most durable form of wealth doesn't sit locked in a vault, nor does it hide behind shell companies or encrypted hardware wallets. It isn't nestled in property deeds or shielded by trusts. No—its foundation lies elsewhere: in your ability to remain lucid when the pressure mounts, to act with independence when options seem limited, and to recalibrate your position without sacrificing principle. True financial sovereignty—resilient, enduring, untouchable—is not some grand structure you erect. It is a fortress you carry within.

This book has avoided offering formulas. It hasn't dangled promises of security through polished financial products or foolproof portfolios. What it has offered is subtler, and perhaps more enduring: a framework for adaptive permanence. A deliberately balanced mix of assets, jurisdictions, rituals, and philosophies—all aimed at keeping you not just financially intact, but personally sovereign, regardless of what system happens to be in charge. And now, at the end, we return to the unspoken thread that has quietly bound every chapter together: What survives when the scaffolding around us begins to shift?

Because shift it will. That's not fatalism—it's history speaking in patterns. Economies centralise, collapse, and centralise again. Empires overstretch, then retreat. Technologies democratise access, only to reconsolidate control. Legal frameworks stretch to accommodate change, then harden into orthodoxy. No static system—however secure it may feel—remains invulnerable. In fact, the very appearance of stability is often the prelude to decay. So the real question is no longer "Where is your wealth?" but "How does it move with you?"

To speak of a "fortress you can carry" is not to reach for metaphor—it is to describe a lived posture. It is the embodiment of certain principles—legal, behavioural, psychological, even spiritual—that let you shift your resources, your strategy, your stance without waiting for permission. You can relocate, adjust, reframe, recover. You are not beholden to bureaucracies that neither see you nor serve you.

You are not trapped within the confines of a single currency, court system, or asset class. You hold options—and that, precisely, is the advantage.

This final chapter is not a deepening of complexity. It is a narrowing toward essence. You've now encountered the core tenets behind the Backup Plan Portfolio: decentralised stores of value designed to endure economic distress; mobility structures that turn geography into strategy; legacy systems that bypass brittle institutions; and daily rituals that convert abstract "wealth" into something alive, practical, and responsive.

Now, we turn inward. Not for summary, but for integration. The fortress you carry begins in the unseen spaces—in thought, in design, in the silent architecture of action. It is not some paranoid bunker mentality. It is a system built for motion.

We start with the terrain of psychological autonomy. Resilience, after all, is rooted less in the size of your holdings than in the clarity of your thinking. Minimal dependencies. A trained eye for patterns. The refusal to be startled by the obvious. Then we turn to the art of signal-based readiness: how to pick out the relevant from the flood of noise, and how to shape a posture that evolves in response—not in panic.

From there, we return to ritualised review. Not as a productivity trick, but as an operating ethic. Regular check-ins—weekly, quarterly, and triggered by thresholds—aren't chores. They're acts of sovereignty. They are how you keep drift from becoming derailment. How you spot inertia before it solidifies. These aren't mechanical. They are discipline turned into resilience.

And then, compression. The ability to distil your entire architecture—your logic, your priorities, your contingency triggers—into a single page. A Wealth Compass. Not a sentimental summary, but a tool. A guide. Something you can reach for when institutions lock up, when borders harden, when stories disintegrate. Not because it holds every answer, but because it reminds you of the questions that matter.

That's what it means to carry a fortress. You move through the world with your strategy intact. You're not starting over with every surprise. You've anticipated what others ignore. You've rehearsed reversibility. You've traded illusions of permanence for something far more powerful: a living system that can flex.

Now, one might ask—perhaps with a sceptical eyebrow—"Is this all just a high-functioning form of paranoia?" It's a fair question. And it deserves a serious answer. There is, indeed, a difference—an immense, moral difference—between fear-driven hoarding and sovereignty-driven design. One contracts the mind. The other expands your capacity to navigate. The fortress-carrier isn't bracing for doom. They are simply refusing fragility as the default.

Too many today are rich in structure but poor in strategy. They own assets they don't understand, obey laws they've never questioned, and anchor their lives in systems that can't explain themselves. Wealth without design becomes theatre. It looks formidable—until it meets pressure. Then it collapses, because it was built for compliance, not evolution.

This is a chapter about the intellectual durability of your financial life. Not about technical knowledge, and certainly not about credentials. But about resilience of thought. Can your system bend without breaking? Can your children comprehend it? Can your capital move? Can your values withstand digitisation, exodus, inflation, control?

Can you make a move without needing to log in?

As you read, you'll be invited to subtract more than you add. To sharpen instead of accumulate. To remove the fluff and focus on what your system is *for*. Not just what it holds, but what it is designed to resist.

Every section is written with intent. Each one is a signal you can return to—not as dogma, but as a point of reference.

Because you are not here to collect symbols of wealth. You are here to craft a living system of value—mobile, coherent, and durable. One that not only survives the world but understands it. That's what wealth means now. And that's where this ends. Or rather, where it truly begins—not in fear, but in clarity.

The Backup Plan as Worldview

The point was never to predict the future. That's a game for speculators, ideologues, and gamblers—those with a fragile sense of control and an unhealthy appetite for certainty. Prediction flatters the ego but insults reality. It assumes that markets will obey modelling, that governments will behave rationally, and that systems built for profit will protect those without leverage. The truth is sharper, but also more liberating: *the future isn't knowable, but your posture toward it is entirely within your control.*

The final insight of this book is a reframe, not a forecast. It is the shift from anxiety to agency. From hoping that the system will hold, to designing your life so that it doesn't matter if it doesn't. From staring at charts and news cycles for comfort, to building a personal infrastructure that renders predictions largely irrelevant. *The backup plan is not an accessory to your financial life—it is a lens through which you now see the world.*

This reframing matters because we live in a cultural context where collapse narratives dominate. The algorithms that shape public thought are biased toward extremes: economic apocalypse or boundless tech utopia, hyperinflation or zero-interest euphoria. But both ends of the spectrum are traps. They paralyse action. They reduce human agency to blind reaction. And most dangerously, they teach people to feel either helpless or invincible—two mindsets that destroy strategic thinking.

The reframed mindset sees the future not as a looming crisis but as a test of preparation. Not as a battlefield to win or lose, but as a terrain to navigate intelligently. It places less faith in macroeconomic narratives and more in micro-level control. Your banking relationships, your jurisdictional exposure, your personal liquidity, your capacity to leave, adapt, pause, restart—*these are not tactical footnotes. They are the primary metrics of resilience.*

This perspective does not guarantee immunity from shocks. But it transforms your relationship to them. A sudden capital control isn't devastating—it's inconvenient. A currency devaluation isn't paralysing—it's a prompt to relocate or rebalance. A cyber event that wipes digital access isn't ruinous—it's a stress test for your decentralised asset map. *You don't panic because you've designed with asymmetry in mind: low downside, high optionality.*

Optionality, in this frame, becomes moral. Not just strategic. The person who has planned well does not hoard knowledge or isolate behind gated wealth. They become an example, and in some cases a lifeline, to others who did not see it coming. Quiet confidence is not performative—it's the residue of preparation. It is what allows you to keep others calm, to lead with clarity, to act when institutions freeze. *True security compounds into ethical leadership.*

What does this look like practically? It looks like the entrepreneur who keeps two passports, not to evade taxes but to keep their team and family safe in the event of political rupture. It looks like the parent who raises children not to inherit wealth blindly, but to understand risk, read contracts, and navigate systems with strategic detachment. It looks like the investor who doesn't just chase alpha but designs liquidity ladders, capital control contingencies, and off-grid redundancies. It looks like the family who meets quarterly not to count net worth, but to align values and update strategy documents. *These actions are not reactive—they are ceremonial. They encode clarity.*

Some will dismiss this as overengineering. But that dismissal is often a defence against discomfort. The deeper reality is that most people do not want to think this clearly about fragility because doing so exposes just how little genuine control they have. Their wealth is optimised for convenience, not survivability. Their identity is tied to systems they neither understand nor influence. They confuse complexity for sophistication. *The backup planner sees through this illusion, not cynically, but responsibly.*

To live with this worldview is not to detach from society—it is to participate in it with lucid eyes and stable footing. You vote, you build, you collaborate. But you do so without naivety. You understand that systems serve their creators first, and that laws change when it suits the powerful. So you act with discipline. You diversify without paranoia. You relocate without drama. You secure your data, your documents, and your values—because you understand that *freedom is not a feeling; it is an architecture.*

This architecture is not final. The worldview of the backup plan is iterative. It rewards reflection, revision, and humility. It rejects dogma in favour of dynamic logic. As such, the real skill you've built across these chapters is not financial literacy or geopolitical awareness, though those matter. It is *personal governance.* The ability to make, audit, and revise decisions under shifting conditions. That is what survives.

At the end of this book, there are no 10-year predictions. There is no master asset allocation. No secret jurisdiction. No gospel about crypto or gold or real estate. Why? Because the map is not the territory. Because wisdom doesn't scale by formula—it scales by awareness. And because, ultimately, *this isn't a book about money. It's a book about strategic clarity under pressure.*

If the only thing this book has done is make you harder to surprise, it has succeeded. If it has moved you from passive participation to sovereign design, it has done its job. If it has reminded you that intelligence is not the same as preparedness—and that preparedness is not hoarding but *designing for dignity under duress*—then it was worth writing.

There are no endings here. Only recalibrations. The backup plan is not a destination. It is a rhythm. A reflex. A posture. It does not make you invincible. It makes you *unshakable where it counts.* And when the noise grows loud, and the headlines lurch from crisis to boom and back again, you will not need to predict. You will only need to listen—to the system you've built, and the clarity you've earned.

That is the fortress you carry now. Not a bunker. Not a bet. *But a worldview, lived deliberately.*

About the Author

Adrian Kassem von Rensselaer is a global wealth strategist and philosophical investor with over two decades of experience advising individuals, families, and sovereign clients on asset protection, decentralised finance, and legacy-building. Educated in Zurich and Tokyo, his perspective blends European financial tradition with Eastern resilience and post-digital pragmatism. Adrian has lived in five countries, navigated three economic crises, and helped thousands secure their futures beyond borders and bank accounts. His work dismantles illusions of safety in modern finance and replaces them with clarity, strategy, and sovereignty. The Backup Plan Portfolio is the culmination of a life spent preparing not just for profit—but for permanence.

www.ingramcontent.com/pod-product-compliance
Lightning Source LLC
Chambersburg PA
CBHW031339230926
51848CB00002B/301